Clauvergne .

Humanitarianism, Identity, and Nation

Law and Society Series
W. Wesley Pue, General Editor

A list of other books in this series appears at the end of the book.

Catherine Dauvergne

Humanitarianism, Identity, and Nation: Migration Laws of Australia and Canada

UBCPress · Vancouver · Toronto

15 14 13 12 11 10 09 08 07 06 05   5 4 3 2 1

Printed in Canada on acid-free paper

Library and Archives Canada Cataloguing in Publication
Dauvergne, Catherine, 1965-
  Humanitarianism, identity, and nation : migration laws of Australia and Canada / Catherine Dauvergne.

(Law and society)
Includes bibliographical references and index.
ISBN 0-7748-1112-9

  1. Emigration and immigration law – Canada. 2. Emigration and immigration law – Australia. 3. Humanitarianism. 4. National characteristics, Canadian. 5. National characteristics, Australian. I. Title. II. Series: Law and society series (Vancouver, B.C.)

KE4472.D39 2005   342.7108'2   C2004-906772-9   KF4483.I5D39 2005

Canadä

UBC Press gratefully acknowledges the financial support for our publishing program of the Government of Canada through the Book Publishing Industry Development Program (BPIDP), and of the Canada Council for the Arts, and the British Columbia Arts Council.

This book has been published with the help of a grant from the Canadian Federation for the Humanities and Social Sciences, through the Aid to Scholarly Publications Programme, using funds provided by the Social Sciences and Humanities Research Council of Canada, and with the help of the K.D. Srivastava Fund.

Printed and bound in Canada by Friesens
Set in Stone by Artegraphica Design Co. Ltd.
Copy editor: Francis Chow
Proofreader: Anna Friedlander
Indexer: Patricia Buchanan

UBC Press
The University of British Columbia
2029 West Mall
Vancouver, BC V6T 1Z2
604-822-5959 / Fax: 604-822-6083
www.ubcpress.ca

Contents

Acknowledgments

I first worked on this book as a member of the Faculty of Law at the University of Sydney, and completed the task after taking up a position at the Faculty of Law, University of British Columbia. I am indebted to colleagues and friends in both places for the supportive atmospheres in which to reflect on the Australian and Canadian nations.

As part of the research for this book, I attended refugee hearings at the Canadian Immigration and Refugee Board and at the Australian Refugee Review Tribunal. Board members and staff welcomed me and shared their time and insights. My greatest debt in this regard, however, is to the claimants who allowed me to attend their hearings as an observer. These experiences enriched my understanding enormously.

Peter Fitzpatrick, Sally Merry, Jenni Millbank, and Jeremy Webber each helped me by reading, suggesting, and encouraging me towards completing the enterprise. Kirsten Anker, Sally Bolam, Danya Chaikel, Janaya Flower, Julia Grix, and Agnes Huang provided research and production assistance.

Peter Dauvergne has read many versions and tolerated much. I am grateful.

Catherine Dauvergne
Vancouver
April 2004

Part 1
Reading Migration Laws

1
Introduction

Human migration occupies a curious place in our collective imagination at this juncture in history. The case that more people are on the move than ever before is a difficult one to make, considering how many more people there are in the world now and that the twentieth century saw a tremendous growth in the regulation, and concomitant restriction, of population movements. Restrictions transform the issue of migration, bringing a legal framework to travel that would have been analyzed differently at earlier points in time. Entire nations understand themselves as nations of immigration or, in a related way, as multicultural nations because of the influence and importance of immigration to their populations. The myth of the global village represents a collapsing of boundaries and spaces between people. A wide array of technologies for compressing space and time by speeding communication and travel have remoulded our perceptions of the world. The past decade has also brought a series of large-scale environmental disasters that have caused people to move from their homes in huge numbers. The simmering war on terror that marks the opening of the twenty-first century has altered border crossing regulations around the world. Reflecting and contributing to all of these factors, migration occupies an important place in global public discourses.

This book develops a framework for understanding the relationships between migration law and national identity. It highlights the importance of humanitarianism to this relationship, emphasizing that humanitarianism is a central concept both in theoretical analyses of migration provisions and in laws controlling migration. At the opening of the twenty-first century, asylum seekers around the globe are the crucial political crisis point in migration regulation, putting humanitarian ideals under intense scrutiny. Understanding the place of humanitarianism in migration laws is vital to making sense of the overall structure of migration laws and in analyzing how migration law functions as a crucial site for the construction of national identity. Far from being an exception to the notion that migration laws are tools of nation building, humanitarian admissions to the polity confirm and reify the identity of the nation as good, prosperous, and generous. These attributes affirm the essence of nation.

Conceptualizing the relationship between migration law and national identity requires an understanding of how identity has been used as an explanatory variable in contemporary legal theory, and an appreciation of the relationship between law and nation. The relationship this book analyzes is a subset of both of these others: law and identity, and law and nation. I draw on the literature about the interrelationships between law and identity to articulate the relationship between one particular kind of law – migration law – and one particular kind of identity – national identity. Using identity as an analytic tool is particularly appropriate for migration law because of the critique of law and legal reasoning that is embedded in theories of law and identity. The attention this draws to hierarchies, categories, and silences is especially apt at revealing the contours of migration law and the gradients of member-ship it contains. Considering the interrelationship of migration law and national identity contributes to that literature and refines that critique. Making identity the focus of the analysis of law calls attention to how an "other" is implicit in the structuring of identity and to how an image of self reflects the contours of the other. This analysis is particularly useful for understanding humanitarianism as the mirror in which the nation seeks a reflection of its beneficence. In addition, a law and identity analysis reveals important features of rights discourses that are themselves central to the migration setting where the nation itself is constructed as a right holder. This analysis, then, also contributes to the debate about the role of rights.

The relationship between law and nation is one of mutual determination. The paradigmatic denomination of law is national. Law is assumed to coincide with national limits unless otherwise stated to be some variant, such as international, natural, Islamic, or customary. Similarly, law contributes the structures that provide limits to the nation. Without legal texts in which to inscribe borders and their protection, the nation would have no end, no limit, and thus would be unimaginable. Describing the relationship between law and nation in this way goes directly to the issue of understanding nation. I draw on work that calls our attention to how nations are defined by myth, invented tradition, and imaginary dimensions. I also consider how the postmodern turn in scholarship disturbs even this understanding of nations as fixed entities. A focus on law and identity highlights the contingent nature of both, and this perspective extends to the nation as well. A nation, then, can be understood, in Brubaker's words, as a practical category, an institutional form, and an event.[1] This does not diminish the importance

---

1 William Rogers Brubaker, *Nationalism Reframed: Nationhood and the National Question in the New Europe* (Cambridge: Cambridge University Press, 1996) c. 1.

of myth, tradition, or imagination, but rather highlights how they are brought into play in a given setting. This combined understanding of nation fits well within my analytic framework, where migration law is one site – but not the only site – in which nationhood is formulated. Attention to the texts and applications of migration law necessarily draws attention to the incessant reconstruction and inherently contradictory aspects of nation. A focus on humanitarianism makes this insight even more acute because of the contradictions it highlights.

The argument that migration law and national identity exist in a symbiotic relationship, and that each reveals something about the other, holds as a general proposition. Nonetheless, the contours of the relationship are easiest to see in nations where immigration is an important part of the national ethos. For these "immigrant nations," the relationships between migration law and national identity are heightened in intensity because in these nations, which have to some extent been "created" through migration, the importance of migration law as a site for the construction and reconstruction of national identities is enhanced. The mythology of migration is directly evident in accounts of the nation. For this reason, I have chosen to use two nations of the "New World" – Australia and Canada – as the empirical examples in this book. The framework, however, has relevance beyond these new nations. The analysis, which could begin by considering the formidable legal hurdles to permanent immigration to Japan,[2] or the symbolic importance of the German legal commitment to membership for ethnic Germans,[3] or the response played out in British nationality law to the dismantling of the British Empire,[4] would reveal some aspect of the intertwining of migration, nation, and identity. A study of the legal construction of migration in Fortress Europe would reveal much of the enduring logic of nation in the face of globalizing challenges.

The importance of humanitarianism in this picture derives from the place of humanitarianism in established immigration programs. In countries with large numbers of immigrants, whether or not they are self-styled "immigrant nations," people are admitted to stay permanently for four reasons: historical or cultural ties, economic reasons, family reasons, or humanitarian reasons.

2 Jean Hampton, "Immigration, Identity and Justice" in Warren F. Schwartz, ed., *Justice in Immigration* (Cambridge and New York: Cambridge University Press, 1995) 67. It was not until the 1990s that fourth-generation Japanese-born Koreans, whose ancestors had been brought to Japan as slaves, were given citizenship.

3 Jules L. Coleman and Sandra K. Harding, "Citizenship, the Demands of Justice and the Moral Relevance of Political Borders" in Schwartz, *ibid.* at 18.

4 Ann Dummett and Andrew Nicol, *Subjects, Citizens, Aliens and Others: Nationality and Immigration Law* (London: Weidenfeld and Nicolson, 1990); Abdul Paliwala, "Law and the Constitution of the 'Immigrant' in Europe: A United Kingdom Policy Perspective" in Peter Fitzpatrick, ed., *Nationalism, Racism and the Rule of Law* (Aldershot, UK: Dartmouth Press, 1995) 74.

In the case of the first three of these, the relationship between migration law and national identity is straightforward at one level.[5] When Israel makes a commitment to admit all Jews, it relies on an idea of already existing membership – of a community identity that is well established and that is then reified and "nationalized" by law. When family reunification provisions are written into the migration laws of the United States, they communicate to the world at large an American vision of family: a statement of values, belonging, and financial obligations (as conveyed by sponsorship requirements) that is not naturally occurring or shared worldwide. When Australia awards additional points to anyone with training in information technology and subtracts points from any general practitioner physician, a message about desirability and the economic vision of the nation is presented. National priorities as economic values are written into the law. Furthermore, the way these priorities are mixed in the migrant stream also conveys a picture of the nation. Historical and cultural ties are not a significant part of the migration programs of the United States, Canada, or Australia. Family migration is the overwhelmingly largest category of the American migration program, but for Australia and Canada it was moved to second priority in the mid-1990s, behind economic migration, signifying that building the economy takes precedence over reunifying families.[6] Shifts between parts of the migration program occur regularly in these three countries to accommodate subtly shifting national visions.

Humanitarian migration is more difficult to fit into this picture. By humanitarian migration I mean those who are admitted to, or allowed to remain in, a country for reasons that tap into a notion of compassion in some way. I include the formal categories of refugees and asylees,[7] those who are allowed to stay because of their "refugee-like" circumstances, and others who are allowed to stay in spite of not fitting within the normally applicable legal requirements but because of a sense that to reject or expel them would contravene a nebulous sense of humanity. For the most part, migrants admitted on humanitarian grounds are allowed to remain permanently,

---

5 I analyze this argument in greater detail in Catherine Dauvergne, "Beyond Justice: The Consequences of Liberalism for Immigration Law" (1997) 10 Can. J.L. & Jur. 323.

6 This happened in Canada in 1995 and in Australia in 1997.

7 These two groups are sometimes distinguished on the basis that refugees are admitted from outside the country and asylees arrive first and then ask permission to remain. Sometimes the distinction reflects a view that asylum is related to political opinion whereas refugee status is not necessarily. In the *Universal Declaration of Human Rights*, 10 December 1948, adopted and proclaimed by General Assembly Resolution 217 A (III), the right provided is that to "seek" and "enjoy" asylum (Article 14), not refugee status, which is available only in countries that are signatories to the *Convention Relating to the Status of Refugees*, 1951, 189 U.N.T.S. 150 (entered into force 22 April 1954), as amended by the *Protocol Relating to the Status of Refugees*, 1967, 606 U.N.T.S. 267 (entered into force 4 October 1967) [*Refugee Convention*]. The distinction is vague, and in practical terms the law that provides for asylum is the law of refugee status.

just as economic, family, or cultural migrants. Humanitarian admission does not serve the national need by "filling gaps" in the economy – admitting people because of the value they bring "us." Nor does it fit in with an ideological vision of community or family – admitting people because they are "us." It does, however, mark the nation as good, prosperous, and generous. This contribution is vital.

The principal reason for the central role of humanitarianism is that nations are part of a liberal paradigm, and when liberal thinkers consider what is just and fair in immigration questions, humanitarianism is the only conclusion they reach. Liberal conceptions of justice are not able to provide answers to the important questions of principle in the realm of migration: Who should be admitted? And how many? Instead, both liberals who advocate that the borders of the community can be justly closed and those who argue that morally borders must be open, agree that at some point, and in some circumstances, needy individuals must be admitted. I have named this agreement liberalism's humanitarian consensus. Despite the fact that humanitarian migration is by far the smallest category in most nations with developed migration programs,[8] humanitarian admissions receive the most attention in theoretical accounts of migration and in political contestations focusing on asylum. Humanitarianism is an impoverished stand-in for justice. Its role in the popular, political, and legal discourses of migration goes a long way towards explaining the intransigence of debates about questions of justice in migration. There are no answers to which the baseline moral consensus of liberal nations can lead. Instead, there is humanitarianism's appeal to all that is best in us. Identifying and describing the place of humanitarianism in migration law is central to clarifying the migration law–national identity relationship.

The main contributions the book makes are in locating and describing this humanitarian consensus. This involves clarifying the place of migration law in the liberal nation and articulating the migration law–national identity relationship. The argument includes insights about the relationship between law and identity construction, about identities and rights discourses, and about the place of migration in liberal theory. This is the first work to join these elements of contemporary legal and political theory in this way. Using the insights about the boundary of the liberal community found in the work of Rawls, Dworkin, Walzer, Carens, Galloway, and others, I conclude that liberalism cannot answer the most fundamental questions about justice in migration law. I therefore turn to the critical theoretical work of scholars like Minow, Williams, and Fitzpatrick as a starting point for assessing migration laws in the face of liberalism's inadequacies. The answers my framework generates are outside the contours of liberalism, as of

8 See Appendix A for a statistical overview.

course they must be. Nonetheless, I acknowledge the vital role of those contours in setting the terms of the debate. This framework provides an original explanation for the long-established intransigence of liberal debates about just migration. By acknowledging their importance, it provides a way of moving beyond them.

The book has a two-part structure. The first part sets out the framework for a reading of the migration law–national identity relationship. The three chapters in this part deal in turn with the elements of the theoretical work I am drawing together. Chapter 2 looks at the trends in legal analysis of identity and highlights the insights that this scholarship can bring to the migration arena. The next chapter outlines the relationship of law and nation, and locates migration law as a particular, and foundational, subset of this interrelationship. The final chapter in this part explains why liberalism is the appropriate paradigm for this analysis and why it fails to produce a justice standard. It then outlines the content, contours, and meaning of liberalism's humanitarian consensus.

Part 2 applies these propositions to a comparative analysis of three aspects of humanitarian admissions to Canada and Australia. Chapter 5 examines the construction of the refugee as the ultimate other to the nation and uses the empirical focus on refugee admissions to underscore how attuning to identity draws attention to what is left out of and silenced by legal discourse. In Chapter 6, the empirical focus is on humanitarian admissions that are outside the restrictive framework of refugee law. This chapter looks at how the rhetoric of humanitarianism is used both in the law and alongside the law to reflect an image of these nations as beneficent. The final empirical chapter considers the way identities, rights discourses, and humanitarian discourses are brought together in the decision making of the highest courts. The way these courts resolve disputes about humanitarian admissions sets the legal limits within which these determinations can be resolved in the future. The work of these courts provides a contrast to administrative and executive decision making about humanitarian admission requests. It also allows me to demonstrate how rights discourses operate in migration law.

The empirical work serves in the first instance to illustrate and amplify the theoretical propositions. It also gathers together new material and puts it in a framework that yields fresh insights. This book does not aim to cover the full range of either country's immigration program, although the theoretical framework could be used in this way.[9] Nor does the empirical work make a historical argument, although the argument that migration law plays

9 A number of works provide comparative overviews. Two leading books are Freda Hawkins, *Critical Years in Immigration: Canada and Australia Compared* (Sydney: UNSW Press, 1989), which focuses on the 1972-86 time period from a sociological perspective, and Howard Adelman et al., eds., *Immigration and Refugee Policy: Australia and Canada Compared*

a vital role in constituting new nations clearly can be used with historical resonance. My use of particular aspects of Canadian and Australian migration law is in the nature of strategic sampling. Rather than providing the whole picture, which I believe is well done by others, I examine some areas in detail. For this close scrutiny, I have selected areas that lend themselves to extending the critical literature on law and identity: the domestic refugee decision making that engages questions of identity construction in legal process; other humanitarian decision making that engages key jurisprudential issues; and the role of rights, which returns to the impetus for much of the law and identity critique. None of the earlier comparative studies considers any aspect of Australian and Canadian migration law in this degree of detail.

The empirical evidence raises a clarification in analyzing the intertwining of migration law and national identity. Like law and nation, migration law and national identity are symbiotically overlapping. Migration law does not determine national identity, nor is the reverse true. Instead, migration law provides a rich site in which to search for images of national identity, and in which national identity can be reinvented, reconstructed, reimagined. Similarly, national identity is not a fixed or determinate quantity. Many Canadians and some Australians disavow any sense of national identity – which is one of the reasons why its appearance in migration law texts is so analytically compelling. Nonetheless, I want to take care not to suggest that a view of national identity, settled or otherwise, determines the way a particular bureaucrat, politician, or judge approaches a migration law question. Instead, I argue that cumulatively the mass of these decisions as read from laws, judicial reasoning, bureaucratic policy advice, and political talk generally reflects a vision of national identity. A host of factors influence migration decision making both in particular cases and at a legal policy level. Similarly, a national identity is constructed over myriad locations, not only in this one type of legal text. What I am arguing is that a sense of national identification can explain some persistent characteristics of law in this area, and in particular contributes to explaining the striking differences between Australian and Canadian humanitarianism.

These different approaches to, and applications of, the humanitarian consensus are one of the principal reasons for locating the empirical work in this comparative setting. Australia and Canada are similarly situated nations

---

(Melbourne: Melbourne University Press, 1994), gathering together twenty-two chapters co-written by Australian and Canadian academics and bureaucrats.

In addition to these two studies, Sean Brawley's book *The White Peril: Foreign Relations and Asian Immigration to Australia and North America* (Sydney: UNSW Press, 1995) considers immigration in the foreign relations of Australia, Canada, New Zealand, and the United States over the twentieth century. Charles Sinclair's PhD thesis, *Who Would Want to Be a Refugee? A Comparative Analysis of Refugee Policy and Law in Australia and Canada* (University of New England, 1995), considers refugee policy and law making in both countries in some detail.

sharing a population pattern and an approach to "nation building" through immigration. The overall conclusion, played out with differing aspects of the law in each of the empirical chapters, is that the migration law of a nation is best understood, interpreted, and manipulated through close attention to that nation's understanding of itself. Differences in Australian and Canadian national identifications are made visible through migration law, and in turn differences in the law and its application in each country are explained by reference to national identities. This is an important conclusion in the face of increasing forces of globalization; it contributes to an understanding of the resilience of the nation to these forces. My research for this book was conducted over a period of time when the two nations made significant changes to their migration laws. These changes were an important test for my analytic framework, proving its reliability and its explanatory capacity.

Australia and Canada are provocative examples for this argument because people in both places display a degree of angst about their national identity. Queries about the meaning of Canadian identity are arguably as much a marker of being Canadian as any other single factor. In Australia, national identity is contested, and even the celebration of a national day is a source of introspection and debate.[10] Given this, the coherent national images that are presented in migration law settings are all the more intriguing.

Canada and Australia are not, of course, the only nations that draw strongly on immigration in their national mythology. The United States and New Zealand share this history. Israel provides some close parallels. Germany and Britain are increasingly being transformed into Old World nations of immigration. Canada and Australia are, however, the best comparators because of their size and their international positioning and posturing regarding humanitarian migration. These two nations are large enough to have well-developed migration programs that have both endured and adapted over the past century, yet not so large as to prevent detailed analysis covering, for example, all relevant decisions of the highest-level appellate court. Further, both of these nations have been longtime key supporters of the international refugee law regime that is vital to understanding the role of humanitarian admissions. Each nation has sought to position itself internationally as a leader in humanitarian actions.

For both Australia and Canada, migration law is of more practical consequence than citizenship law for questions of membership.[11] In real terms,

---

10 In recent years, Australia Day celebrations commemorating the arrival of the first Colonial Governor have been the subject of debate. Re-enactments of Governor Phillip walking ashore and planting the British flag are gradually being replaced by celebrations of aboriginal heritage.

11 This is a contrast with the conclusion William Rogers Brubaker draws in comparing France and Germany. See Williams Rogers Brubaker, *Citizenship and Nationhood in France*

there are few distinctions between permanent residents and citizens in these two countries. The most meaningful membership distinctions are the hurdles set within the migration law. After permanent residency has been achieved within the migration law framework, citizenship is largely a matter of choice. In both countries, only citizens can vote, and in Canada only citizens have the constitutionally guaranteed right to "enter, remain in and leave Canada."[12] Permanent residents convicted of serious crimes are to be deported. In Australia, permanent employment in the national civil service is restricted to citizens.[13] Most importantly, however, the hurdle for becoming a citizen in both countries is low; one must be a permanent resident for a set number of years.[14] Decisions about whether one is acceptable as a member of the community are made at the migration stage rather than later. Migration law rather than citizenship law constitutes the community and contains the most significant distinctions between members and others.[15] This "us" and "them" distinction is the crux of the relationship between migration law and national identity.

---

and Germany (Cambridge, MA: Harvard University Press, 1992) at 181-82; Catherine Dauvergne, "Citizenship, Migration Laws and Women: Gendering Permanent Residency Statistics" (2000) 24 Melbourne U.L. Rev. 280 [Dauvergne, "Citizenship"].

12 *Canadian Charter of Rights and Freedoms*, Part 1 of the *Constitution Act, 1982*, being Schedule B to the *Canada Act 1982* (U.K.), 1982, c. 11, s. 6.

13 For an in-depth discussion of the incoherent map of entitlements that Australian citizenship entails, see Kim Rubenstein, *Australian Citizenship Law in Context* (Sydney: Law Book Company, 2002).

14 In Australia, two years of permanent residency is required: *Australian Citizenship Act 1948* (Cth.), s. 13. In Canada, three years of permanent residency is required: *Citizenship Act*, S.C. 1974-75-76, c. 108.

15 My concerns in this book cover some of the same areas as citizenship theory, but are for the most part more narrowly focused on law and on admittance to the polity rather than on the subsequent questions of types of membership and participation. For examples of citizenship analyses, see: T. Alexander Aleinikoff, *Semblances of Sovereignty: The Constitution, the State and American Citizenship* (Cambridge, MA: Harvard University Press, 2002); Geoff Andrews, ed., *Citizenship* (London: Lawrence and Wishart, 1991); J. M. Barbalet, *Citizenship: Rights, Struggle and Class Inequality* (Milton Keynes, UK: Open University Press, 1988); Seyla Benhabib, *The Claims of Culture: Equality and Diversity in the Global Era* (Princeton, NJ: Princeton University Press, 2002); Joseph H. Carens, "Who Belongs? Theoretical and Legal Questions about Birthright Citizenship in the United States" (1987) 37 U.T.L.J. 413; Davina Cooper, "The Citizen's Charter and Radical Democracy: Empowerment and Exclusion within Citizenship Discourse" (1993) 2 Social and Legal Studies 149; Jurgen Habermas, "Citizenship and National Identity" in *Between Facts and Norms: Contributions to a Discourse Theory of Law and Democracy* (Cambridge, MA: MIT Press, 1996); Stuart Hall and David Held, "Citizens and Citizenship" in Stuart Hall and Martin Jacques, eds., *New Times: The Changing Face of Politics in the 1990s* (London: Lawrence and Wishart, 1989); Will Kymlicka, *Multicultural Citizenship: A Liberal Theory of Minority Rights* (Oxford: Clarendon Press, 1995); Will Kymlicka, *Recent Work in Citizenship Theory* (Toronto: Faculty of Law Workshop Series, University of Toronto, 1992); Iris Marion Young, "Polity and Group Difference: A Critique of the Ideal of Universal Citizenship" (1989) 99 Ethics 250.

Finally, comparing Australia and Canada contributes not only to the body of work analyzing immigration and refugee law but also to a body of work comparing these two legal settings. The similar histories and legal cultures have led to a body of work comparing diverse areas of law ranging from native title to constitutional law to administrative review. There are academic organizations in each country devoted to study of the other, which contributes also to a growing number of comparative conferences and other linkages. The contrast between Canadian and Australian identities revealed in this study makes a challenging contribution to this scholarship, as well as to the scholarship of identity itself.

Frameworks of Migration Law in Australia and Canada

As the empirical analysis in this book does not aspire to present a complete picture of the migration provisions in either country, it is useful to have an overview of the framework of migration law in each country, especially for readers who are not familiar with either legal setting. The case for comparison in some way derives from the similarities observable at this scale, in contrast to the differences in detail presented in the second half of this book. Canada is larger geographically and in population, with a current population of approximately 30 million, compared with Australia's 19 million. This makes each a relatively empty space in comparison with most of the earth. Australia's population is concentrated on the eastern and southeastern coasts of the continent, and about 90 percent of Canada's population lives within 100 kilometres of the American border.

Canada and Australia are nations of immigration. In each case, the indigenous population was decimated and dominated by early colonists to such an extent that First Nations peoples in Canada are now between 3 and 4 percent of the population and aboriginal Australians are between 2 and 3 percent.[16] Each country bears the contemporary scars of this experience, with a vital part of its population suffering the ongoing effects of dispossession and dislocation. There is neither a political nor a legal formulation for reconciling this past, despite ongoing attempts. It may properly be irreconcilable. The national mythologies of migration have served to reinforce this disenfranchisement, as the vision of a nation made of migrants makes indigenous peoples – "first nations" – invisible.

In both Australia and Canada, at different points throughout history, migration has been used to increase the population in general, or to increase the population in particular parts of the country or the economy. In the postwar period, assisted-passage programs brought British immigrants to

---

16 Canadian data come from the 2001 census data reported by Statistics Canada. Australian data from the 2001 census come from Australian Bureau of Statistics, Press Release, 4705.0, "Population Distribution: Indigenous Australians" (2002).

Australia, as part of a strategy of increasing the population through an immigrant intake of up to 170,000 per year.[17] In Canada, Chinese workers were "imported" to provide the hard labour to fulfill the national dream of a cross-Canada railway link,[18] and federal immigration arrangements provide for Quebec to manage the flow of immigrants to that province, acknowledging the importance of migration to the culture and future of the nation. For other reasons, more provinces are also pursuing these arrangements. All of these policies were or are facilitated by the migration laws of each country. In this way, migration laws have contributed to the literal construction of the nation by providing the mechanism through which people who would later come to think of themselves as Australians or Canadians were recruited or lured.

Migration to Australia is controlled by the *Migration Act*[19] and to Canada by the *Immigration and Refugee Protection Act,*[20] which replaced the *Immigration Act*[21] in mid-2002. Each act governs permanent and temporary entry provisions. The legislative framework in each country underwent a major overhaul in the 1970s aimed at making the law more "neutral" and "removing" racism.[22] In Australia, this change is associated with the end of the infamous "White Australia" policy. The "White Canada" policy was never as coherent, but migration restrictions in the first decades of the twentieth century did include at times a complete ban on Chinese immigration, a "head tax," and targeted use of language testing, all standard features of White Australia.[23] Canadian provinces asserted themselves more vigorously than Australian states in the migration area, and the ensuing legal battles meant that the Canadian national government could often further its interest in controlling the legislative power by arguing against racist provincial regulation. Lawmaking practices have been considerably refined since then, but language skills and money, and the race and gender biases they mask, remain important predictors of successful permanent entry to each country.[24]

The *Migration Act,* as well as both present and past versions of the Canadian legislation, open with statements of objectives that are ultimately completely manipulable. Section 3 of the Canadian act enumerates twenty-five

---

17 Ann Marie Jordens, *Redefining Australians: Immigration Citizenship and National Identity* (Sydney: Hale and Iremonger, 1995) at c. 2, "Seeking Workers for a New Australia."
18 Hawkins, *supra* note 9 at xv-xvii; Donald Galloway, *Essentials of Canadian Law: Immigration Law* (Concord, ON: Irwin Law, 1997) [Galloway, *Essentials*] at 10-15.
19 1958 (Cth).
20 S.C. 2001, c. 27.
21 R.S.C. 1985, c. I-2.
22 The changes came into effect in Canada in 1978 and in Australia in 1980.
23 Galloway, *Essentials, supra* note 18 at 12. See also Ninette Kelley and Michael Trebilcock, *The Making of the Mosaic: A History of Canadian Immigration Policy* (Toronto: University of Toronto Press, 1998).
24 I discuss some of these biases in Dauvergne, "Citizenship," *supra* note 11.

separate objectives under the headings immigration, refugees, and application. These range from pursuing maximum social, cultural, and economic benefits and supporting a strong and prosperous economy to protecting the health and safety of Canadians, maintaining the security of Canadian society, expressing Canada's fundamental humanitarian ideals, and furthering the domestic and international interests of Canada.[25] While these objectives are highly detailed, there are so many that almost any decision under the act would conform with at least some of them, without even minimal interpretive wordplay. At the same time, it would be almost impossible to conceive of a decision that would conform with *all* the objectives in either the immigration or refugee area. The Australian *Migration Act* takes a more direct route to the same end. Section 4 of that act provides that "the object of this Act is to regulate, in the national interest, the coming into, and presence in, Australia of non-citizens."[26] This statement is bolstered by three subsections providing specific examples of how non-citizens are to be controlled. The guiding principle is the national interest and the primary mechanism is control. Both acts share the emphasis on the national interest, conforming overtly with the instrumental and constitutive role of migration law in liberal settler societies.

The difference between the two sets of objectives is primarily one of tone. Both acts put the national interest first and foremost, but the Australian formulation links this in a rigorous way to control. As Chapters 5, 6, and 7 demonstrate, Australian migration law and the mythology that surrounds

25 The full text of s. 3 runs to three pages and includes references to social, economic, and cultural benefits; the federal, bilingual, and multicultural character of Canada; minority official language communities; economic development across regions; family reunion; successful integration into Canada; consistent standards and prompt processing; trade, commerce, tourism, and international understanding; protecting health and safety; international justice and respect for human rights; cooperation with the provinces regarding foreign credentials; saving the lives of displaced and persecuted persons; international legal obligations; humanitarian ideals; offering a safe haven; fair and efficient processes that maintain integrity, self-sufficiency, and well-being of refugees; domestic and international interests; accountability and transparency; cooperation between governments within Canada and internationally; the *Canadian Charter of Rights and Freedoms;* and international human rights instruments.

26 The full text of s. 4 reads:
  (1) The object of this Act is to regulate, in the national interest, the coming into, and presence in, Australia of non-citizens.
  (2) To advance its object, this Act provides for visas permitting non-citizens to enter or remain in Australia and the Parliament intends that this Act be the only source of the right of non-citizens to so enter or remain.
  (3) To advance its object, this Act requires persons, whether citizens or non-citizens, entering Australia to identify themselves so that the Commonwealth government can know who are the non-citizens so entering.
  (4) To advance its object, this Act provides for the removal or deportation from Australia of non-citizens whose presence in Australia is not permitted by this Act.

and supports it are dominated by a control emphasis. While control is also important in the Canadian law, it is subverted and hidden to a much greater extent. This in turn points to differences between Canadian and Australian national identities, and to differences in national migration mythologies. These objectives are not substantive provisions, but they do guide interpretation of the laws and formally constrain discretionary decision making.

Moving beyond their objectives, the migration legislation of Australia and Canada share other features as well. One of the central tools of the migration scheme in each country is the use of a "point system" for economic category applicants. An applicant is assigned a certain number of points over a range of criteria,[27] which are then added up to determine eligibility. The point system is applied differentially in subgroups of the economic stream. While the point system does not apply to refugees applying onshore or inland, those who are seeking resettlement from abroad are sometimes assessed on similar criteria as indicators of their ability to settle easily in Australia or Canada.[28] The point system provides migration law with a veneer of neutrality, although of course the criteria that merit points replicate biases of earlier formulae. As well, the point system is easily adjusted to meet particular policy goals. The Australian policy of awarding "–10" points to physicians at some points in time is a good example of how this can be accomplished.[29]

The point system ensures that the malleability of the law is not only at the level of broadly worded objectives. In Canada, the details of the system – the actual points to be awarded – are contained in the *Immigration and Refugee Protection Regulations*.[30] The Australian point system is not as deeply buried as the Canadian; it appears in the *Migration Act,* Division 3, Subdivision 3. Nonetheless, the legislative provisions create only a framework, into which regulations insert substance. While regulatory changes are reviewed by parliamentary committee and are open to public review, they do not usually attract the same degree of democratic scrutiny as changes in the law. In both countries, the "pass" mark in any category – the true who-gets-in

---

27 The Canadian criteria are education, English or French language proficiency, work experience, age, arranged employment, and adaptability, with some variations for different subclasses within the economic migration stream: *Immigration and Refugee Protection Regulations,* Pt. 6, Div. 1. The Australian criteria are employment, age, language skill, family relationships, length of sponsor's Australian citizenship, and location of sponsor: *Migration Regulations,* para. 2.26-2.27, Schedule 6.

28 Those with relatives or other ties to Australia currently have priorities "one" and "two" in Australia's humanitarian program. Those with "resettlement potential" are priority "three."

29 This was a deduction from points given under "employment qualification": *Migration Regulations,* para. 2.26(3)(c).

30 S.O.R./2002-27.

measure – is determined by the responsible minister and gazetted, with a requirement that they later be presented to Parliament.[31]

The equally vital numbers to be admitted are similarly not set out in the text of the law.[32] In both countries, the target numbers, or quotas, that determine how many migrants in which categories are to be admitted are made by the responsible minister.[33] In times when migration levels are a contentious political issue, these numbers are undoubtedly subject to scrutiny by Cabinet at the very least, but clearly the executive has direct control over this number. The procedure surrounding these vital numbers highlights a difference between Australian and Canadian provisions. The Australian act establishes a legal requirement that the target numbers cannot be exceeded and that excess applications will be "taken not to have been made."[34] The Canadian act provides only for "estimates." Here again the Australian act takes a more overtly controlling tone than the Canadian. The Canadian requirement that the numbers be tabled in Parliament is of little import, as no opportunity is provided for review or comment by parliamentarians. Interestingly, a duty to consult with provincial governments has now been introduced in Canada and may lead to additional public consultation.

The combined effect of the point system and the target or quota numbers means that all important provisions that influence the day-to-day decisions about who will be permitted entry and who will be excluded are not contained in the act but in regulations and in executive pronouncements. Both the *Immigration and Refugee Protection Act* and the *Migration Act* establish frameworks for migration policy in the national interest. Rather than providing a statement of the relevant law, each provides a sieve into which a changing view of the national interest can be poured and thereby made law.

The biggest contrast between the two legal schemes is that in 1989 the Australian Parliament attempted to eliminate discretionary decision making under the act.[35] Discretion is an important feature of any administrative regime, and is particularly vital if migration law is to respond to and reflect perceived national need. There are two results of the 1989 changes. First, the attempt to eliminate discretion is, of course, futile. Discretion insinuates

---

31 In Australia, a movable "pool" number is also used as part of the point system process to determine the eligible pool of applicants.

32 This is in sharp contrast to the American legislation, where a formula for calculating admission numbers is written into the *Immigration and Nationality Act*, 8 U.S.C. 1952.

33 In Australia, these numbers must be gazetted, pursuant to s. 39 of the *Migration Act*. In Canada, they must be tabled in Parliament as part of the Annual Immigration Plan, pursuant to s. 94 of the *Immigration and Refugee Protection Act*.

34 See *Migration Act*, ss. 76(2), 108(2)-(4).

35 *Migration Legislation Amendment Act 1989* (Cth). One of the recommendations of Canada's 1999 legislative review was to sharply curtail discretionary decision making under the act. The new legislation takes some steps in this direction, but is not a stringent as either the review suggested or as the Australian act.

itself into all bureaucratic decision making. The 1989 changes merely narrow discretion and rest more of it at the highest levels of decision making. Second, the *Migration Act* is frequently amended to tailor it to national need as the scope for broad discretionary adjustments is reduced. The *Migration Act* was amended by over sixty separate acts between 1995 and 2003. The Canadian legislation, in contrast, has been amended less than one-quarter as often. However, as Chapter 7 in particular demonstrates, there is a greater range of discretionary decision making under the Canadian act.

In Canada, migration is managed by the national government department now known as Citizenship and Immigration Canada (CIC).[36] The corresponding department in Australia is presently the Department of Immigration and Multicultural and Indigenous Affairs (DIMIA).[37] Migration decisions are made within the departments and by tribunals. In Australia, the two relevant tribunals are the Migration Review Tribunal (MRT) and the Refugee Review Tribunal (RRT). Both conduct merit reviews and, under Australia's strict separation-of-powers doctrine, exercise executive rather than judicial power. In Canada, the four-division Immigration and Refugee Board (IRB) determines refugee applications at first instance and reviews other decisions in the immigration portfolio. In both countries, the supervising court is known as the Federal Court.[38]

In both Canada and Australia, migration and the law and policy that surround it have been under almost constant public scrutiny since the early 1990s. The negotiation about the border of the nation, the line between "us" and "them," is ongoing. Since 1994, Canada has undergone an almost unceasing process of public consultation about potential changes to its immigration law. In 1994, consultations across the country were held and were later incorporated into the extended version of the 1995 Immigration Plan entitled *Into the 21st Century: A Strategy for Immigration and Citizenship*,[39] released in late 1994. These plans generated further public discussion, and were followed in late 1996 with the appointment of a three-member legislative review panel that again conducted country-wide consultations with a mandate to propose a major overhaul of the immigration legislation. These proposals were presented late in 1997 under the title *Not Just Numbers: A Canadian Framework for Future Immigration*.[40] The government then

---

36 Formerly Employment and Immigration Canada.
37 Formerly Immigration and Multicultural Affairs and also Immigration and Ethnic Affairs.
38 See Appendix B. Only three divisions of the IRB operate at present. Implementation of the Refugee Appeal Division has been indefinitely postponed.
39 Canada, Citizenship and Immigration Canada, *Into the 21st Century: A Strategy for Immigration and Citizenship* (Hull, QC: Minister of Supply and Services, 1994).
40 Canada, Immigration Legislative Review Advisory Group, *Not Just Numbers: A Canadian Framework for Future Immigration* (Ottawa: Citizenship and Immigration Canada, 1997).

conducted further consultations about the recommendations, and issued a response entitled *Building a Strong Foundation for the 21st Century*[41] in early 1999. This became the basis of the bill to replace the former *Immigration Act,* which was first tabled in early 2000. The tabling led to further public consultations and extensive public comment before the bill died on the Order Paper when Parliament was dissolved in late 2000. After the government was returned, amended legislation was introduced and passed in 2001. The process of developing regulations to accompany the new law involved another round of consultation and corresponding attention, before the act took effect in June 2002.

The extent of public consultation signifies the importance of migration issues to the public agenda. Public consultation assists the government in asserting that changes in either policy (e.g., the *Into the 21st Century* documents) or law (as proposed in *Not Just Numbers*) respond to what the nation, as constituted by individual voices, wants. National interest is crucial to the law, and therefore no changes will be made without extensive high-profile attention to it. The devotion of such intense resources to these public processes also signifies the intertwining of the public, political, and legal discourses of migration. While consultation functions to gather public information, it also promotes the government's view and the government's ability to form the agenda. It fosters overlap between public and legal discourse, and can also serve to highlight when the dissonance between the two is used by governments to meet their goals. Interestingly, the government was quick to reject the *Not Just Numbers* recommendation that migration issues be divided into two pieces of legislation, one dealing with immigrants and the other with those whom the nation seeks to protect. The logic of this recommendation is compelling, but following through on it would reduce the potential for the government to harness humanitarian admissions, as well as economic and family admissions, to the needs and priorities of the nation.

The level of attention paid to migration law in Australia has been, if anything, more intense than in Canada, at least since 1999, when a sharp increase in the number of people arriving by unauthorized boat sparked a debate that reached the dimensions of a moral panic by 2001. The total unauthorized boat arrivals for 1999-2000 reached 4,175,[42] a small percentage of total migration for the year, even if all had been allowed to stay. This sudden increase sparked a flurry of legislative changes, including the introduction for the first time of a temporary visa – with reduced access to

41 Canada, Citizenship and Immigration Canada, *Building a Strong Foundation for the 21st Century* (Hull, QC: Minister of Supply and Services, 1999).
42 "Fact Sheet: Unauthorised Arrivals by Air and Sea" (revised 15 October 2002), online: The Department of Immigration and Multicultural and Indigenous Affairs (Australia) <http://www.immi.gov.au/facts/74unauthorised.htm>.

various welfare state supports and no possibility of family reunion – for refugees who arrive by boat.[43] Legislation increasing the state's powers to warn off boats before they enter territorial waters and to penalize people smugglers more severely was introduced.[44] Beginning in 1999, the government increased the number of detention centres to support Australia's mandatory detention scheme for unauthorized arrivals,[45] and has embarked upon an aggressive politics of immigration.

This politics came to a head in August and September 2001 when the Norwegian container ship *MV Tampa* rescued 438 people from a sinking ship in waters north of Australia. In light of the looming national election, the centre-right coalition government decided to make the *Tampa* incident its line in the sand. The government closed Australia's territorial sea to the *Tampa* and later ordered elite SAS troops to board the ship.[46] The government's actions were challenged in a Federal Court habeas corpus claim, but were upheld on appeal.[47] Given what was perceived to be strong public support for the government's actions and the election scheduled for two months later, the opposition Labour party supported the government's stance and in the aftermath of the crisis joined in passing a series of amendments to the *Migration Act* that it had opposed for, in some cases, several years.[48] One extraordinary amendment excised sovereign territory from the Australian "migration zone" – a legal fiction of Australian migration law that purports to determine where refugee claims can be made.[49] The rescuees were moved to New Zealand and Nauru in what the government originally labelled its "Pacific Solution."[50] Since August 2001, asylum seekers heading to Australia in boats have primarily been diverted elsewhere, including to Nauru and Manus Island, Papua New Guinea. Many Australians believe that the government's tough stance against the *Tampa* was a significant factor in the

43 Visa subclass 785.
44 *Border Protection Legislation Amendment Act 1999* (Cth.); *Crimes at Sea Act 1999* (Cth.).
45 *Migration Act,* Div. 6.
46 Many accounts of the *Tampa* incident have now been published. For example, Catherine Dauvergne, "Making People Illegal" in Peter Fitzpatrick and Patricia Tuitt, eds., *Critical Beings: Law, Nation and the Global Subject* (Aldershot, UK: Ashgate Press, 2004); Pene Mathew, "Australian Refugee Protection in the Wake of the Tampa" (2002) 96 Am. J. Int'l L. 661; Donald Rothwell, "The Law of the Sea and the *MV Tampa* Incident: Reconciling Maritime Principles with Coastal State Sovereignty" (2002) 13 Public Law Review 118; Mary Crock, "In the Wake of the Tampa: Conflicting Visions of International Refugee Law in the Management of Refugee Flows" (2003) 12 Pac. Rim L. & Pol'y J. 49.
47 *Ruddock v. Vardalis,* [2001] F.C.A. 1329.
48 Such as the privative clause introduced by the *Migration Legislation Amendment Act (No. 1) 2001* (Cth.), first proposed in 1998.
49 This fiction is undoubtedly a transgression of the *Refugee Convention* but there is no practical way for a refugee claimant to seek a remedy to this. See the *Migration Amendment Act (Excision from Migration Zone) Act 2001* (Cth.).
50 Of the original *Tampa* refugee claimants, 27 were eventually accepted for resettlement in Australia. The government has since renamed its program the Pacific Strategy.

November 2001 election, which returned it to a third consecutive majority.[51] This series of events brought Australian migration law and politics into the international spotlight in an unprecedented way, and moved humanitarian migration to centre stage in domestic political debate.

These patterns of similarity form the background to the empirical work of the second half of this book, the setting for illustrating and elaborating the theoretical framework for investigating and describing the interrelationship between migration law and national identity. In both Australia and Canada, the place of the liberal humanitarian consensus is key to understanding migration law and the politics that provide its content. I turn now to the three chapters that spell out the elements of my analysis: identity, nation, and humanitarianism.

51 "A Victory Crafted by John Howard" *The Age* (12 November 2001) 22; "Refugees and Others" *Sydney Morning Herald* (28 December 2001) 14; "*Tampa* Crisis Won't Be a Slur on Australia, Claims Howard" *The West Australian* (9 March 2001); Mairi Barton "Ruddock Warns Off UN" *The West Australian* (9 January 2002); Andrew Clennel "New Zealand Denies It's a New Magnet for People Smugglers" *Sydney Morning Herald* (18 January 2002) 4; Gerard Henderson "Too Late for PM to Abandon Refugees Ship" *Sydney Morning Herald* (13 November 2001) 14.

2
The Insights of Identity

This chapter explores the potency of identity as the central pillar of my theoretical framework for understanding migration law. Identity's explanatory capacity for this work is derived from its development in social and psychological theory and its more recent deployment by legal scholars. The adoption and adaptation of identity by the legal academy has, of course, moved it apart in some respects from its location in other disciplines. In the process, a new tradition of law and identity scholarship is emerging. In this chapter, I outline the contours of the new tradition, defining law and identity scholarship by its rich account of categorizations, hierarchies, and boundaries, and their interrelationships within the law. I then explain how a focus on identity is situated within the debate about rights discourses that animates much of the tension between critical legal studies and other "new" legal theory. The debate about the utility of rights to redress racializing legal practice and other discriminations has now travelled to all corners of the Anglo-American legal sphere and beyond. The deployment of identity as an analytic tool within that debate has shaped the law and identity tradition and is important to how identity now provides vital insights into migration law.

In popular discourse, the term "identity" has risen to prominence in connection with identity politics – that is, politics organized around demographic attributes of individuals that have been and continue to be the basis of discrimination. The last decade of the twentieth century saw the notion of identity politics dragged into the abyss of political correctness. As a result, Minow's description of identity politics as "the mobilization around gender, racial and similar group-based categories in order to shape or alter the exercise of power to benefit group members,"[1] and Perry's assertion that identity politics "expresses a widely felt, weary cosmopolitan disdain for a

1 Martha Minow, "Not Only for Myself: Identity, Politics and Law" (1996) 75 Or. L. Rev. 647 at 648.

certain sort of claim made against the state or its bureaucratic agencies on behalf of a broad range of collectivities,"[2] both ring true. In short, identity politics have sufficient currency to attract disdain.

The importance of identity politics for my project is twofold. First, identity politics brought identity in an analytic and politicized sense into popular discourse. This in turn reflected and heightened the importance of scholarly efforts to interpret and explain identities. That the politics of migration appear to be only tangentially linked to identity politics is directly related to my use of identity as a theoretical concept, and to why identity needs to be interrogated rather than assumed at the outset. In the migration context, it is national identity that matters most. National identity is not usually at stake in identity politics (despite the fact that ethnicity or nationalism may be) because identity politics tend to refer to debates within a national community. While the debate may be about the meaning of that community, it is also, and significantly, about exclusion.[3] Accordingly, the community is assumed to exist and to have some meaning and some established membership. The phrase "identity politics" is linked with advocacy by groups marginalized in different ways.

My inquiry is directed primarily to the meaning of the national community itself rather than to debates within it. The two necessarily overlap. Contestations about exclusion and marginalization within the national community crystallize in the community's definition, whether that is self-definition or description by outsiders.[4] The voices of excluded groups raise important issues about migration law, and migration law is itself a site of exclusions. The values that find expression in migration law are those that prevail in internal contestations.

For all these reasons, it is important to inquire why national identity and identity politics do not have more points of convergence. The response to this leads in two directions that are equally important in this book: first, into understanding that identity is defined and experienced situationally, and that one of the vital insights identity brings to migration law is that in the migration setting, national identities come to the fore; and, second, that the role of the boundary of the community in shaping debates about

---

2 Richard Warren Perry, "The Logic of the Modern Nation-State and the Legal Construction of Native American Tribal Identity" (1995) 28 Ind. L. Rev. 547 at 552-53.

3 This is the defining characteristic of identity politics in Wendy Brown's analysis in "Wounded Attachments: Late Modern Oppositional Political Formations" in John Rajchman, ed., *The Identity in Question* (New York: Routledge, 1995). She argues that capitalism and disciplinarity "breed the emergence of politicized identity, rooted in disciplinary productions, but oriented by liberal discourse towards protest against exclusion from a discursive formation of universal justice."

4 Sherene Razack explores one example of this process in Sherene Razack, "Domestic Violence as Gender Persecution: Policing the Borders of Nation, Race and Gender" (1995) 8 C.J.W.L. 45.

justice and equality – the debates that animate identity politics – is vital to how migration discourses, laws, and politics are framed in liberal nations. This chapter traces the argument in the first of these directions. The next two chapters follow the second direction.

The Essentials of Identity

While legal scholars increasingly write about both identity and its importance, we have little to say about what it is. This is partly because of the commitment to social constructionism in legal scholarship, which I will come to shortly, and partly because legal scholars are simply not well equipped for the task. The latter reason also partially accounts for the former: when the essence of identity is treated as elusive, a commitment to social constructionism may be more apparent than fully embraced. Some understanding of how identity has taken shape in disciplines where it has a longer history is useful in developing its analytic potential. It also frames the essentialist-versus-constructivist debate that is impossible to bypass when engaging identity and that cuts through identity scholarship.

Some background to the theoretical position of my argument lies in social psychology and in social theory. From social psychology, I have borrowed an explanation of the interaction between individual self-identification and the behaviour of a group as large as a nation.[5] While psychological processes belong only to individuals, it is nonetheless appropriate to consider group behaviour as separate and distinct, and this behaviour can be explained by considering how individuals react and identify in group settings. Social psychologists acknowledge and explain that even in very large groups, individuals can have a sense of identity, and that this sense can affect the way members of the group behave.[6] Further, they demonstrate that in different settings, different identities will be most important. This is important for an argument about national identity focusing on Australia and Canada, where many individuals associate "nationalism" with Old World rivalries or wars in emerging states. It provides a foundation for arguing that national identity can be an important force even in places where many

---

5 This argument draws primarily from the work of John Turner in John Turner, *Rediscovering the Social Group: A Self-Categorization Theory* (Oxford and New York: Blackwell, 1987) [Turner, *Rediscovering*]. His ideas are further developed in John Turner, *Social Influence* (Milton Keynes, UK: Open University Press, 1991).

6 Turner explains the effect this way: "That psychological processes belong only to individuals is fully compatible with the idea of a psychological discontinuity between individuals acting as 'individuals' and as group members. Group behaviour is psychologically different from and irreducible to interpersonal relationships and yet this need involve no metaphysical notions of a group mind. If the theory proves valid, then the group has *psychological reality* in the sense that there is a specific psychological process, a self-grouping process, which corresponds to and underlies the distinctive features of group behaviour" (*Rediscovering, ibid.* at 66).

individuals disavow its existence or dispute its content. Further, this account grounds my assertion that legislative, judicial, and administrative decision making reflects images of national identity without requiring that each individual, and each individual decision, would always and consciously reflect this identity.

Social theory has been much more preoccupied with identity than legal scholarship has, and has contributed considerably more detailed accounts of its nature. These accounts of identity are very similar to those used, less self-consciously, in studies of law and identity. The common theme is that however much identity is considered to fluctuate and to be socially constructed, it is nonetheless crucial to how individuals make sense of their lives. A sense of identity gives meaning to one's life and this meaning has a collective aspect to the extent that identity is derived from comparisons of oneself with others. This collective dimension of identity means that identity has an inbuilt political potential.[7] That is, identity connects an individual to the setting in which they live. Even in conceptions of identity that emphasize its fluidity, the emphasis on identity as social connector is at the forefront. Craig Calhoun, after outlining the potential pitfalls of taking either a purely essentialist or a purely constructivist view of identity, asserts that identity always embodies a tension between the individual and collective levels and that it is never successfully equated with self-interest. These tensions and inconsistencies form Calhoun's explanation for the fluctuating nature of identity.[8]

This insight captures our sense of the extent to which any "identity-box" never feels like a complete description of oneself, for as individuals we have many different labels, and experience ourselves as more than the sum of these disparate parts. While I may analyze some aspects of my experiences as typical of a woman's experience or a Canadian's view of the world, others are much less so, or are completely atypical. Thus, to speak of an experience of national identity will never completely capture how a given individual will describe their own identity.

---

7 Homi Bhabha asserts that "within the pluralist framework that seeks to contain and resolve the debate, identity is taken as the referential sign of a fixed set of customs, practices and meanings, an enduring heritage, a readily identifiable sociological category, a set of shared traits or experiences": Homi Bhabha, "Commitment to Theory" in *Third Cinema Reader* (1989) 111 at 125, cited by J.W. Scott in "Multiculturalism and the Politics of Identity" in Rajchman, *supra* note 3.

8 Calhoun writes: "To see identities only as reflections of 'objective' social positions or circumstances is to see them always retrospectively. It does not make sense of the dynamic potential impact – for better or worse – in the tensions within persons and among the contending cultural discourses that locate persons. Identities are often personal and political projects in which we participate, empowered to greater or lesser extents by resources of experience and ability, culture and social organization": Craig Calhoun, ed., *Social Theory and the Politics of Identity* (Oxford and Cambridge, MA: Blackwell, 1994) at 28.

Social theorists call our attention to the comparative, contingent, and political nature of identity, all of which are central to law and identity scholarship and to my argument concerning migration law and national identity. This body of scholarship also engages directly the tension between essentialist and constructivist accounts of identity that polarizes this theory. This debate is, for the most part, sidelined in legal scholarship for the reasons I suggested at the outset, and it is therefore not crucial to resolve the issue to give an account of law and identity scholarship. What is interesting, and possible, for legal scholars is to analyze the legal (and therefore social) constructions of identity, even if identity also has essential aspects. An identity-focused analysis of the law necessarily lines up on the constructivist side of the debate. The pitfall for legal analysts is not so much being entangled in the essentialist–constructivist debate that we are ill-equipped to navigate, but rather falling into a version of social constructionism that is completely circular. That is, we risk presenting an analysis in which law constructs society, which in turn constructs law, without providing any way to break the chain of "infinite regress."[9]

Peter Fitzpatrick's critique of this tendency in contemporary legal theorizing contains an important lesson for my theoretical framework, and at the same time a justification for its basic premise. He calls on legal scholars to use a constructivist method that embraces the lessons of deconstruction.[10] In particular, deconstruction is not simply a dissolution into nihilism but rather an analysis that reveals the process of making a particular construction. Deconstruction also serves to bring a construction into relation with others. With these two insights, Fitzpatrick calls for a social constructionism that makes a broad account of interpretation and the social, and within which dichotomous pairings such as power and agency, law and society, can be opened up to each other.

In the process of developing this critique, Fitzpatrick demonstrates the viability of bypassing the essentialist–constructivist dilemma. In his words, constructionism can be "rescued" from within rather than from an engagement with essentialism.[11] It is precisely this engaged constructionism that underlies my analytic framework here. While allowing that identity has an existence or even an essence *outside* the law, I examine its place within the law. Migration law and national identity have locations and relationships outside those that they share. However, looking at them as a pairing serves to highlight the ways in which each is constructed on an ongoing basis and

---

9 I borrow this term from Peter Fitzpatrick, whose argument I draw on throughout this section: Peter Fitzpatrick, "Distant Relations: The New Constructionism in Critical and Social Legal Studies" in Philip A. Thomas, ed., *Socio-Legal Studies* (Aldershot, UK and Brookfield, MA: Dartmouth Press, 1997) 145.

10 *Ibid.* at 158-59.

11 Or perhaps more accurately, it can be rescued from "beside" by deconstruction.

to reveal the relationship between the two. Accordingly, my framework aims at the two lessons of deconstruction that Fitzpatrick highlights. I do not assert that there is nothing to national identity beyond migration law, or the inverse, or indeed that one can causally account for the other. Instead, I argue that there is much to be learned about each from the other. This lesson is significant and underexplored. The claim need not be exaggerated. There is much to be learned in tracing the patterns and processes of a particular construction, such as migration law, and in demonstrating its relation to another, such as national identity.

Theorizing Law and Identity

My framework for analyzing the migration law–national identity relationship builds on the insights of the emerging body of law and identity theorization. Within this body of work, we find both a description of the law and identity relationship in differing contexts, and a critique of legal method. Both of these are important to my analysis, the first because given the place of migration law in the liberal nation, national identity is the most powerful variable for giving an account of this law's features, changes, and applications; the second because the law and identity critique of legal method is particularly useful for explaining how the "us" and "them" categories at the heart of migration law ground the functioning of diverse aspects of the law.

Legal analysts who use identity as an organizing concept in their work share the perspective that identity is not a fixed essence but a variable, a site of struggle, a contingent result of contestation over meaning. Thus, Martha Minow refers to "the negotiated quality of identities," and the "kaleidoscopic nature" of identity.[12] As identity is negotiated and malleable, it follows that there must also be at least the potential for multiple identities. Dan Danielson and Karen Engle argue that "in order to generate more effective legal strategies, legal consciousness should take account of the role of law in the constitution of identities and in the simultaneity of multiple identities and perspectives."[13] Elizabeth Mertz takes a similar position when she describes "the complex and mutually constitutive relationships that form between legal processes and social identities."[14] Duncan Kennedy takes an optimistic view of the role of an individual in negotiating identity, stating, "My view is that the identities celebrated both in modern multicultural rhetoric and in the traditionalist rhetoric of the mainstream are best seen as

12   Martha Minow, "Identities" (1991) 3 Yale J.L. & Human. 97 at 99 and 112 [Minow, "Identities"].

13   Dan Danielson and Karen Engle, "Introduction" in Dan Danielson and Karen Engle, eds., *After Identity: A Reader in Law and Culture* (New York and London: Routledge, 1995) at xiii [Danielson and Engle, *After Identity*].

14   Elizabeth Mertz, "Introduction to Symposium Issue: Legal Loci and Places in the Heart: Community and Identity in Sociolegal Studies" (1994) 28 Law & Soc'y Rev. 971 at 972.

'positions' or 'situations' within which people operate as free agents."[15] In theorizing the relationship between law and identity, identity is never a given. It is a question, an object of analysis. It is bounded, but its boundaries are to be explored and explained.

Putting identity at the centre of the inquiry into how law works does not, however, make it the end product or the dependent result of legal process. Rather, identity is in a middle position, neither a dependent nor an independent variable. It is, therefore, a useful concept for understanding both law's potential for social transformation and its inherent conservatism. When law requires the construction of an identity, it is always for some particular purpose. The dilemma is that of the particle physicist: if she seeks a singular entity, she will find one; if she calibrates her instruments to chart the motion of a wave, they will do so.[16] Any inquiry into law and identity must begin with the caution that law can both constrain identities and liberate them. Directing attention to identity, therefore, requires us to consider how this constraint or liberation operates, to investigate its mechanics. It also requires us to examine conditions under which law becomes either constrictive or liberating, and to analyze to what extent and by whom these conditions may be strategically manipulated. Migration is a highly politicized area of law at present and, as a consequence, political and public debate is directed towards manipulation of the identities shaped in this law. As I detail in the next chapter, migration law is structured to accommodate political ebbs and flows by easily constricting or expanding the national identity it portrays.

The assertion that law is implicated in the construction of identity belongs to a broader argument that law has a role in social construction. This argument has been taken up in diverse settings, but the subset of work that analyzes the law and identity linkage is probably the largest area. Alan Hunt has developed the most fully articulated account of a constitutive theory of law, drawing on theoretical trends in the sociology of law, the critical legal

---

15 Duncan Kennedy, *Sexy Dressing, Etc.* (Cambridge: Harvard University Press, 1993) at viii. He continues: "Of course, the freedom is relative to the position or situation. But freedom does mean that we sometimes get to choose how to handle things after taking our identities into account. It does not mean that we can get beyond contextual constraint and do or be anything we want. And we can also choose to be loyal and true to our constrained identity positions, choose to be as little free as possible."

16 Martha Minow expresses this conundrum this way: "I suggest that the question about the identity of a group ... will always be befuddling if it is detached from the purposes for which the question is being asked. Once the purposes are disclosed, the perspective of the inquirer and the perspective of the evaluator become critical. For some purposes, self-proclaimed identity will be most significant; for others, external community responses and understandings. But the perceptions of outsiders are not 'objective' or removed from the interests of the outsiders themselves": Martha Minow, ed., *Making All the Difference: Inclusion, Exclusion and American Law* (Ithaca, NY: Cornell University Press, 1990) at 355 [Minow, *Making All the Difference*].

studies movement, Marxist theory, and Foucauldian social theory.[17] A range of other contemporary legal scholars have worked on delineating the place of law in social construction, and this has been particularly important in analyses of American civil rights law. Hunt chastises critical legal scholars for failing to take theory seriously and for not paying sufficient attention to the problem of mediation, through which legal ideology and legal consciousness influence mass or popular consciousness. The question of mediation is one I take up throughout this book, by using a narrower theoretical framework than Hunt's, tailored to examining some legal discourses and some legal outcomes. Hunt argues that the "thesis that law both constitutes and is constituted has to be pressed further. In this form it verges on the vacuous."[18] This concern is important to me, as my analysis of migration law and national identity forms one response to it. I am concerned with *how* and *why* migration law contributes to an articulation of national identity and to the overt and subtle ways in which national identity in turn shapes the law.

In her influential voice, Patricia Williams has summarized the central role for law in building social delineations, arguing:

> Our system of jurisprudence is constantly negotiating the bounds of our communal civic body in the context of disputes about the limits of our physical edges (such as experimentation with fetal tissue, sales of body parts, and sterilization), the limits of identity (male–female, citizen–non-citizen, and so on) and the limits of life itself (wrongful death cases, right to die, and executions). Law negotiates these boundaries by constructing verbal guideposts and a whole range of representational lenses and filters through which we see each other.[19]

Her analysis highlights the central place of the law and identity relationship in legal accounts of social constructionism and also points to the role of an identity-focused critique of legal method. Most analyses of law and identity, as Williams indicates, focus on how the two are related within a "communal civic body." By moving the level of analysis to the question of national identity, my framework considers how the community itself is constituted. The boundary my work focuses on is that which is most often assumed or ignored – the one that delimits a sphere of relevance within which a "social" can be interpreted.

17   Alan Hunt, *Explorations in Law and Society: Toward a Constitutive Theory of Law* (London and New York: Routledge, 1993) at 149.
18   *Ibid.* at 175.
19   Patricia J. Williams, *The Rooster's Egg* (Cambridge, MA: Harvard University Press, 1995) at 230-31.

Another key theme in law and identity scholarship that I draw on to build my theoretical perspective is the insight that identity is relational. This perspective on identity, which can trace its roots to Hegel's philosophy and Lacan's psychoanalysis, is used in a relatively straightforward way in most legal analysis. One identity emerges only in contrast to another. This "other" is most frequently overlooked or submerged in legal reasoning. Attention to the way law constructs identities enables a consideration of these implicit others whose presence structures legal analysis. There are numerous examples of work taking this view as a starting point. Gary Peller, for example, points to the way the black civil rights movement in the United States drew attention to racial difference and the constructed nature of race and how, as a consequence of this, the constructed nature of white identity was also put at issue.[20] The relational aspect of identity is most often hidden, and is the object of inquiry for those exploring the identities created in law. In this vein, Martin Chanock challenges the assertion that the South African common law is racially neutral, arguing that, "the creation of self and the exclusion of 'other' is basic to the nature of South Africa's laws in a more fundamental way than simply in the passing of discriminatory statutes."[21] A theoretical focus on identity facilitates unearthing of the racism obscured by law's neutral and liberal language.

The relational nature and malleability of identity are also linked to the observer's expectations. In Martha Minow's account, identity is constructed both in contrast to another and in response to pre-existing expectations. In many legal instances, these two influences on identity will be combined; for example, when a refugee lawyer interviews a potential client for the first time, her assessment of her client's story will be influenced by her expectations based on other experiences with refugee clients and on her understanding of the legal category of "refugee," which will operate either as an "other" (because she assesses that the client does not fit within that identity) or as an expectation (because as the conversation continues, she forms the view that the client will be able to make a successful claim).[22] To examine identity in law is also to consider who is doing the identifying and how that process affects them, aspects that are raised as part of the identity-based critique of legal method.

---

20 Gary Peller, "Race Consciousness" (1990) Duke L.J. 758.
21 Martin Chanock, "Race and Nation in South African Common Law" in P. Fitzpatrick, ed., *Nationalism, Racism and the Rule of Law* (Aldershot, UK: Dartmouth Press, 1995) 195 at 197.
22 Minow uses a similar example in discussing the story of a guardianship application for a special needs child. She states: "The judge, the lawyers, and the parties in effect showed how an individual like Philip has an identity only in relation to others and how the description of his situation depends upon who is offering the observations": Minow, *Making All the Difference, supra* note 16 at 351.

The perceptivity of the relational nature of identity also brings insights when the image is inverted. This capacity to bring focus to the mirror image or silenced voice is vital to my use of identity. Marlee Kline's work on motherhood provides an example here, as she argues that "the expectations of 'good' mothering are presented as natural, necessary, and universal. The 'bad mother,' by corollary, is constructed as the 'photographic negative' of the 'good mother,' again with the operation of racism and other such factors rendered invisible."[23] The photographic negative metaphor is particularly apt as the assumed or implicit "other" is often hard to make out and is rarely the focus of attention. Pushing this analysis further, Michel Rosenfeld argues that the constitutional subject in American law can be approached and understood only in the negative, that it is much easier to determine what the constitutional subject *is not* than what it is.[24] His analysis depends on the relational nature of identity, as it requires that we understand the constitutional subject by looking at what it exists in contrast to – that is, that we develop the photograph from its negative. In my work, this perspective means that it is sometimes easiest to understand what it is to be Australian or Canadian by considering what it is not. This is a vital insight for assessments of national identity that are often contested or disavowed. While it is always difficult and contentious to "name" the characteristics of a nation or its people, the texts of migration laws reveal these, sometimes unknowingly.

The relational quality of identity makes it a key concept for considering national identity and migration law. Migration law is directed outwards, at those beyond the nation's borders. In labelling and controlling these others, it builds a reflected image of the nation and those who are insiders. In addition, the relational nature of identity makes it a good tool in the search for exclusions and silences in law. Paying attention to the identities that are represented in and through legal discourses reminds us to search for the others against which these identities derive their content. This perspective, therefore, draws attention to those most completely excluded by the law. This characteristic of identity creates an important intersection with legal reasoning, and is the key factor uniting several of the criticisms of legal reasoning examined in law and identity theory.

Identity's Critique of Legal Method

In addition to describing the contingent and relational nature of identity and focusing on how law positions it socially, law and identity scholarship also contains a critique of legal method. This critique is apposite for describing how law functions in the migration realm. In broad terms, the

---

23 Marlee Kline, "Complicating the Ideology of Motherhood: Child Welfare Law and First Nation Women" (1993) 18 Queen's L.J. 306 at 315.
24 Michel Rosenfeld, "The Identity of the Constitutional Subject" (1995) 16 Cardozo L. Rev. 1049.

argument is that legal reasoning is acutely categorical, and through its categorizations it creates, defines, and constrains identities. The categorization effect is related to the binary "either–or" mechanics of legal reasoning. The resulting categories have structured boundaries and are hierarchically related. Legal reasoning is also shaped by the identities of the individuals participating in it and the relative power they are able to deploy. I now consider each of these features in turn and how my empirical work draws from them.

Categorization

Legal reasoning has a binary structure. It works through a series of either–or choices, leading to an ultimate pronouncement in the same framework: guilty–not guilty, liable–not liable, eligible–ineligible. This structure alone is not unique. In legal reasoning, however, the process is simplified. There are ultimately only two alternatives, which are diametrically opposed to each other. Everything outside that narrow framework becomes irrelevant, either through formal rules of evidence and admissibility or through subtler techniques by which lawyers mould stories told to them about individuals into legal arguments. There is little room for compromise, for considering multiple alternatives, or for examining the ways in which the legal choices available obscure complicated situations. One of the most important skills learned by law students is how to analyze a complex hypothetical scenario and identify within it the legal issues arising. Instructors make an effort to pack exam questions with extraneous detail, imitating "real life," so that bright students can distinguish themselves by strategically jettisoning much of the story. The legal argument narrows the factors to consider, thereby making the question amenable to an either–or resolution. Patricia Williams describes this characteristic of legal reasoning when she argues that "theoretical legal understanding" in Anglo-American jurisprudence is characterized by "the hypostatization of exclusive categories and clear taxonomies that purport to make life simpler in the face of life's complication: rights/needs, moral/immoral, public/private, white/black."[25]

Binary categories are important to an identity-based analysis of legal discourse because so many of the categories are used to identify individuals. The white–black categorization that Williams refers to is only one of these. Other key legally bounded identities are innocent–guilty, sane–insane, adult–child. Each of these categorizations simplifies and fixes reality in an artificial way, particularly in cases at the margins: the woman who put a blouse in her shopping bag, forgot about it, and left the shop (not guilty), the hermit who mails explosives to distant cities in protest against civilization

---

25 Patricia J. Williams, *The Alchemy of Race and Rights* (Cambridge, MA: Harvard University Press, 1991) at 8 [Williams, *Alchemy*].

(sane), the fifteen-year-old who lives on her own, caring for her child and completing high school by correspondence (child). And each of these identity labels has consequences in the lives of these individuals, consequences that affect their realities, even if the labels do not accurately reflect those realities. In migration law, the principal distinction is between citizens and others, "us" and "them." Beyond this, however, migration law creates a long list of categorizations and corresponding entitlements for groups such as residents, visitors, foreign students, and refugees.

Hierarchy

The oversimplification of realities by legal categories has various effects. One of the most important of these is that the categories have a hierarchical relationship with each other. To use Minow's words: "When we identify one thing as unlike the others, we are dividing the world; we use our language to exclude, to distinguish – to discriminate."[26] Categorization in legal discourses rarely lives up to its assertion of neutrality both because of the consequences attached to legal categories and because the categories are frequently constructed through assumption of a background norm that is necessarily privileged in the process. The background norm, as an unstated category, occupies the most privileged position. The hierarchical nature of legal categories is embedded in the way they are formed and in who does the forming. While much of the analysis of categorization is linked to work on discrimination law, the argument is equally apposite to legal categories not already linked to discrimination. The labels "migrant," "citizen," "resident," and "alien" also contain an implicit hierarchy that derives from submergence of the point of view against which these labels are affixed.

Issues of voice, visibility, and hierarchy are all important aspects of legal reasoning that are brought to light by a focus on identity. Expressing a similar argument in the context of the law of intellectual and cultural property, Rosemary Coombe states that "only by situating these claims in this context [of historical experience and contemporary political struggle] can we understand how supposedly abstract, general and universal principles (like authorship, art, culture, and identity) may operate to construct systematic structures of domination and exclusion in ... society."[27] The hierarchical nature of legal categorizations, and the implicit background norms that ground them, make legal discourse particularly suited for domination and exclusion, and mask these effects at the same time. The critical perspective on legal reasoning employed by theorists of law and identity aids in lifting this mask.

26   Minow, *Making All the Difference, supra* note 16 at 3.
27   Rosemary J. Coombe, "The Properties of Culture and the Politics of Possessing Identity: Native Claims in the Cultural Appropriation Controversy" in Danielson and Engle, *After Identity, supra* note 13 at 276.

Boundaries

Law's categorical reasoning reifies boundaries. In order for categories to be meaningful, they must be clearly demarcated. An analytic focus on identity brings boundaries into question as identities themselves are bounded. The two terms often occur together, each highlighting a different aspect of the law's identity-labelling role. In migration law, which describes a border for the polity and specifies who may cross it, the concept of boundary is particularly important. In an overt way, migration law is about boundaries, and the identities that emerge on either side of them. Theorists concerned with law and identity consider ways in which identities are contested. One important way in which an identity can be contested is at its boundary – that is, whether one is inside or outside a given identity group can be debated.[28] The importance of boundaries in legal reasoning contributes to the inflexibility of the categories that are created. In Minow's analysis, the law has difficulty addressing conflicts within relationships because its focus is the boundaries between people rather than the relationships that necessarily emerge on either side of a boundary as an expression of that boundary. This insight is vital in adapting this framework to considering migration law.

Boundaries are also important because categorical reasoning relies on being able to treat certain questions as beyond the scope of inquiry or not at issue. That is, some things are clearly out of bounds. This mechanism works in many ways in the law, which also adopts and enshrines societal boundaries. Considering the law's methods for excluding and limiting, arguments often raise the issue of boundary construction.[29] An analysis of identity in the law, then, introduces the concept of boundary in considering the contested bounds of identity, and in doing so draws attention to other boundaries reified by the law. Both of these aspects of boundary are important to my study. Migration law establishes clear boundaries around identities such as citizen, resident, and visitor. It sets strict limits on categories such as

28 The other principal way in which identities are contested is through debates over the meaning or expression of the particular identity, treating group membership as settled; for example, asking "what does it mean to be a citizen?" These two types of contestations can, of course, occur at the same time.

29 For example, in considering the effectiveness, for the capitalist class, of the nineteenth-century distinction between "citizens" and "workers," Hunt, *supra* note 17 at 325, states:

There is a literal sense in which law, and most explicitly property law, demarcates and enforces boundaries; but this notion of boundary maintenance has wider significance. In the case of the workplace boundaries have special import precisely because of the critical significance of the division between work and politics within capitalist economies; it is here that there is the distinction between the incorporation of the working class within the polity while excluding workers from full participation in the workplace ... It is not that law creates this boundary but rather that once in place it is protected and reinforced by both legal ideology and legal practice.

"bona fide spouse" or "refugee," and provides tools for policing those bound-aries. It is the principal site for constructing the border or boundary of the nation, and the ways of crossing it. Migration law determines who is let in and who is kept out, and the categories that constitute explanations for these outcomes.

People

A consideration of law and identity also yields insights about individuals who engage the legal process, both as professional actors – lawyers, judges, scholars – and individuals seeking legal outcomes. The process itself limits the identities of the roles these individuals can play and determines which roles will be most powerful. The legal process does not determine identities of advocates, decision makers, or plaintiffs, but it limits the choices avail-able to individuals in these roles. Choice is also an important element in analyzing identities in the legal process. Those with more power exercise more control over the roles they play in legal processes and over the way their own actions will intersect with a set script for their role.

In considering law as narrative and asking lawyers to reflect on the stories told in and by law, Bellow and Minow aimed to raise questions about how identities are constructed, accommodated, and challenged by and for indi-viduals in legal practices.[30] They concluded that "as they engage a legal problem, clients and legal workers experience shifts in the ways they see themselves and others and changes in the way they relate to and are seen by others."[31] The form of legal reasoning means that one of a lawyer's most important tasks is to shape her client's identity into one that fits within a desirable legal category: not guilty, competent, refugee. In order to accom-plish this, some aspects of that identity must be highlighted, others down-played. In migration law, successful outcomes mean being able to fit a particular identity label such as "bona fide spouse" or "dependent relative."

The lawyers building these cases and the decision makers presiding over them also project and are limited by identities cast for them as professional roles. Unlike the clients, however, these are identities that the professionals choose for themselves, whose contours they are trained and socialized to acquire. The identities of the individuals playing out roles on legal stages are important to explaining legal outcomes, but the variance between these identities is sharp. It is important to consider the pattern of power relation-ships that underlie the emergence of particular identities. In Minow's words, "Who picks a given identity and who is consigned to it?"[32] One may "win"

30 Gary Bellow and Martha Minow, eds., *Law Stories* (Ann Arbor: University of Michigan Press, 1996).
31 *Ibid.* at 3.
32 Minow, "Identities," *supra* note 12 at 112.

a legal result by successfully fitting the identity mould of "incompetent" or "abused wife," but fitting this mould carries its own legal and non-legal consequences.

This again points to the intermediate positioning of identity as neither wholly determinative nor wholly determined. The value of examining the identities of individuals in legal processes, however, is not that it can necessarily predict outcomes for us but rather that it is instructive in showing how those with power over the process – the lawyers and judges – choose to construct themselves, and how the legal setting shapes the options they choose from. It also guides us in examining how legal discourse transforms one's experience of self into a legally mediated outcome. A theoretical perspective linking law and identity provides room, therefore, for considering these aspects of the legal process, as well as drawing critical attention to the categorical and hierarchical characteristics of legal reasoning. It also necessarily brings us to an engagement with one paradigmatic facet of legal reasoning: the role of rights.

Rights, Critics, and Identities

My analysis and use of an identity perspective can be situated within contemporary critical legal scholarship, particularly within the debate about rights. The "rights debate" is an argument among reasonably likeminded theorists – sharing the views that social transformation is necessary to achieve justice and that law has only infrequently been an important tool for just social outcomes – about the utility of rights for achieving social change. To grossly oversimplify, there are three types of responses to the question. The first is to argue that rights are the key tools for achieving legal milestones, and legal milestones are in themselves an important change. Few progressive theorists would make this response, for it is this classic liberal legal response that is the cause for a rights debate in the first place. A second type of response is to argue that rights are a potentially valuable tool for social change, but that they represent an engagement with the legal system that must be treated cautiously. Finally, another type of response is to state that rights claims are damaging to progressive causes because they narrow and depoliticize the terms of debate, they provide formal rather than substantive remedies, and they truncate further and better arguments for redress.

The first reason to situate my analysis of migration law and identity in relation to this debate is that much of the law and identity scholarship I draw on and refine has developed within this context. Responses to the central issue of rights utility are often framed in identity terms. Fudge and Glasbeek, for example, argue that contemporary "new social movements" lack political transformational power because of their focus on identity and their use of rights discourses.[33] Nitya Iyer similarly details her objections to rights discourse in identity terms. Considering the protected grounds formulations used in equality rights instruments, she argues that a category-based approach will always obscure the complexity of social relations and thus limit the possibility of redressing inequality.[34] In other words, the price to be paid for using rights instruments as a legal strategy is that the identities that can be portrayed in rights arguments are limited. Some aspects of social reality will be lost in the process, and some social realities will just not fit into the boxes provided. In Iyer's analysis, rights narrow identities and arguments about them in particular ways that are related directly to the centrality of rights discourse to legal discourse. In defending critical legal studies' strong critique of rights discourse, which embraces the positions seen in Fudge and Glasbeek's and Iyer's work, Robert Gordon links the "dangerously double-edged" rhetoric of rights to power differentials between individuals and to procedural constraints of the legal process.[35] Both these points are well-established themes in law and identity scholarship.

On the other side of the rights utility argument, an identity-based analysis is equally important to making the argument that rights have an enduring transformative role to play. Patricia Williams reasons, for example, that rights in themselves provide important markers of identity: "To be unrighted is to be disempowered, and the line between rights and no-rights is most often the line between dominators and oppressors. Rights contain images of power and manipulating those images, either visually or linguistically, is central in the making and maintenance of rights."[36] She links rights with the labels "dominators" and "oppressors," and suggests that rights are generally empowering and can be created out of nothing. Rights are associated with particular identities, dominator and oppressor, but this structure has built-

33 Judy Fudge and Harry Glasbeek, "The Politics of Rights: A Politics with Little Class" (1992) 1 *Social and Legal Studies* 45. At 61 they state: "The new social movements theory, then, seems to lack the underpinning of a normative theory, a prerequisite for any coherent form of politics. In this sense there appears to be a congruence between the politics of identity and culture and the furtherance of fragmentation which is valorized by the liberal state."

34 An example of the categorization she criticizes is the equality rights guarantee found in s. 15(1) of the *Canadian Charter of Rights and Freedoms*, which states: "Every individual is equal before and under the law and has the right to the equal protection and equal benefit of the law without discrimination and, in particular, without discrimination based on race, national or ethnic origin, colour, religion, sex, age or mental or physical disability." One of Iyer's points is that even when the list of categories of protection is open-ended, it is still a list and still categorically grounded: Nitya Iyer, "Categorical Denials: Equality Rights and the Shaping of Social Identity" (1993) 19 *Queen's L.J.* 179.

35 Robert W. Gordon, "Some Critical Theories of Law and Their Critics" in David Kairys, ed., *The Politics of Law: A Progressive Critique*, 3rd ed. (New York: Basic Books, 1998) 641 at 657.

36 Williams, *Alchemy, supra* note 25 at 233-34.

in flexibility. She concludes, therefore, that "the more dizzyingly diverse the images that are propagated, the more empowered we will be as a society."[37] Alan Hunt, who urges a strong role for rights in his constitutive theory of law, links the importance of rights to the way that identities coalesce around them: "Rights-in-action involve an articulation and mobilization of forms of collective identities. This does not imply that they need take the form of 'collective rights,' but simply that they play a part in constituting social actors, whether individual or collective, whose identity is changed by and through the mobilization of some particular rights discourse."[38]

Rights are a form of collective identity because a "right holder" necessarily designates a group of individuals, even when the right is expressed as an individual right. While rights are most often or most successfully asserted by individuals,[39] they belong to categories. The "accused," the "contracting party," the "plaintiff" can each exercise rights, but each of these legal categories can be filled by any individual whose identity is adaptable to the confines of the category. For those who assert, as Hunt does, that rights contain the potential for social transformation, the mechanics for such a transformation are therefore a manipulation of the identities of the right holder and the creation of new right-bearing identities, forming the dizzying array called for by Williams. Richard Delgado's response to critical legal theory's rights analysis is set in terms that draw directly on the principle that rights and collective identities are intertwined. In response to the criticism that rights atomize and isolate individuals, he asserts that for minorities, rights have been a "rallying point" and have formed "cloaks of safety."[40] The importance of identity is the crux of his call to critical theorists to understand that different groups see and use rights differently. The relationship between law and identity is vital to an informed reading of the rights debate, and hence to all progressive theoretical approaches to rights analysis.

The second reason to relate my work to the rights debate is that thoughtful engagement with the role of rights necessarily takes up the concepts that are central to my migration law framework. The importance of communities, boundaries, and identities is a marker of work in this area. In Jeremy Waldron's response to the critical legal studies assertion that a discourse of needs is a better tool for social change than one of rights,[41] he

---

37 *Ibid.*
38 *Supra* note 17 at 247.
39 Catherine Dauvergne, "A Reassessment of the Effects of a Constitutional Charter of Rights on the Discourse of Sexual Violence in Canada" (1994) 22 Int'l J. Soc. L. 291.
40 Richard Delgado, "The Ethereal Scholar: Does Critical Legal Studies Have What Minorities Want?" (1987) 2 Harv. C.R.-C.L.L. Rev. 301 at 305-6.
41 Waldron is responding specifically to Mark Tushnet's analysis in Mark Tushnet, "An Essay on Rights" (1984) 62 Tex. L. Rev. 1394.

maintains that the power of rights is found in their relationships with our understanding of "personhood [identity], citizenship, universality, community, and equality."[42] Each of these relationships is crucial to interpreting the migration law–national identity linkages in this book. The two are linked because of the concepts of citizenship, personhood, community, equality, and universality. Martha Minow's work similarly focuses on relationships and communities and how rights discourses mediate the two. Her attention to these aspects leads her to conclude that rights discourse is marked by a inherent instability, which derives from the idea that everyone enjoys the same rights but in some instances special rights are necessary to achieve equality.[43] The instability of rights discourse is part of Minow's analysis of how rights and the relationships and identities they encode come into conflict within communities. In drawing on this analysis, I look at how rights discourses are played out across the border of the national community creating the "us" and "them" of migration law. Considering the place of rights within liberal migration law taps into how the call for attention to the historical and contextual grounding of rights is part of the rights debate.

The third reason to engage the rights debate here is that much of the work of minority rights scholars that responds to the central tenets of critical legal studies, thereby marking out one of the key poles in this debate, focuses on exclusions. My argument is that migration law texts constitute community boundaries and are a principal and *prior* site of exclusion. There is much in migration law's repertoire of exclusion that is about race. Although the texts of many migration laws until the 1970s were more directly racializing than their contemporary counterparts, racialization and exclusion still coincide in many admissions regimes. Their coincidence is especially troubling in the humanitarian admissions that are my principal concern. Recent scholarship analyzing law and race highlights how exclusion, power, and identity are linked. Critical race scholars have been especially attentive to the strategic role of rights discourses, to understanding why rights discourses retain their relevance in the face of claims of indeterminacy.[44] These insights can be adapted to the consideration of migration law's role in exclusions and to an understanding of the place of rights discourses in migration law.

Finally, my analysis of humanitarianism, identity, and nation contributes to our understanding of the place and utility of rights. The conclusion

---

42 Jeremy Waldron, "Rights and Needs: The Myth of Disjunction" in Austin Sarat and Thomas R. Kearns, eds., *Legal Rights: Historical and Philosophical Perspectives* (Ann Arbor: University of Michigan Press, 1996) 87 at 108.

43 Minow, *Making All the Difference, supra* note 16 at 108.

44 One leading example of this is Mari Matsuda's argument that critical legal scholarship could enhance its analytic power by considering the perspectives of those who have experienced exclusion and discrimination: Mari Matsuda, "Looking to the Bottom: Critical Legal Studies and Reparations" (1987) 2 Harv. C.R.-C.L.L. Rev. 323.

that humanitarian admissions to prosperous nations are legally outside of, and in opposition to, a rights discourse, is one of the principal contributions of this framework. The key planks in the argument that leads to this understanding of humanitarianism and its relationship to identity, and especially national identity, are the hegemonic *right* of a liberal nation to close its borders – a right at the boundary that therefore trumps all others – and the situation of *nation* within a liberal and not-yet-post, modern paradigm. I develop these two aspects of the argument over the next two chapters. Overall, my reading of migration laws asserts a limited role for rights because of the power they encode. Nonetheless, close attention to rights and the identities that they assist in constructing tells us much about how and why this power is embedded in the law. These insights are among the most important insights of identity in building strategies to change the shape of our law.

3
Nation and Migration

This chapter describes the framework for my analysis linking migration law and national identity. The framework builds on the insights of identity outlined in Chapter 2 and adds an understanding of nation that draws on recent scholarship about nations and on a scrutiny of the place of migration law provisions in liberal communities. One approach to the national identity–migration law relationship is to reflect on the ways that migration has been used in the construction of the "New World" nations. This history presents many ways of approaching the analysis of migration law and national identity: it gathers together elements of "truth" and of "myth"; it contains aspects of law; it encodes relationships between differing parts of the world. Adding to this story, the insights of identity draw attention to the silencing and "othering" that are also part of the story, and to the role of law in constructing the categories and boundaries that this mythology relies upon.

This framework is constructed in three phases. I consider the implications of contemporary understandings of nation for the relationship between nation and law. I then consider the place of migration laws in liberal communities, drawing on a parallel strain of scholarship in which the nation and the liberal community are coterminous. These two aspects of my analysis are complementary. The logic of liberal legalism is vital for understanding the functions of persistently modern migration law. While the nation remains elusive and contested, its political importance is intertwined with the hegemonic sway of liberalism. The boundaries that are established by migration laws are made sense of within a liberal framework, and debates about changes to these laws often take place within a broad liberal consensus, even though individuals participating in the debate are not necessarily committed to liberalism themselves. In the final part of the chapter, I combine the first two, as well as the identity scholarship in Chapter 2, to outline a framework for interpreting the linkages between migration law and national identity. The special place of humanitarianism in this framework is so vital to both the theoretical analysis and the empirical aims of the book that it is presented separately in Chapter 4, rounding out Part 1 of the book.

Nation, Myth, Law

Nation persists. In the last few decades of the twentieth century, two scholarly trends challenged the endurance of nation as a conceptual category. First was the insistence in disciplines such as political science and international relations on emphasizing state rather than nation, or on compromising through the use of the couplet "nation-state." Among those who considered nation itself, the threat to its persistence was in highlighting the fragility of nation with attention to its instability, its fragile or nonexistent foundations, and most recently its contingent nature. Employing the term "nation" at this point in time, therefore, requires some attention to these challenges. My choice of the concept is grounded in the reason for its persistence – the occasional and recurring importance of national identity, even for those individuals most likely to deny it.

The political nation is a product of modernity, emerging in Enlightenment Europe and solidified by the 1648 Treaty of Westphalia. The early twenty-first-century era of globalization is marked by challenges to the vitality and sovereignty of the nation, which may be markers of an imminent passage from modernity to a postmodern era.[1] Whether this may be the case is not yet clear. The political alignments of modernity centring around nations and states in turn remain dominant. Scholarly interpretations of nation were once dominated by ethnic primordialism – a view that a nation was and could be only a group united by history, culture, and place. This understanding of nation probably still retains a commonsense appeal, particularly in its association with the nationalisms of post-communist Europe. An ethnic-centred view of the nation has also been dominant in Canadian scholarship, where the "two nations" thesis has been an influential explanation of the French and English relationship within Canada.

This scholarship gave way in the 1980s to a reading of nation as nonprimordial, but instead as mythological, symbolic, or imagined. These readings of nation are central to understanding how law, in its own resolute

1 Whether the capacity of the nation or, more often, the nation-state is eroded by globalizing forces is one of the most significant debates among theorists of globalization. Kenichi Ohmae argues that the nation-state has already become redundant, in Kenichi Ohmae, *End of the Nation State* (London: HarperCollins, 1995). Paul Hirst and Grahame Thompson argue that the nation's capacity is altered but not removed, in Paul Hirst and Grahame Thompson, *Globalization in Question,* 2d ed. (Malden, MA: Polity Press, 1999). Linda Weiss asserts that nations are stronger than ever, in Linda Weiss, *The Myth of the Powerless State: Governing the Economy in a Global Era* (Cambridge: Polity Press, 1998). I have surveyed globalization theory in "Sovereignty and Illegal Migration" in Catherine Dauvergne, ed., *Jurisprudence for an Interconnected Globe* (Aldershot, UK: Ashgate Press, 2003) 187.

modernity, is linked with nation. They are also vital to an understanding of what more recent readings of nation have contributed.

Anthony Smith's influential work is at the border of primordial interpretations and those that turn entirely to a non-ethnic explanation. Smith asserts that all nations have at least some ethnic component and argues that "conceptually, the nation has come to blend two sets of dimensions, the one civic and territorial, the other ethnic and genealogical, in varying proportions in particular cases."[2] Smith categorizes nations into those based primarily on territory and those based primarily on descent, and argues that nations without ethnic cores must "re-invent" them.[3] While he states that myth and memory are the sine qua non of nation, he never departs from the view that an ethnic core is associated with true nationhood. He implies that any reinvented ethnicity cannot be as successful in defining nation as an ethnicity with established historical roots in a "homeland."[4] In his 1991 analysis, he described America, Argentina, and Australia as "being formed through an attempt to coalesce the cultures of successive waves of (mainly European) immigrants" rather than as fully established nations, revealing his commitment to a partial primordialism despite his emphasis on myth.[5]

Among the other luminaries of nation, however, primordialism has no place at all. Hobsbawm argues that while an ethnic base may be necessary for nationalist movements, it is not sufficient to create a nation, and "not essential for the formation of national patriotism and loyalty once a state has been founded ... Nations are more often the consequence of setting up a state than they are its foundation."[6] Hobsbawm makes the important point that the concept of nation is bound up with the idea of mass participation. In his words, "whatever else a nation was, the element of citizenship and mass participation or choice was never absent from it."[7] This, then, becomes part of the story of why nations emerged at the beginning of the modern

2 Anthony D. Smith, *National Identity* (London and New York: Penguin, 1991) [Smith, *National Identity*].
3 Anthony D. Smith, *The Ethnic Origins of Nations* (Oxford and New York: Blackwell, 1986) *passim* and at 212.
4 For example, he states that in the struggle against decentralization and ethnic–national forces, "state elites employ the tactic of 'bureaucratic nationalism': they claim that their state constitutes a 'nation,' and the nation is sovereign and therefore integral and alone legitimate, with the result that nationalism becomes an 'official' doctrine and the nation is taken over by the territorial and bureaucratic state": *ibid.* at 221.
5 Smith, *National Identity, supra* note 2 at 40. This core of Anthony Smith's analysis persists in his more recent work; see, for example, *Myths and Memories of the Nation* (Oxford and New York: Oxford University Press, 1999) and *Nationalism: Theory, Ideology, History* (Cambridge, UK, and Malden, MA: Polity Press, 2001).
6 Eric J. Hobsbawm, *Nations and Nationalism since 1780: Programme, Myth, Reality,* 2d ed. (Cambridge: Cambridge University Press, 1992) at 78 [Hobsbawm, *Nations*].
7 *Ibid.* at 19.

era, as a sense of political consciousness at a mass level emerged. Hobsbawm concludes that the formation of nations required a massive exercise in social engineering, which he terms "the invention of tradition" because modern nations claim to be, *but are not,* rooted in antiquity.[8] He claims that because the modern "nation" consists of so many invented or constructed components and is associated with so many recent symbols and "suitably tailored discourses (such as 'national history'), the national phenomenon cannot be adequately investigated without careful attention to the 'invention of tradition.'"[9] In Hobsbawm's words, "the force of the sentiments which lead groups of 'us' to give themselves an 'ethnic'/linguistic identity against the foreign and threatening 'them' cannot be denied."[10]

Importantly for my analysis, Hobsbawm links the emergence of American national identity to massive migration to the United States: "Americans had to be made. The invented traditions of the USA in this period [1870-1914] were primarily designed to achieve this object."[11] Migration law and its associated rituals, such as border examinations and oath swearing, is one vital site for the invention of tradition. It is also an important location for the construction of "us" and "them" images. These images are bound up in the existence of the nation at its broadest political level, and also in the experiences of the individuals pledging and saluting.

Benedict Anderson's account of nations as imagined communities is perhaps the best known among this late-twentieth-century turn in scholarship. Drawing on a detailed historical examination of South American nations, Anderson describes nation as "an imagined political community – and imagined as both inherently limited and sovereign."[12] Anderson's use of "imaginary" as a descriptor of the national community is important for linking nation and identity on both the individual and the collective planes. He asserts that "all communities larger than primordial villages of face-to-face contact (and perhaps even these) are imagined. Communities are to be distinguished, not by their falsity/genuineness, but by the style in which they are imagined particularistically – as indefinitely stretchable nets of kinship and clientship."[13] In Anderson's analysis, the administrative arrangements that fostered a collective imagining, along with the printing technology that made the mass spread of information possible, were vital

---

8 Eric J. Hobsbawm, "Introduction" in Eric J. Hobsbawm and Terence Ranger, eds., *The Invention of Tradition* (Cambridge: Cambridge University Press, 1983) at 13-14.
9 *Ibid.*
10 Hobsbawm, *Nations, supra* note 6 at 170.
11 E.J. Hobsbawm, "Mass-Producing Traditions: Europe 1870-1914" in Hobsbawm and Ranger, *supra* note 8, 263 at 279.
12 Benedict Anderson, *Imagined Communities: Reflections on the Origin and Spread of Nationalism,* rev. ed. (London and New York: Verso, 1991) at 6.
13 *Ibid.*

in assuring that nations coalesced as imagined communities in South America before they did in Europe.

The importance of these key readings of nation is their success in reinterpreting the nation away from ethnic origins, and in providing an account of the persistence of nation beyond its European origins, an account that therefore could make sense in settler and postcolonial societies as well. This shift is vital in understanding the relationship between law and the nation, and in understanding national identity as distinct from nationalism. If nation were a mere alternate to ethnicity, it could not develop the relationship with law that is central to understanding both terms. If nation were primarily an institutional form of ethnicity, national identity would not make sense for nations such as the United States, Australia, and Canada.

The influence of postmodern social theory points up, however, that despite their focus on the invented, the symbolic, and the mythological, these interpretations persist in reifying the nation, in treating it as an existing and coherent collectivity.[14] For Anderson, Gellner, Hobsbawm, and, most especially, Smith, the persistence of nation is explained partly by its existence, even if no one were to pay it attention. The role of mythology, tradition, and collective imagination are important to my reading of nation in relation to migration law because of the evocative appeal of the image they create. I also draw, however, on a newer reading of nation that calls attention to its constructed, contingent nature. Interpreting nation in this way provides the closest parallel to law and identity scholarship. A focus on identity calls our attention to boundaries and relationships across those boundaries. Coupling this with nation calls our attention to how the nation itself, and national identity, are constituted by the presence of a boundary. Reading nation with attention to its incoherence and its contradictions does not require that we jettison the role of mythology, tradition, or imagination. Instead, it requires reinterpreting how and why these function in diverse political settings, how they are contradictory or incoherent, how they are constructed, and what lies behind their construction. It is precisely these kinds of ruptures that are necessary to understanding migration laws across their legislative, executive, judicial, and administrative settings. In its persistence, nation clings to modernity. It is appropriate, therefore, to consider how late modern readings of nation retain their relevance.

14 This view is elaborated by Brubaker in William Rogers Brubaker, *Nationalism Reframed: Nationhood and the National Question in the New Europe* (Cambridge: Cambridge University Press, 1996). Peter Fitzpatrick also makes this point, particularly in relation to Anderson's analysis that labelling the nation as an imagined community fails to account for the widely and readily recognized existence of nations "even with the manifest absence of a commonality of consciousness": Peter Fitzpatrick, *Modernism and the Grounds of Law* (Cambridge: Cambridge University Press, 2001) at 117 [Fitzpatrick, *Modernism*].

Brubaker's analysis of nation grapples with how to "reconceptualize" the reality of nationhood in order to focus on it as a conceptual variable that is not a real collectivity but instead an institutionalized form, a practical category, or a contingent event – and possibly all three.[15] Brubaker does not dispute "the reality of nationhood,"[16] nor by implication its analytic importance, but he urges that those who study nation endeavour to avoid "unintentionally *reproducing* or *reinforcing* th[e] reification of nation in practice with a reification of nations in theory."[17] This caution is one I engage directly in my analysis through the argument that migration law is a particular site where manifestations of nation are likely to be present. The relationship between migration law and the nation is mutually constituting, but not exclusively so on either side of the equation. Migration law is a site where nation comes into being as practical category and an institutionalized form, and where events giving rise to nation-ness occasionally erupt. One such eruption was the saga of the container ship *MV Tampa* in August and September 2001. Despite directing the rescue of a group of asylum seekers making their way to the Australian territory of Christmas Island from Indonesia, Australian authorities then refused the boat entry to their territorial sea. The *Tampa* story was played out in Australian courts, in a national election, and in international forums, each evoking and altering the meaning of the Australian nation.[18]

The relationship between law and nation is not limited to migration law. Law and nation are intertwined in many ways, each depending on the other for its present shape. One of the transformations of the nineteenth century that made the state the main arena for most activities was the standardization of administration and law throughout states. The existence of administrative, and hence legal, units in the Americas was key to the emergence of a sense of nationhood in those states, in Anderson's analysis. Today we make the assumption that law is associated with nation; that when we say "the law," we mean the law in the place we are speaking of. Speaking of law that is not national requires a qualifier, as in "international law," "Islamic law," "the common law," and "customary law." Peter Fitzpatrick expresses the relationship this way: "Modern law necessarily clings to nation as its epitome. From the early nineteenth century, law is seen as definitely attached to a rigidly demarcated national territory and as expressing the interests of a particular nation."[19] Both law and sustaining myth are important

---

15 *Ibid.* at 16.
16 *Ibid.*
17 *Ibid.* [emphasis in original].
18 I have written about the *Tampa* in "Making People Illegal" in Peter Fitzpatrick and Patricia Tuitt, eds., *Critical Beings: Law, Nation and the Global Subject* (Aldershot, UK: Ashgate Press, 2004) 83.
19 See Peter Fitzpatrick, "Introduction" in Peter Fitzpatrick, ed., *Nationalism, Racism and the Rule of Law* (Aldershot, UK: Dartmouth Press, 1995) xiii at xv [Fitzpatrick, *Nationalism*].

to the emergence of nations. This equation highlights the mythic dimension of law,[20] that law is interwoven in the way we imagine our world and our place in it. When we talk about what it means to be an American or an Argentine, thus tapping into the mythic dimension in which those identities exist, we also tap into the legal framework that provides those places with borders and constitutions, with citizens and with rights. Law, therefore, is deeply implicated in the essence of the nation. It provides the baseline mechanical criteria for the existence of a state, and it is one source of the unifying mythology that provides staying power for the state by instituting a sense of nation. This is true of all law associated with the state, of which migration law is a highly visible instance.[21]

The delineation of a universe of meaning works in both directions in the law-and-nation pairing. The nation and the law each provide a setting in which the other is meaningful. In Fitzpatrick's analysis, this is because both law and nation are marked by a tension between the universal and the particular. Both aspire to be universal, but need to have a limit, a particularity, in which they can be meaningful.[22] He describes their relationship as one of "complementarity," in which law and nation each provide an essential missing element to the other.[23] Fitzpatrick draws on identity to articulate the law-and-nation relationship: "The irresolution of nation's identity is 'overcome' by law, and the irresolution of law's identity is 'overcome' by nation."[24] This interaction is most easily observed in those areas where law addresses nation overtly: constitutional law and migration law. Both are sites where constituting the nation is the transparent concern of the law. While these areas of the law overtly aim to delineate a universe of meaning with national limits, the meanings they generate work below the surface as well.

The coexistence of law and nation is crystallized in considering the place of First Nations[25] when discussing migration law and national mythology,

---

20 On this point, see Peter Fitzpatrick, *The Mythology of Modern Law* (London and New York: Routledge, 1992), especially c. 2, "Law as Myth."

21 Joel Migdal asserts that law is one of three crucial areas of state and society relations that ensure the endurance of state structures in the face of increasing globalizing forces. He argues that this is in part because "much of what law – state and others – does is delineate a universe of meaning for people": Joel S. Migdal, "Why Do So Many States Stay Intact?" in Peter Dauvergne, ed., *Weak and Strong States in Asia Pacific Societies* (Sydney: Allen and Unwin, 1998) 11 at 26.

22 These themes have been explored by Peter Fitzpatrick in many settings. For a recent and comprehensive analysis, see Fitzpatrick, *Modernism, supra* note 14, especially c. 4, "Nationalism."

23 *Ibid.* at 129.

24 *Ibid.*

25 The emotive power of the word "nation," its imagery of sovereignty and unity, is seen when the term is taken up by groups seeking to evoke that mythology. The terms "black nationalism," "queer nation," and "deaf nation" make this political statement. In the Canadian political context, an important example of the use of "nation" is the term "First Nations" to refer to Canada's indigenous peoples. The accuracy of the term

for, salubrious linguistic innovation notwithstanding, the aboriginal peoples of both Canada and Australia are absent from the mythology of these "nations of immigrants." Using the latter phrase explicitly denies the presence of the First Nations. The myth of a nation of immigrants is intertwined with visions of conquering a vast and empty land, and of "peopling" it with people from elsewhere, primarily Europe. Until very recently, this myth was supported by the legal doctrine of *terra nullius*,[26] itself overturned only once its true usefulness had passed – that is, once the spread of European civilization was so complete that even removing its own account of self-justification could not threaten its hegemony. Despite the fears raised in some quarters by the *Wik*[27] decision in Australia that large tracts of land would be returned to traditional owners to the detriment of the now dominant population, and the prospect of massive compensation payments following *Delgamuukw*[28] in Canada, both Australia and Canada are nations of immigrants because the mythology and law that make them nations belong to these immigrants. The First Nations are first in linguistic retrospect only. The silence to which the mythology of migration law and of nationhood confines aboriginal peoples speaks its own powerful truth. These spaces were overtaken by migrants and made into nations by migration. Migration law and the mythology it engenders reflect the historical and legal oblivion that indigenous peoples in these nations are now railing against.

Another aspect of nation is territory. A nation is also a piece of land, a space on a map. Even in this territorial dimension, however, both law and myth are implicated. The border that encloses the nation, that gives effect to the imaginary lines separating one nation's rocks and trees and fish from those of another, is a legal one. It is migration law that determines who can cross that line and under what conditions. It is migration law, therefore, that imbues that line with meaning in human terms. The territory of a nation is vitally bound up in its mythology. We cannot *think* Canada without also thinking of the cold, the rugged terrain of the Canadian Shield, the

---

is undeniable, highlighting the historical precedence of the indigenes and emphasizing that white Canada has had a negligent tendency to think of all indigenous people as one cultural group rather than many independent peoples. The successful integration of the term into popular Canadian discourse is in part due to the clarity its use brings in referring to groups such as the Assembly of First Nations (the largest national council of leaders) or the Saanich Nation or Gitskan Nation (where "nation" is an alternative to "people" or the legislatively created "band").

26 This doctrine was rejected by the Australian High Court in *Mabo v. Queensland (No. 2)* (1991), 175 C.L.R. 1. The rejection was finalized in the Supreme Court of Canada in *Delgamuukw v. British Columbia*, [1997] 3 SCR 1010 [*Delgamuukw*].

27 *Wik Peoples v. Queensland* (1996), 141 A.L.R. 248 (H.C.A.) [*Wik*]. In *Wik*, the High Court held that a pastoral lease would not necessarily extinguish native title to land. The decision was followed by an intense and acrimonious debate and by legislation restricting the reach of the Court's ruling.

28 *Delgamuukw, supra* note 26.

immense stretch of wheat-filled prairie, the North that stretches all the way to the pole. The word "Australia" raises a cloud of red dust in the mind, along with, incongruously, long stretches of sandy beach and an endless blue horizon. The Bush, which is not bushy but dusty and dry, is woven into the mental landscape of even those Sydneysiders who have never been further than twenty kilometres from the ocean. Thus, even conceiving of nation in purely geographic terms, we confront the importance of law and myth to understanding it.

Nation and Identity

An individual's national identity is her sense of belonging to a nation, of being a part of a political, territorial, and mythic unit. It is also the image of the nation projected in its mythology, presumed in this mythology to be shared by the putative collectivity. This image is reified, enshrined, and adapted each time a politician appeals to national sentiment or an opinion leader calls on the populace to act as "good Australians." It is tested and refined each time a diplomatic delegation represents "Japan" in an international forum. National identity functions in all these dimensions simultaneously. Anthony Smith defines it as "complex and abstract," "fundamentally multi-dimensional ... it can never be reduced to a single element, even by particular factions of nationalists, nor can it be easily or swiftly induced in a population by artificial means."[29] Hobsbawm makes the point that while it is widely accepted that a mass level "national consciousness" accompanied the emergence of nations, little is known about what that meant to the masses involved.[30]

It is crucial in linking national identity to the incoherence and contradictions of nation to recall that any individual's identification with a given group may not be the most significant aspect of their identity – or even part of their self-identity – at any given point in time. This comes to the fore in discussing Australian and Canadian identity because many people in each place assert that other identities are more important to them most or even all of the time, and undoubtedly some never think of national identity at all. This does not necessarily mean, however, that they do not have a sense of national identity that could become important in some situations. It may be that they only subjectively identify as Australian when unexpectedly jailed in a foreign country or when detained at a border crossing.

The situations in which most individuals *would* strongly assert their national identity lead to two points. The first is that national identity and nationalism are related but not indistinguishable phenomena. Nationalism has a political agenda, and has often been associated with an ethnic

29   Smith, *National Identity, supra* note 2 at 14.
30   Hobsbawm, *Nations, supra* note 6 at 130.

identity.[31] As nationalism requires this element of ideological commitment, it becomes an important aspect of an individual's self-identification in different settings than national identity. By talking about Australian or Canadian national identity, I do not mean a commitment on behalf of a mass of the population to advance a particular set of interests, nor do I mean patriotism. Rather, I mean that most individuals in these places, who are not visitors or temporary residents of some sort, locate themselves in the world with some reference to the mythic dimensions of the Canadian or Australian nation. I mean that these individuals can make sense of a politician's exhortation to support the Aussie battler or to make sacrifices in the name of Canadian humanitarianism. Aleinikoff gives an example that draws out the extent to which national identity and sense of self are interwoven:

> Imagine that you awake one morning to find that your American citizenship has been taken away. What springs to mind? That travel to Europe may be difficult without an American passport? That no country will seek your release if you become a hostage overseas? That it will be impossible to vote in the next presidential election? I doubt that any of these issues are on the top of your concern list. More likely you feel violated, naked. You ask, how can I not be an American? What am I, then? A part of oneself is gone.[32]

This illustration is valuable because it contrasts those situations where most people would likely consciously claim their national affiliations and the foundational level at which individuals integrate a sense of national identity into their understanding of self. In the not-yet-post modern world, it remains difficult to imagine ourselves as individuals without national attachments.

The second point raised by the apparent "weakness" of Australian and Canadian national identities is that, as emphasized in the literature on law and identity, identity emerges in contrast to an "other." Even someone who rarely feels Canadian and who would argue that their Canadian identity is of no importance to their life, would likely claim to be Canadian at a border crossing or in a war zone. Fitzpatrick makes the point that for a nation to exist, there must be others, and because of this, the nation exists in a relationship with those others: "As universal, the nation can have no positive

31 Smith defines nationalism as "an ideological movement," which captures what distinguishes it from national identity: Smith, *National Identity, supra* note 2 at 73. He acknowledges that the term has led to as much confusion as "nation" itself. Brubaker categorizes nationalisms as nationalizing, external, and minority, which also serves to clearly demarcate nationalism and national identity: *supra* note 14 at 4-5.
32 T. Alexander Aleinikoff, "Theories of Loss of Citizenship" (1986) 84 Mich. L.R. 1471 at 1495-96.

limits and would, without more, lack identity ... This dynamic of identity inevitably results in the 'failure' of the nation as universal. The nation must exclude the other – and so be non-universal – in order to be universal."[33] Migration law is a discourse that brings nation and the other into contact, thereby creating images and reflections of each. It is therefore a logical site to find representations of national identity – of the nation and of the other.

Liberal Limits

Migration law is an important site in searching for an understanding of national identity both because it is an interface between insiders and others and because of the specific role that migration law plays in liberal thought. My assertion here is that liberal theory is the most important body of political theory in which to locate the nation and its migration laws. There are three reasons for this. First is that the idea of nation emerged historically alongside that of liberalism and the two have been interrelated, mutually adaptive, and persistent since that time. Second is that the two types of nation for which this framework is most important are settler societies and states with established immigration programs which are predominantly liberal regimes in the contemporary world. Third is that even states that do not currently have, or have never had, a liberal governing regime are part of an international system that is shaped by liberal values. This is increasingly so given current globalizing trends.

The importance of migration law to settler societies, or nations of immigrants, is obvious in one sense. In cases where the majority of those who constitute the dominant culture and the elite of a nation consider themselves to have come from elsewhere, migration law plays a primary role in determining who those people, and therefore the culture and the elite of the nation, will be. Migration law literally constitutes the community, setting out the rules for who will be members of the community, who will be eligible to become members, and who will be excluded.

For Australia and Canada, and for other settler societies such as Argentina, the United States, and New Zealand, immigration and the law regulating it have been central concerns of nation building from the outset. While the migration law of settler societies may today resemble similar provisions in other countries, the role of this law in nation building and national mythology is very different. Brubaker makes this point in introducing his comparative study of European and North American migration laws: "There is a basic difference between nations constituted by immigration and countries in which occasional immigration has been incidental to nation-building. Canada and the United States have a continuous tradition of immigration.

---

33 Peter Fitzpatrick, "'We Know What It Is When You Do Not Ask Us': Nationalism as Racism" in Fitzpatrick, *Nationalism, supra* note 19, 3 at 10.

They were formed and reformed as nations through immigration, and immigration figures prominently in their national myths."[34] The building of a national identity for immigrant nations requires the integration of the experience of migration into national mythology. Discussing the role of English constitutional law in the construction of New Zealand, Kelsey writes that "creating the settler nation required something more. Its boundaries had to coincide not just with a particular territory, but with a given people who constituted a *nation* – an entity which would provide the sources of their identity and the sole legitimate object of their political allegiance."[35] In settler societies, migration law and the mythology constructed in and around it is a prior condition to the community. As such, it is *foundational,* and constitutes the community in a way that *constitutional* law alone cannot.

Migration law is a prior foundational element to constitutional law because nations are established on a liberal model and liberalism presumes the existence of communities and assumes those communities to have closed borders.[36] Rawls theorizes justice within an imagined society that he describes as a "closed system isolated from other societies."[37] Individuals enter the community at birth and leave at death. It provides "a complete self-sufficient scheme of cooperation, making room for all the necessities and activities of life ... citizens do not join voluntarily but are born into it, where ... we assume they are to live their lives."[38] Dworkin's community of principle is marked by its closed borders and clear distinctions between insiders and outsiders.[39] He asserts: "We treat community as prior to justice and fairness in the sense that questions of justice and fairness are regarded as questions of what would be fair or just within a particular political group."[40] Walzer confronts the issues of membership in the liberal community more directly than Rawls or Dworkin, and argues that the question of membership precedes that of justice. While membership is the chief good to be distributed by a community, it is not subject to the constraints of his distributive justice model.[41]

---

34 William Rogers Brubaker, "Introduction" in Williams Rogers Brubaker, ed., *Immigration and the Politics of Citizenship in Europe and North America* (Lanham, MD: University Press of America, 1989) 1 at 7 [Brubaker, *Immigration*].

35 Jane Kelsey, "Restructuring the Nation: The Decline of the Colonial Nation-State and Competing Nationalisms in Aotearoa/New Zealand" in Fitzpatrick, *Nationalism, supra* note 19, 177 at 183 (emphasis in original).

36 I elaborate this argument in Catherine Dauvergne, "Beyond Justice: The Consequences of Liberalism for Immigration Law" (1997) 10 Can. J.L. & Jur. 323.

37 John Rawls, *Theory of Justice* (Oxford: Oxford University Press, 1971) at 8.

38 John Rawls, "Justice as Fairness: Political Not Metaphysical" (1985) 14 Philosophy and Public Affairs 223.

39 Ronald Dworkin, *Law's Empire* (Cambridge, MA: Belknap Press, 1986).

40 *Ibid.* at 208.

41 Michael Walzer, *Spheres of Justice: A Defense of Pluralism and Equality* (New York: Basic Books, 1983); see c. 2, "Membership."

Various theorists have made arguments extrapolating liberal tenets to the migration law context, but there is little agreement about whether liberalism requires open borders or closed borders.[42] The only point of agreement among liberals is that borders must be opened to the extent required by humanitarianism.[43] These features of liberal theory have two important consequences for migration law. The first is that liberal theory does not give a standard by which we can assess how many migrants, if any, a society that grounds its moral consensus in liberalism must admit. This contributes, from both an international and a domestic perspective, to the view that immigration and the nation's sovereignty are directly linked. The power to control migration is directly associated with sovereignty.[44] In the common law tradition of the United Kingdom, powers over migration questions derive from the prerogative powers of the Crown. This strong association with the Crown as the legal symbol of sovereignty is reflected in a number of migration law doctrines.[45]

This linkage is hardly surprising for a type of law over which the executive retains close control and that falls outside democratic theory. Unlike other laws in a democracy, migration law regulates primarily those outside

42   Walzer argues that closed borders are required for justice: *ibid.* Donald Galloway also argues that liberalism supports a closed border position: see "Liberalism, Globalism and Immigration" (1993) 18 Queen's L.J. 266, and "Strangers and Members: Equality in an Immigration Setting" (1994) 7 Can. J.L. & Jur. 149. For a contrasting view, see Joseph Carens's various articles, including "Aliens and Citizens: The Case for Open Borders" (1987) 49 The Review of Politics 251; "Membership and Morality: Admission to Citizenship in Liberal Democratic States" in Brubaker, *Immigration, supra* note 34; "Refugees and the Limits of Obligation" (1992) 6 Public Affairs Quarterly 31; and "Who Belongs? Theoretical and Legal Questions about Birthright Citizenship in the United States" (1987) 37 U.T.L.J. 413.

43   I discuss this in detail in Catherine Dauvergne, "Amorality and Humanitarianism in Immigration Law" (1999) 37 Osgoode Hall L.J. 597. Walzer and Galloway both take this position, and Carens reinforces this as a minimal requirement. See also John A. Scanlan and O.T. Kent, "The Force of Moral Arguments for a Just Immigration Policy in a Hobbesian Universe" in Mark Gibney, ed., *Open Borders? Closed Societies? The Ethical and Political Issues* (New York: Greenwood Press, 1988); Peter Singer and Renata Singer, "The Ethics of Refugee Policy" in M. Gibney, *ibid.*

44   Indeed, for some writers control over the border and the population is the crux of sovereignty itself. See, for example, David Jacobson, *Rights across Borders: Immigration and the Decline of Citizenship* (Baltimore and London: The Johns Hopkins University Press, 1995); Christian Joppke, "Why Liberal States Accept Unwanted Immigration" (1998) 50 World Politics 266; Kim Rubenstein, "Citizenship in a Borderless World" in Anthony Anghie and Garry Sturgess, eds., *Legal Visions of the 21st Century: Essays in Honour of Judge Christopher Weeramantry* (The Hague: Kluwer Law International Publishers, 1998).

45   This is the cornerstone of Stephen Legomsky's explanation for the inordinate deference of British and American courts to immigration decisions of the executive. See Stephen H. Legomsky, *Immigration and the Judiciary: Law and Politics in Britain and America* (New York and Oxford: Clarendon Press and Oxford University Press, 1997). See further discussion in Chapter 6 at pp. 157-61.

the polity, either because they are seeking entry or because they do not have the full political membership symbolized by citizenship. The usual democratic arguments in support of laws – that they reflect the will of the people, that they have been passed in a constitutional manner by duly elected representatives, that the government has a legitimate mandate to enact them – are applied in the migration law context in a fashion that again points to the role of migration law in the liberal nation. The interests that are reflected through the democratic calculus in the migration law of a democratic nation are those of the members of the nation, of people who already clearly belong to that polity. Migration law serves their needs and regulates others, outsiders, to achieve that end. Those the law applies to do not democratically approve it.

The second consequence of liberalism for migration law is that humanitarianism dominates theoretical discussions of migration, even though the vast majority of immigrants to those nations with established migration programs are not admitted on a humanitarian basis.[46] This feature of liberal theory is taken up in Chapter 4, as it is vital in shaping liberal migration laws and the public discourse that surrounds them.

The absence of a liberal justice standard for immigration decision making means that migration laws can be assessed only in terms of the values they inscribe along the "us–them" line – the things they tell us about ourselves. The boundary that migration law provides for liberal immigrant nations serves the needs of those polities in various ways. In the first instance, it is crucially bound up in the identity of the nation because it constitutes the community for which questions of justice and equality will be meaningful. It draws the line between "us" and "them," bringing an "us" into being. The sovereignty of the nation thus conjured means that this boundary can be manipulated to serve its needs. At one level, this is what is at stake when immigration levels are raised to boost the population, or when skilled migrants are recruited to a given sector of the economy. In a less overt way, however, the us–them line is manipulated to serve more deeply submerged needs of the "us" group. The humanitarianism that is enmeshed in liberal migration law nourishes images of the nation as powerful and good. The line between insiders and outsiders serves to galvanize national identity and unify disparate views. The boundary provides convenient scapegoats in times of high unemployment or stress on the public purse. In order to meet these diverse needs, migration laws have particular characteristics.

As the needs of the nation with respect to migration are changeable, in response to conditions within the country and interpretations of what those conditions mean, the boundary of the nation must, as a first priority, be malleable. At the same time, it retains an appearance of stability required in

46 See Appendix A.

its role as limit of the nation. The image of the other, the outsider, is manipulated in order that the reflected picture of those who belong can appear constant. In this way, changes in migration law help ensure that national identities have some constancy. Fitzpatrick comments on the malleability of the nation's limits: "The ruptured or radical double marks the point of constant, and unmediated exclusion, the point of ultimate alterity. The protean double is forever in transition from such ultimate alterity to the realized pure form of nation."[47] Migration law, which is renowned for its frequent changes in both Australia and Canada, achieves this through its stated aims and its structure. In both these places, the objectives of legislation are open enough that contradictory actions can come within them, and crucial determinations about how the law will be put into practice are buried in the regulations or in executive fiat.

The Identities Emerging
The boundary provided by migration law facilitates the emergence of "us" and "them" identities on either side of that line. This process is a vital concern of law and identity theory. The boundary line acts as a reflecting mirror, in which we can see, depending on our vantage point, images of ourselves – whomever we are – and images of the excluded "aliens." These images necessarily exist together. While migration law is not the only site for finding images of a nation's members and the excluded outsiders, it is important because of migration law's constitutive role in the national community, and it provides particularly clear reflections because it brings insiders and outsiders into close proximity. Members and others are intertwined in the text of a migration law, and in each of its applications. The policy statements in the Canadian *Immigration and Refugee Protection Act* provide a powerful example. While the law itself is directed almost exclusively towards outsiders, the objectives refer overwhelmingly to Canada and Canadians.[48] Canada has a social and cultural fabric, minority language communities, a *Charter of Rights and Freedoms,* and humanitarian ideals. The aims of the act carefully portray an image of Canadians; the outsiders targeted by the law are absent.

The identities that emerge around the boundary are a function of that boundary itself and of what migration law aims to achieve. Edward Morgan states: "In a nutshell, the goal of the legal process, in the immigration context, might be said to be to distinguish between peoples – to differentiate

---

47 *Fitzpatrick,* "'We Know What It Is When You Do Not Ask Us': Nationalism as Racism" in *supra* note 19 at 11.
48 This was also true of the *Immigration Act,* R.S.C. 1985 c. I-2, which controlled immigration from the late 1970s until June 2002. The expanded objectives provisions of the new legislation include some references to those affected by the law that the former legislation did not.

citizens from foreigners, or "us" from "them" – in a world of supposedly undifferentiated persons to whom human rights are due."[49] Different aspects of our identity become important in different settings; in migration law, national identity becomes key. But this effect at the level of legal discourse is supported by our own non-legal, non-analytic experiences of feeling more Canadian when we are abroad, or cheering reflexively for each Australian athlete in the Olympics.[50]

Migration law also reflects some of the tensions that Australians and Canadians feel about their national identities; some of the ambiguities and uncertainties are echoed in contradictory legal provisions and frequent shifts. Morgan states:

> In domestic and international legal discourse, aliens are a reflection of ourselves. Ultimately, it is because we cannot focus on a single, determinative self-conception that we cannot in a determinate way pronounce on the stature of foreigners caught up in our legal system. At one moment we think of ourselves as individuals, undifferentiated in nature, and therefore, rights, from the universe of persons whom the state might happen to confront. At the very next instant, we conceive of ourselves as nationals, with a differentiated stature from each polity's members that accords with the separate existences and equal rights enjoyed by the world's nations. Since we are simultaneously human persons and national peoples, it is little wonder that aliens are both included and excluded from our norms. They are our mirror image.[51]

Morgan captures a key feature of the us–them distinction here. While the outsider is a reflection of "us," it is a difficult identity to pin down and describe because our own self-perception is ever shifting. This parallels the point that migration law is highly flexible to accommodate unceasing reshaping of the national interest. It is a text in which both nation and identity are in flux.

Understanding the role and relationships on either side of a boundary is always easier when the boundary is absolute. Migration law provides a boundary, but also ways of crossing it. Crossing the boundary is particularly

---

49 Edward M. Morgan, "Aliens and Process Rights: The Open and Shut Case of Legal Sovereignty" (1988) 7 Wis. Int'l L.J. 107.
50 Martha Minow expresses this feeling this way: "Encounters with people of more varied ethnic, racial, religious and class backgrounds challenge an individual's sense of self and community. Perhaps identity becomes important when it becomes a question, and it becomes a question when individuals and groups are mobile and able to change some of their identifying traits. When people come in frequent contact with others unlike themselves they can both heighten and submerge their sense of distinctiveness": Martha Minow "Identities" (1991) 3 Yale J.L. & Human. 97.
51 Morgan, *supra* note 49 at 147.

important for nations of immigrants. In addition to the "us" and "them" identities ensconced in migration law, other identity categories emerge. "Temporary" or "permanent resident," "refugee," and "visitor" are common labels, and each nation with an ongoing migration program generates its own variations. These identities provide bridges between us and them. They also ensure that some who are *inside* remain firmly identified as *outsiders*. This ensures that making the boundary relatively easy to cross will not erode its role in providing a reliable and predictable limit to the community.

Reading Border Laws

Three elements contribute to my framework for reading migration laws: the critical insights of law and identity scholarship; an understanding of nation as a contested element that relies upon myth, tradition, and symbol (often mediated by the law); and an appreciation of how liberal assumptions underpin both nation and migration. A critical focus on identity provides an ideal avenue of inquiry into migration law. The term "identity" brings with it the insights of analysis of the role of law in social construction and the pedigree of critical race studies. Both of these aspects enrich an examination of migration law. The first does so because migration law is quite literally essential to the construction of nations. It puts a border around the community, constituting those for whom laws will be meaningful. In settler societies such as Australia and Canada, this role is enhanced, as they have been peopled by individuals who have entered the community through provisions in the migration law, or, more rarely, in spite of provisions in the migration law prohibiting them. In either case, migration law is the newcomer's first encounter with the nation, and the label it puts on an individual provides a context for their life within that country. Further, as liberalism provides no justice standard against which migration laws can be assessed, exploring the contours of the national identifications these laws construct is the best way of assessing the provisions. Although we cannot conclude that a given law is just or unjust in a traditional liberal sense, we can state what the law leads us to conclude about the nation, about what Australia and Canada value or find meaningful. This mapping is important to making future policy choices, and to understanding the persistent failure of political consensus that surrounds migration law.

Crucially, identity is neither determinative of the law nor determined by it, but an intermediate position. To make use of this insight, we must consider why it is so and how this position means that the law can be manipulated. Migration law is not the only source of national identity, even in settler societies. It is a site that reflects aspects of that identity, but that is also well adapted to accommodating changes in identity perceptions that occur elsewhere. At an individual level, the consequences of conforming to "refugee" or "entrepreneur" identity are always complicated and are only ever a starting point for one's experiences within the nation. The identity labels of migration law code particular power dynamics, but also interact with other sources of power. Migration law communicates some messages about the values of being Australian or Canadian. It is also transformed and affected, in both its letter and its interpretation, by values and perspectives from other arenas of national public life. Migration law reflects a picture of how the nation identifies itself, and in doing so reifies those aspects of national identity. To accomplish this role in the nation, migration provisions are highly malleable, accommodating and masking shifts in the national interest. Law and identity literature focuses on the fluid and negotiated quality of legally constructed identity, which is so central to this setting and thus is ideally suited for this framework.

The association of legal identity analyses with critical race studies brings an important perspective to an examination of migration laws because these laws are designed to discriminate and to exclude. Migration law is a bold expression of the sovereign power of the nation, and of its absolute ability to control, to choose, who will be admitted to the community. This function is *discriminating* in the most neutral sense of the word. But it is much more than that as well. The histories of immigration to Australia and Canada are replete with overt racial discrimination. At present, the racial and gender biases of migration laws are obscured by genuine improvements compared with past practice and by neutral language. By putting identity in the centre of the analysis, the discriminatory effects of the law can be laid bare. The concerns of identity politics are appropriately raised in studies of migration provisions. The role of migration law in silencing and excluding some experiences remains important.

Analyses of law and identity have also been used to explore implications of categories, hierarchies, and boundaries in legal reasoning. This analysis is incisive in migration law, which is both overtly and implicitly involved in creating clearly bounded categories hierarchically related to one another. In migration law, where categories and boundaries are so patently exposed, it is crucial to push this analysis of legal reasoning further. Doing so allows us to examine not only the label on a given category, such as refugee or temporary worker, but also the subtle ways in which this label moulds the identity and therefore the experiences of the individual who either chooses or is consigned to that label. Careful attention also gives us information about the society itself that generates these categories. The boundary created by migration law reveals much about those who erect it around themselves. The essential us–them hierarchy is replicated in a multitude of binary categories that make up the day-to-day functioning of migration law. Rights discourse is also of pressing importance in the migration law context, which forces the confrontation between members' rights and the potential human rights of outsiders. The discourse of rights in migration law is diverse and contains lessons that move beyond a monolithic understanding of the roles and functions of rights.

The term "identity" enriches the study of nation because a nation is anchored in part in individual beliefs and in part in mythology. National identity, the sense an individual has of belonging to a particular geopolitical configuration, is a modern phenomenon. But the state as a collective or formal government apparatus does not have a sense of self – a sense of identity; this can belong only to individuals. What is labelled national consciousness is generated through individual identification with symbols and myths portraying the nation. Migration law is implicated in this process in several ways. For Australians and Canadians, New Zealanders and Americans, part of our understanding of self consists of belonging to a nation of immigrants, of people from all corners of the world who have gathered in search of a better life. This is, at its core, a migration myth. Migration law also expresses images of ourselves and of our collective values. It contains definitions of "family," of "skilled," of "deserving." These definitions portray us to the world at large and also perform a double reflecting function. They reflect already existing beliefs and they reify those beliefs against further change. In this way, the identities in migration law are neither determined nor determining, but have a role to play in both processes, depending on the evolution of societal beliefs.

A focus on law and identity also highlights two central aspects of liberal theory. The emergence and importance of the sovereign nation is historically intertwined with the dominance of liberalism as an individual and political philosophy. The sovereignty of the liberal nation is nowhere more clearly expressed than in its control over its borders and its membership. The closed community that functions as a base assumption of liberal theorists is the working model for modern nations. The ability to determine who will be let in, both territorially and to citizenship, is a closely guarded power of the state. By considering how the state exercises this power, we can trace imprints of how the state identifies itself and its members.

In addition, liberalism is the basis for the association of humanitarianism with migration law. The role of humanitarianism in migration law is complex. The liberal consensus that some individuals ought to be given the assistance of prosperous nations is one factor providing for the international consensus that refugees are "owed" some protection. But this consensus is closely framed by the nation's sovereignty and carefully constrained by national goals and domestic political imperatives. Thus, there is an ongoing tension in the nation's desire to be perceived as humanitarian and good yet firmly in control of its sovereign borders. The humanitarianism of migration laws is the hardest part of the migration law–national identity puzzle to fit together. But in liberal analyses of borders, and in terms of international legal provisions, it is the most demanding of attention. Humanitarianism is the only real challenge to population control as the last bastion of sovereignty in global times. I consider it fully in the next chapter.

4
Humanitarianism and Identity

In Chapter 3, I examined liberal approaches to questions of immigration and concluded that liberalism does not produce a justice standard for assessing immigration provisions. One consequence of this is that immigration laws are tied directly to the "us" and "them" identities that are related to each other by the national boundary and that are given shape within migration law texts. Family immigration, for example, reveals much about the values, priorities, family identities, and exclusions of the "us" group. Economic migration conveys a picture of current needs and market valuations of individuals, of what is good for our economy. Humanitarianism is easily perceived at first instance as being an exception to this principle. This first impression is incorrect, however. Rather than weakening the national identity–migration law linkage, humanitarian admissions confirm and reinforce it. Understanding humanitarianism is vital to understanding the particular role that humanitarian admissions play in established migration systems, in understanding how migration laws project liberal tenets in the absence of a justice standard, and in understanding why political debates about immigration are likely to remain intransigent.

For all these reasons, this chapter is the heart of this book. It sets out the most challenging elements of the theoretical framework, which in turn ground each of the empirical illustrations in Part 2. This chapter examines what I have named the humanitarian consensus in the liberal debate about whether a community's borders ought to be open or closed. It then considers the consequences of this consensus for migration laws by looking at the how humanitarianism can be pragmatic or political and how it relates to internal standards of justice. Finally, it explores the meaning of humanitarianism and looks at how it is related to other aspects of migration.

The Humanitarian Consensus
Liberal theorists agree that a just nation must open its borders to some

needy outsiders. This agreement is articulated differently in the work of closed-border theorists than in the work of those advocating open borders. The various ways that this humanitarian commitment is expressed are important to understanding its role in migration laws and its relationship to national self-identifications. It is also useful to consider how the rhetoric of humanitarianism masks other issues, and historical shifts, in migration to Australia and Canada.

For Walzer, whose seminal work *Spheres of Justice* presents a comprehensive defence of closed borders as a necessary condition for the just liberal community, the principle of mutual aid generates particular duties to admit some outsiders.[1] Acknowledging that the requirements of mutual aid are indeterminate, Walzer argues that the duty to provide mutual aid arises in cases of need or urgent need and when the risks or costs of providing such aid are relatively low.[2] While this duty can sometimes be met by yielding territory – that is, by changing the geography rather than the composition of the community – or by exporting wealth,[3] the needs of some outsiders are for membership itself and can therefore be met only by allowing them to join the community.[4] The guidance that this principle provides to the hypothetical liberal community is limited because Walzer asserts that at some unspecified point, the community will be justified in closing its borders even to those who have a need for membership itself. The community faced with more needy outsiders than it can admit ought to then choose from among them on the basis of their connection with the community – that is, there is a higher obligation to those whose plight we are responsible for[5] or who are persecuted because they are like us in some way.[6] Walzer's principles for humanitarian admission are thus limited to those who cannot

---

1 Michael Walzer, *Spheres of Justice: A Defense of Pluralism and Equality* (New York: Basic Books, 1983); see especially c. 2, "Membership."
2 *Ibid.* at 33-34.
3 Massive increases in foreign aid are often hypothesized as the just alternative to massive increases in migration to prosperous Western nations. This is part of Walzer's argument as well. What these arguments ignore is that the political sentiments opposing open borders are equally opposed to implementing increases in foreign aid. Louis Michael Seidman discusses this in "Fear and Loathing at the Border" in Warren F. Schwartz, ed., *Justice in Immigration* (Cambridge and New York: Cambridge University Press, 1995) 136 at 142 and following [Schwartz, *Justice*].
4 Walzer, *supra* note 1 at 48.
5 The culturally specific and necessarily dated example that Walzer refers to are Vietnamese refugees: *ibid.* at 49.
6 Walzer distinguishes between refugees and asylees by referring to refugees as those who have not yet entered the nation and asylees as those who meet the neediness standard that triggers the mutual aid principle and have already entered the country. The obligation to asylees is higher because "its denial would require us to use force against helpless and desperate people, and because the numbers likely to be involved, except in unusual cases, are small and the people are easily absorbed": *ibid.* at 51.

be assisted in other ways and who can be admitted with little impact on the community.

Not surprisingly, given both the minimal and the indeterminate nature of this commitment, most Australian and Canadian contemporary humanitarian admissions policies fit within these theoretical parameters. Walzer concludes that "the principle of mutual aid can only modify and not transform admissions policies rooted in a particular community's understanding of itself."[7] In Walzer's communitarian analysis, admission policies and community identity are, predictably, linked directly.[8] Turning to other, avowedly non-communitarian perspectives, however, this link remains crucial. Furthermore, while I agree with Walzer that humanitarian admissions can modify a community's understanding of itself, this modification is always accompanied and superseded by the nation's identity as humanitarian. This is the point I will return to after examining some other perspectives on the duty to admit needy outsiders.

Galloway's articulation of this argument is important because he advocates closed borders without embracing communitarianism.[9] In Galloway's view, the liberal state ought to function as a "self-help device for moral individuals."[10] It is this function of the state that leads to the requirement that some humanitarian migrants must be accepted. While the state is morally free to close its borders to claims raised from outside, when its own members seek the admission of outsiders as a fulfillment of their own personal moral duties, then the state ought allow these admissions. He summarizes the proposition this way:

> It may be the case that some members of a community rightly identify it to be their moral duty to render assistance to an alien in need, not by giving that person money or other resources, but by providing shelter and a human support network. If the state prevented the admission of people for whom provision would be made by a member, it would be hindering that member's

---

7 *Ibid.*
8 Coleman and Harding take a similar communitarian position, arguing that political communities are entitled to exclude because of their characteristics as communities, in Jules L. Coleman and Sandra K. Harding, "Citizenship, the Demands of Justice and the Moral Relevance of Political Borders" in Schwartz, *Justice, supra* note 3. They also assert that "refugees have a right to immigrate" (at 46). Their conclusions are based on a survey of current immigration laws and policies in eight nations. Their assertion of a right to immigrate does not accord with international law: see Chapter 5 of this book.
9 Galloway asserts that "closed borders are consistent with 'pure' [rather than communitarian] liberalism": Donald Galloway, "Liberalism, Globalism and Immigration" (1993) 18 Queen's L.J. 266 [Galloway, "Liberalism"]. Galloway's analysis of liberalism in immigration law is further developed in "Three Models of (in)Equality" (1993) 38 McGill L.J. 64; and in "Strangers and Members: Equality in an Immigration Setting" (1994) 7 Can. J.L. & Jur. 149.
10 Galloway, "Liberalism," *ibid.* at 294.

fulfilment of her moral duty. A liberal would be justified in criticizing an immigration scheme which did not allow for private sponsorships.[11]

In Galloway's analysis, the commitment to humanitarianism draws its principal support not from the need or other characteristics of those seeking to be admitted but from the individual moralities of those who are members of the community. The identity that matters in this equation is that of the member, not that of the outsider. This demonstrates another aspect of humanitarianism that figures in my analysis. For Galloway, the personal moral duty to assist an outsider through physical support that could not be provided outside the community tells us something about the morality of the individual who holds this duty. That individual is someone we would call good, generous, or even (erroneously) selfless. This level of moral commitment is higher than what is required of members of the liberal community that Galloway describes, and would necessarily, in his analysis, be outside the norm.[12] Humanitarianism is more than is expected, more than justice demands; it tells us several things about those who offer it and little about those who receive its benefits.

The assertion that liberalism mandates open borders, on the other hand, begins from the commitment to individual freedom and equality. With these values as a focus, the open-borders position is treated almost as a self-evident presumption by some theorists. Frederick Whelan expresses the logic of the argument this way: "It seems clear from the outset that a moral theory that sets out to attend to the claims of all human beings as such, on an equal basis, is going to have some difficulty in justifying borders that set off groups of people from each other and act as barriers to the free movement of individuals."[13] This assertion is most acceptable when liberalism is treated as primarily a moral rather than a political theory, a distinction that Whelan explores in some detail.[14]

---

11 Galloway continues: "Insofar as there are citizens who are willing and able to provide for needy aliens, and who are also able to satisfy the needs of their dependants, it is incumbent on the liberal state not to create barriers which would impede them in their attempt to provide the conditions of autonomy to foreigners": *ibid.* at 295-96.

12 If it were not outside the norm, his defence of closed borders would be internally inconsistent on this standard. This moral commitment crosses what James Fishkin describes as the threshold of heroism: James Fishkin, *The Limits of Obligation* (New Haven, CT: Yale University Press, 1982). See further below at pp. 65-66.

13 Frederick G. Whelan, "Citizenship and Freedom of Movement: An Open Admission Policy?" in Mark Gibney, ed., *Open Borders? Closed Societies? The Ethical and Political Issues* (New York: Greenwood Press, 1988) 3 at 7 [Gibney, *Open Borders*].

14 Whelan argues that liberalism requires that communities have open borders, but when combined with communitarianism, statism, or democracy, closed borders are morally justified: *ibid.* The problem with Whelan's approach is that it divorces liberalism from political context, while it is only in political context that questions of immigration can arise.

For those who advocate open borders to the liberal community, humanitarianism obviously plays a different role in the analysis, as it is not treated as an exception to what is otherwise the rule. Interestingly, however, the open-borders position is often supported through a detailed argument precisely about humanitarianism. Carens is one of the most prolific and theoretically thorough of the open-borders advocates.[15] His argument that liberalism supports open borders draws on his claim that utilitarian, Rawlsian, and Nozickian versions of liberalism converge upon this point and that the argument is further supported by extrapolating Rawls's original position device to the international plane.[16] While his analysis of Nozick's argument is not grounded in a humanitarian argument, it is by considering admissions of a humanitarian character that he builds his conclusions about Rawls and about utilitarianism. Regarding the former, Carens urges that considering the Rawlsian principles of the priority of liberty and the perspective of the worst-off, we would be compelled to admit at least those whose liberty was not protected in their current situations as well as the worst-off of the potential migrant pool.[17] That is, we would be compelled to admit those who in our current migration regimes are considered to be classic political refugees and destitute humanitarian claimants. For the latter, Carens argues that when the greatest good of the greatest number is calculated, particular attention must be paid to those outsiders to the nation who have the most to gain from entry. When their good is entered into the calculus, it is hard to deny admission.[18]

This argument is also concerned with the type of admission that is usually provided for in the various humanitarian categories, rather than under family or economic migration programs. Carens's argument that borders should generally be open,[19] even to those who do not raise humanitarian

---

15 Aspects of this position are elaborated by Joseph Carens in "Aliens and Citizens: The Case for Open Borders" (1987) 49 The Review of Politics 251 [Carens, "Aliens"]; "Open Borders and Liberal Limits" (2000) 34 International Migration Review 636; "Refugees and the Limits of Obligation" (1992) 6 Public Affairs Quarterly 31 at 25; "Migration and Morality: A Liberal Egalitarian Perspective" in Brian Barry and Robert Gordon, eds., *Free Movement: Ethical Issues in the Transnational Migration of People and Money* (University Park, PA: Pennsylvania State University Press, 1992); "Membership and Morality: Admission to Citizenship in Liberal Democratic States" in William Rogers Brubaker, ed., *Immigration and the Politics of Citizenship in Europe and North America* (Lanham, MA: University Press of America, 1989) 31; and "Who Belongs? Theoretical and Legal Questions about Birthright Citizenship in the United States" (1987) 37 U.T.L.J 413. His book *Culture, Citizenship, and Community* (Oxford: Oxford University Press, 2000) takes up other, related concerns.
16 Carens, "Aliens," *ibid.* at 258.
17 *Ibid.* at 260-62.
18 *Ibid.* at 262-63.
19 Carens would allow the least possible restrictions if the sheer numbers seeking admission threaten national security: *ibid.* at 260.

claims, is grounded in the same liberal consensus about humanitarian admission that I am sketching here. In arguing the case for open borders, it is not the spectre of wealthy jet-setters with multiple citizenships, or of investors with financial interests around the globe, that forms the backdrop for the argument. Rather, this argument draws on the emotive power of vast disparities in wealth between nations in the world and the assumption that many people in poorer countries would prefer to live in more prosperous states.[20] To make their case, open-borders advocates appeal to the humanitarian impulse, even though most contemporary migration to prosperous Western nations is approved on family reunion or economic bases and has little to do with humanitarianism.

Peter and Renata Singer offer yet another perspective on the open-borders position that draws strongly on a humanitarian setting. Their version of the utilitarian calculus is that the doubling of refugee admissions to prosperous states could continue for a considerable time before the benefits to those being admitted would outweigh any detriment to the community.[21] In its extreme, this argument is of course controversial and suggests a commitment to radical global redistribution of wealth.[22] Their more modest view is that Walzer's mutual aid principle ought to be viewed much more expansively and that our understanding of "need" should ground a considerable increase in admissions for permanent settlement even with no alterations to family or economic migrant categories. Where their argument parallels Carens's is in its use of the established humanitarian consensus as a building block in an argument for far-reaching change.

The tension in the liberal debate about closed or open borders parallels the central tension in liberalism that James Fishkin considered to constitute the limit of liberal obligations.[23] The immigration debate in liberal societies provides an example of Fishkin's thesis that the core liberal commitments to impartiality and individuality are in unresolvable conflict. The attractiveness of general obligations, of the idea that we are bound to all other individuals through a minimal duty of mutual aid (in Fishkin's terms, "minimal altruism"), is the core of liberal morality. To each person we have a minimal duty to save their life when the cost to us of doing so would be negligible. Yet on a large scale, even such a minimal obligation pushes us to accept heroic personal sacrifice, sacrifice that liberalism's commitment to individual autonomy will not countenance. Fishkin relied on donations to

---

20 The closed-border argument draws on this image as well, of course, to vastly differing ends.

21 Peter Singer and Renate Singer, "The Ethics of Refugee Policy" in Gibney, *Open Borders, supra* note 13 at 111. Their argument is a literal example of lifeboat ethics.

22 To this extent it echoes Carens's view that birth in a prosperous Western nation is the modern equivalent of feudal privilege: Carens, "Aliens," *supra* note 15 at 251-52.

23 Fishkin, *supra* note 12.

famine relief as his primary reasoning device, but the open-borders argument has the same features. The early-twenty-first-century debate about immigration law in liberal democracies takes place against the often unstated, but potentially quite truthful, spectre of millions of individuals wanting to become members of these wealthy societies. At some point, far, far beyond existing immigration quotas in these nations, admitting more people would decrease the standard of living of existing members.

To accept that immigration should be permitted until living conditions have been equalized throughout the world is surely, in Fishkin's terms, a heroic stance. A similar equalization of living standards is postulated at one extreme of the famine relief scenario. Fishkin bases his call for a re-examination of liberal morality on this tension between liberalism's dual commitments to equality and to limits on individual moral sacrifice.[24] The two principles check each other, with the result that we do not require heroism as a standard of moral behaviour and we permit moral individuals a robust sphere of indifference, within which their choice of whether to respond compassionately to those in need is "free" in that it is morally neutral. The border argument fits well on the central axis Fishkin describes: the open-borders argument emphasizes impartiality; the closed-borders position emphasizes the limits to individual sacrifice that are inherent in individualism.

The intractability of the argument, and the central tension in liberalism it mirrors, do not justify rejecting liberal discourse about immigration as a source of insight. Liberal hegemony in domestic and international political spheres requires that we seek to understand immigration debates in liberal terms. The limits of liberal theorizing about immigration are important to this debate. Because international order is built on a liberal infrastructure and the prosperous countries attracting aspiring immigrants are liberal democracies, debates about immigration law and policy use liberal terms whether they take place in the political arena, the supermarket, or the university lecture theatre. Efforts to move the argument away from liberal theory, to a framework where questions of justice could perhaps be more easily answered, lose their resonance in the face of liberalism's hegemony. Real consequences for members of a society, and for new and would-be immigrants, happen more often in the political arena and the supermarket than in the lecture theatre. In the international arena, liberal hegemony means that immigration questions are tightly bound up with state sovereignty. In this context, understanding the contours and limits of liberalism's humani-

---

24 He states: "This argument also has a further implication for political theory in that the overload problem exemplifies the incompatibility, at the large scale, of two central components of liberalism: (a) impartiality or 'equal concern and respect' and (b) individualism. Notions of impartiality ... press us towards acceptance of general obligations. Notions of individualism require, or implicitly assume, limits on the moral demands which can be made of each individual": *ibid.* at 170.

tarian consensus is important to being able to structure arguments that will resonate within that consensus and thereby gain political purchase.

Consequences for Justice

The intractability of the closed-borders–open-borders debate and the humanitarian consensus that accompanies it have in turn shaped liberal thinking about fair immigration rules. In the absence of a justice standard that spans the border, this thinking moves in two directions: first, to emphasizing the pragmatic value of humanitarianism, and second, to the development of "internal" justice standards.

One important avenue of thinking is represented by those who assert on a pragmatic basis that the value of humanitarianism requires that more needy people be admitted to prosperous nations, regardless of our views about the ultimate morality of borders. This argument emphasizes humanitarianism and therefore reveals something about its meaning, and also provides an agenda for political action by taking sovereignty as a given and seeking ways to manipulate politics within that framework.

Writing of the American setting, Scanlan and Kent articulate this position fully. They argue that while liberalism requires open borders, implementing such a policy is politically impossible.[25] They claim that a call for shifting immigration policy on the grounds of a liberal conception of justice will be ever unsuccessful. Rather, given the paramountcy in American culture of the rhetoric of political freedom and human rights, arguments that focus on the these types of claims by migrants will garner support. In other words, Scanlan and Kent assert that only humanitarian rhetoric will support a shift in the law in the United States and other claims, regardless of their philosophical soundness, will fail to win sufficient political support. In their view, those who advocate expansion of admission quotas would do best to draw on the well-established "myth of American generosity."[26] That is, they advocate enhancing and then courting the humanitarian self-identification of the liberal nation.

Seidman's argument that any serious analysis of migration law and policy must take account of the limits of our capacity for empathy is similarly positioned. He argues convincingly that our capacity to care is partially associated with physical location within our borders.[27] Given the curious nature of our compassion – that it seems to diminish at our borders – the politically possible humanitarian option in migration is to continue with restrictive laws but to also permit and accept very lax enforcement of them.

25 John A. Scanlan and O.T. Kent, "The Force of Moral Arguments for a Just Immigration Policy in a Hobbesian Universe" in Gibney, *Open Borders, supra* note 13, 61 at 65.
26 *Ibid.* at 63.
27 Louis Michael Seidman, "Fear and Loathing at the Border" in Schwartz, *Justice, supra* note 3, 142.

This treatment of the issue reveals that humanitarianism may be something that is unworkable as a legal standard. While our impulse may be to make a humanitarian gesture in a given scenario, we may be reluctant to make generosity the rule. This is another reason for its position in the traditional law-versus-discretion dichotomy. Equally, it may be difficult to formulate a rule based on humanitarianism because the concept itself is elusive. Like Scanlan and Kent, Seidman does not argue that this is morally right, but rather that it is politically feasible. In his conclusion, he states: "Membership is important not because it is a moral right that justifies exclusion, but because it is a political reality that blocks inclusion. We should not ignore that reality when we formulate immigration policy. But neither should we reinforce it so as to provide ammunition for those interested in justifying the status quo."[28] Both these analyses emphasize that when we argue for changes in the law to allow increased admissions, it is the language of humanitarianism that is most persuasive in liberal cultures. The humanitarian consensus runs through all strands of liberal theoretical discussions about immigration, which is itself an indicator of the potential instability of its meaning.

A second response to the absence of a liberal standard of justice that informs decisions about what is fair between members and non-members of a society is to articulate standards for principled decision making *within* a particular society. While such standards cannot answer the question of whether liberalism mandates open or closed borders, or whether a particular policy is just from the perspective of an applicant for admission, they provide a guard against capricious or self-serving political decision making. They also conform to the traditional liberal tenet that questions of equality and justice are to be resolved within the community. The justice, or fairness, established by such standards applies to those who are already members of the society. That is, we establish "fair" standards for admission given who we imagine ourselves to be and what our aims as a nation are. This type of fairness standard provides a way of arbitrating disputes about immigration that arise because of the interests of groups *within* the community. These standards of justice are well developed and conform to liberal postulates. The problem is only in their almost xenophobic narrowness. They define justice based on community norms when those to whom just consideration is arguably most important in immigration matters are outside the community.

Scanlan and Kent's argument about pragmatic humanitarianism falls partly into this category because they deliberately draw on American concepts of liberty and equality. The standard for principled policy that they develop depends explicitly on American political history and political culture; it is

---

28 *Ibid.* at 144-45.

designed to rally support among the American populace rather than to act as a standard for liberal societies. I have labelled their justice standard "internal" because its point of departure is, "we are Americans, so this is what fair immigration policy is for us."

A similar internally principled approach is put forward by Shacknove, who stipulates that the principle of mutual aid implies three positive duties towards refugees: (1) to avoid depriving them of basic security, subsistence, and liberty unless some actual proximate and compelling interest of state is implicated; (2) to assume responsibility for our own actions that directly deprive others of their basic needs; and (3) to treat all persons whose lives are in jeopardy as equal before the law.[29] While these duties are articulated in universal terms, they are internally based. In Shacknove's analysis, these principles apply to people who are already within the borders of the nation, awaiting decisions on whether they will be permitted to remain. As with Scanlan and Kent, important principled improvements in actual practice could be made on the basis of Shacknove's three duties. Nonetheless, these duties do not address the important questions of whether refugees should be admitted for permanent settlement at all, who should be considered a refugee, or how many people should be admitted. The case of immigrants is also beyond the scope of these principles, as they derive from liberalism's minimal principle of moral duty rather than from a broad conception of justice. To this extent, Shacknove's argument is pragmatic because he draws on the humanitarian consensus and articulates justice principles from that standpoint. His perspective is internal because in his view compelling state interests trump even the basic subsistence of refugee claimants. The interests of the "us" group have enormous primacy.

Howard Adelman has developed a highly sophisticated model for determining questions of justice in immigration and refugee law that provides an elaborate example of a narrow standard.[30] He asserts that the universality of Rawls's theory of justice means that it ought to be applicable to the immigration and refugee context, yet the rights emphasis of Rawls's theory makes it inappropriate for these questions. Adelman develops a framework for just decision making that shows how immigration and refugee policy meets different aims within a society and that differing conceptions of justice prevail in relation to each of these.[31] He claims that justice is not abstract and that we must look at actual policy decisions and see which

29 Andrew E. Shacknove, "American Duties to Refugees: Their Scope and Limits" in Gibney, *Open Borders, supra* note 13, 131.
30 Howard Adelman, "Justice, Immigration and Refugees" in Howard Adelman et al., eds., *Immigration and Refugee Policy: Australia and Canada Compared* (Melbourne: Melbourne University Press, 1994) 63.
31 A similar type of analysis is seen in Coleman and Harding's essay, where justice is also deduced from current practice: *supra* note 8 at 18.

conceptions of justice underlie them: "In immigration policy, justice is achieved by adjudicating among various utilities and normative rights criteria, as well as the capacity of the society to absorb those immigrants and refugees."[32]

Adelman views justice as a variable concept; its moral content is determined by its context. He examines various types of immigration decisions and considers how justice standards could be inserted into the decision making. This yields a set of principles for policy making, however, rather than a model of liberal justice. While ultimately of great use to decision makers, in many instances his taxonomy of values driving decisions is more explanatory than normative. For example, he discusses how an ecological perspective can lead to support for either more or less immigration depending on whether national or global ecology is emphasized and how economic self-interest can take policy in divergent directions depending upon what other values are also considered. Adelman would agree that his aim is to articulate principles to guide enlightened policy making. The principles he outlines do, in some instances, incorporate the perspective of admission applicants. What Adelman ignores is that Rawlsian justice is inapplicable to the immigration and refugee context because Rawls assumes community and this assumption is not easily cast aside, as the open-borders–closed-borders debate shows. Adelman's own work, like that of Scanlan and Kent and of Shacknove, demonstrates that principled policy making derives from the values of one society and puts the needs of members first. He is compelled to develop flexible principles because no liberal justice standard fits the context he is considering. By arguing that what is just depends upon our goals (including our desire to be humanitarian) in a given context, Adelman demonstrates that there is no one standard that applies to immigration, and that the goals of non-members are irrelevant to "fair" policy making.

Internal standards of justice are a crucially important device. They articulate goals for immigration law and policy that, in practical terms, would be a marked improvement on political reality. These standards contribute more to the debate about pragmatic improvements in the immigration realm than to the more ethereal open-borders–closed-borders debate. They are more compelling to community members who ultimately must make or support rules about admittance to the polity. Their existence does not, however, mean that liberalism provides standards for justice in immigration. Internal justice standards address the question of fairness only from the perspective of society members. They announce that certain laws are fair if they are fair to all of "us." To speak of justice in this narrow sense does not alter the conclusion that immigration law is an amoral realm, beyond or at

32 Adelman, *supra* note 30 at 70.

the border of liberal conceptions of justice. Justice for those who will not be directly touched by these laws is not a full conception of justice. These standards serve to reinforce the central role of the humanitarian consensus.

The Meaning of Humanitarianism

One important reason for the pre-eminent role of humanitarianism in immigration discourses is precisely that it is the point of convergence for those liberals who claim the need for closed borders, those who assert the importance of open borders, and those who claim that this intractable argument must be circumvented to achieve real change. For those who take up the question of just immigration on a theoretical plane, humanitarianism is the crux of the issue. Looking beyond this to specify the meaning of humanitarianism reveals its relationship to national identity in the liberal nation.

Open- and closed-border advocates alike argue that more needy outsiders ought to be admitted to wealthy Western nations.[33] At a minimum, this is the substance of the humanitarian consensus: by *any* liberal standard, contemporary nations are failing in their moral obligations. Beyond this, humanitarianism spells out little. Both Walzer and the Singers would agree that a nation must admit only those it has the capacity to admit, but that capacity would be defined dramatically differently in each argument. For Galloway, the limit of humanitarianism is unknowable, given that it depends on the individual moralities of all members. Carens's restriction for national security concerns is open, at least, to manipulation. In the dangerous times of the early twenty-first century, this is a very significant exception to his principle. For those taking a pragmatic position, the limit of humanitarianism will be drawn when its rhetorical political potential is exhausted. In any given nation, this provides an imaginable limit, but not more. The humanitarian consensus tells us nothing about the numbers of economic or family migrants who ought to be admitted, and therefore adds very little to one of the core issues of popular political debate in many nations with established immigration programs: how many immigrants should be admitted on a regular basis.

Humanitarianism cannot tell us how many immigrants a just nation should admit because at its core it differs profoundly from justice. "Humanitarianism" is the term describing all the best and most generous elements of liberal immigration laws. It sums up the emotional appeal of "give

---

33 Of those discussed above, this is the explicit position of Walzer, Coleman and Harding, Carens, Singer and Singer, Scanlan and Kent, and Seidman. This position is also implied in Galloway's work, especially considering his argument in "Strangers and Members: Equality in an Immigration Setting," *supra* note 9. Others who would support this position include Mark Tushnet, "Immigration Policy in Liberal Political Theory" in Schwartz, *Justice, supra* note 3, 63.

us your huddled masses" and defines our willingness to share our prosperity. Liberal humanitarianism, which is the pride of many nations that have comparatively open borders and are important international actors in questions of refugee assistance, is based on inequality rather than justice. The central role of humanitarianism in immigration law makes the search for fair law and policy more difficult because it emphasizes beneficence despite being ostensibly derived from a duty to needy outsiders.

Humanitarianism provides a stand-in for justice in the immigration realm while reinforcing the boundary between an "us" group and a "them" group. Justice is a standard that implies, and applies, equality between individuals. Humanitarianism is the opposite; it is grounded in a specific type of difference created by material inequality. We have something – in the case of migration law, membership in a prosperous, rights-respecting state – that they do not. Humanitarianism in migration law functions only because of the profound inequalities between members and non-members. When we are humanitarian we bestow, as a gift, something upon others who have no rightful claim to it.

Keeping humanitarianism as the central concept in immigration and refugee law ensures that the law is about what "we" can give to "them." Humanitarianism is not a standard of obligation, as justice would be, but rather of charity. Humanitarianism defines us as good when we are able to meet the standard, and justifiable when we are not. As is the case with the principle of mutual aid, humanitarianism is very flexible. It does not provide principled guidance about whom to admit and when. The obligation is minimal, depending on subjective perceptions of state capacity, of actions that can be taken with no risk or loss. It is well suited to the ways in which liberal societies use migration law to accommodate changing perceptions of national need, and it can expand and contract easily with the domestic political environment. The elasticity of the boundary of the nation has a perfect parallel in the concept of humanitarianism. The standard that humanitarianism provides for migration law is only to lay bare the complete dependence of this branch of the nation's legal framework on political consensus and rhetorical support. That is, this close examination of humanitarianism provides crucial support for the argument that migration law is vital to the ongoing construction and reconstruction, invention and reinvention, of the liberal nation.

The inequality that humanitarianism enshrines reinforces the difference between members and others. Through this function, it contributes to defining the identity of the nation. Part of this shaping of identity is achieved through the "othering" process – that is, we find aspects of identity by looking at those who are excluded or who gain from our beneficence. The humanitarianism of our laws also defines us directly, without any reference to those "others," as good and as generous. The mirror of humanitarianism reflects us as members of a nation that does more than it is required to do, which is more than just, better than fair. This sentiment is reflected in the Australian Minister for Immigration's comments regarding the 1997 Young Australian of the Year, who had come to the country as a refugee from Vietnam: "Those who applauded this young woman, not only applaud her individual courage and achievements, but, I suspect, applauded themselves for being members of a community that, as she said in her acceptance speech, welcomed her so unquestioningly."[34] Part of our humanitarianism is about just that, applauding ourselves. When humanitarianism is used in immigration laws and discourses, it tells us something about ourselves as a nation – that is, the extent of our aspirations to goodness – and something implicit about our national identity – that is, how we go about balancing the needs and claims of insiders and outsiders. The self-conscious construction of ourselves as good becomes clearer through the examination in the second part of the book of how humanitarianism is written into Australian and Canadian law.

It is true that the commitment to protect refugees, which is an important component of humanitarian admissions in most nations with established immigration programs (and even in some nations with no immigration programs at all), is enshrined in international law, and therefore it could be argued that nations undertake this commitment as a matter of law, not as a matter of generosity. This argument, however, fails to fully account for both the nature of international law and the role that liberal humanitarianism has played and continues to play in providing a foundation for international refugee law. The international legal commitment to admit refugees is binding only on those nations that agree to be bound.[35] Furthermore, the humanitarian structure of international refugee law itself draws on liberalism's humanitarian consensus, and undoubtedly drew on this consensus for the support that brought it into being in 1951.[36] Nations that participate in international refugee law may be motivated to do so in part in order to enhance their reputations as humanitarian in the international sphere, or even to enhance their legitimacy as full-fledged members of the international

---

34 Honourable Philip Ruddock, Minister for Immigration, "Immigration Reform: The Unfinished Agenda" (Address at the National Press Club, 18 March 1998), online: <www.minister.immi.gov.au>.

35 While some treaty-based international principles have evolved to become generally applicable principles of international law, this is not generally considered to be the case with the *Convention Relating to the Status of Refugees*, 1951, 189 U.N.T.S. 150 [*Refugee Convention*]. Equally, the *Universal Declaration of Human Rights'* assertion of a right to seek asylum has not been accompanied by a concomitant duty of states.

36 One of the clauses in the Preamble to the *Refugee Convention* states: "*Expressing* the wish that all States, recognizing the social and humanitarian nature of the problem of refugees will do everything within their power to prevent this problem from becoming a cause of tension between States."

community. This also directly links humanitarian commitments to national identification. Finally, international law does not explicitly require that refugees be *admitted;* it prescribes only how they are to be treated once they have arrived. To this extent, then, the international legal standards skirt the direct question of humanitarian admissions entirely.

While I demonstrate that humanitarianism enshrines inequality and circumvents justice, and often holds the position of a self-serving ruse in the law, I would also strongly urge that it is a discourse of immense value in both law reform and national aspiration. Although arguments about what is the just number of migrants to admit will never be resolved in a way that takes account of justice for those outside the nation, aspiring to be generous and good introduces an important value to this law, even if it does not yield precision or clear standards and results in provisions that are difficult to interpret. The value of humanitarianism tempers, without altering, the blatant self-centredness of migration law. In analyzing how this value is translated into legal effect, I conclude that the aspiration to generosity and goodness is often missed, in both Australia and Canada. Nonetheless, the rhetoric of humanitarianism is valuable because it calls on us to think beyond ourselves, even if we do fall short of the mark. While it is fraught with problems, it remains what is best about our liberal migration laws. Precisely because it is the point of liberal consensus, it is strategically, as Scanlan and Kent and Seidman suggest, the discourse that is most likely to be persuasive for those aspiring to change the law to make admissions policies more open or more responsive to those in need.

Bifurcated Migration Laws

The place of humanitarianism in Western migration laws is a comparatively recent development, emerging only in the latter half of the twentieth century. Specific provisions for narrowly defined refugees are one aspect of the broader migration stream encompassed by the term "humanitarian." Two factors account for this emergence. First, it was not until the twentieth century that widespread immigration control and restrictive regimes became the norm.[37] Second, this move to restrictive immigration regimes directly harnessed migration laws to the needs of the sovereign liberal nation. Once this linkage has been made, the rationale for migration must be understood

---

37 Ann Dummett and Andrew Nicol, *Subjects, Citizens, Aliens and Others: Nationality and Immigration Law* (London: Weidenfeld and Nicolson, 1990). John Torpey makes the argument that control over population movement emerged gradually in Europe over the past three centuries and that it is imprecise to describe it as a wholly twentieth-century phenomenon. It is nonetheless accurate that migration control was consolidated and became widespread at the start of the twentieth century: John Torpey, *The Invention of the Passport: Surveillance, Citizenship and the State* (Cambridge: Cambridge University Press, 2000).

in terms of national objectives. In the cases of family reunification migration and economic migration, the linkages are easily drawn.

When migration law is articulated as a means of fulfilling national ends, humanitarian migration emerges both as an exception and as something that must somehow be fitted into the national need spectrum, even if the connection is more subtle in this case. The need that is met by humanitarian migration is the need to define and understand the nation as compassionate and caring. The extent of our collective commitment to these aims is reflected in the amount of humanitarian migration we will tolerate. Humanitarian migration becomes the exception, whereas in earlier times it would have been at least part of the rule. The Irish who fled starvation to the United States and the Canadian colonies, those fleeing persecution as religious minorities who broke the earth of the North American prairies, the former convicts who chose freedom and remained in what was to become Australia, and the post–Second World War migrants who worked to rebuild economies throughout the world would all be humanitarian migrants by today's standards. The nature of migration, of what is at stake, and of what type of person will serve a national need has shifted. In the cases of Australia and Canada, this is partially because they became fully sovereign nations sometime in the middle of the twentieth century and therefore gained complete control of their borders, but the same shift has occurred in Europe and the United States. As migration laws in general stand as bulwarks against globalization, migration increasingly becomes an option for the privileged. There is thus a bifurcation in the law between humanitarian and "other" classes of migration. The notion of privileged and non-privileged migration is replicated within the humanitarian scheme, as it is often the well-off who can pay for passage to a place like Canada or Australia and therefore gain the possibility of lodging a refugee claim and of having the nation treat their presence as a constraint on sovereignty.

Humanitarian and non-humanitarian migrants are governed by different principles. Evidence of this is seen in the Australian separation between its "migration program" and its "humanitarian program,"[38] and in the recommendation of the 1997 Canadian legislative review panel that the immigration regime be replaced with two new acts, one dealing with immigration and citizenship and the other dealing with "protection."[39]

38 "Fact Sheet: Unauthorised Arrivals by Air and Sea" (revised 15 October 2002), online: The Department of Immigration and Multicultural and Indigenous Affairs (Australia) <http://www.immi.gov.au/facts/74unauthorised.htm>.
39 Canada, Immigration Legislative Review Advisory Group, *Not Just Numbers: A Canadian Framework for Future Immigration* (Ottawa: Citizenship and Immigration Canada, 1997). The proposal for two new acts was the centrepiece of the legislative review and was therefore discussed throughout the report. This aspect of the report was rejected but has left its mark in the title of the new legislation: the *Immigration and Refugee Protection Act*, S.C. 2001, c. 27.

Hathaway's proposal to reform international refugee law by implementing a truly temporary standard for refugee protection in other countries also relies crucially on separating responses to those who need humanitarian assistance from the usual concerns of migration law.[40] Whereas in the nineteenth century settler societies were peopled by those we would now call humanitarian migrants, it seems the twenty-first century will bring increased argument that humanitarian migration is not the same as "general" migration. Furthermore, this argument is equally likely from those who advocate humanitarian admissions and those who oppose them.

This bifurcation of the logical underpinning of migration law contributes to the conceptualization of humanitarianism and to the articulation of the relationship between migration law and national identity. Humanitarianism looks as though it is an exception to the rule of migration serving a national agenda, but even at a rhetorical level it must bend to the national agenda in some ways, as becomes clear in Chapter 6 when I examine how humanitarianism is located in Canadian and Australian law.

Situating the humanitarian consensus within the migration law–national identity framework serves to build a unified explanation for migration provisions. Migration laws limit the community and serve the national interest even in their humanitarian instances. Identifying the nation as good is as important as, or even more important than, any other values that are ascribed to it by migration law. This ascription works in both the domestic and international spheres, projecting humanitarianism as a nebulous value that underpins even international agreements in this area. This explanation of migration law runs parallels to Brubaker's explanation of the politics of citizenship as "a *politics of identity,* not a *politics of interest* (in the restricted materialist sense)."[41] Given the intertwining of national interests and migration law, the law itself is highly politicized, so that the distinction between a *politics* of identity and a *law* of identity is minimal.

Understanding humanitarianism is also important to being able to deploy its political potential. As migration law is harnessed solely to national aspirations and is immune from assessments of justice, humanitarian-based arguments are often the most powerful that can be made in this area, as the open-borders advocates have demonstrated. For those who advocate changes in the law, humanitarian arguments are vital. For individuals who seek admission to the state, it is important to be able to fit themselves into an

---

40 James Hathaway, "Preface" in James C. Hathaway, ed., *Reconceiving International Refugee Law* (The Hague and Boston: M. Nijhoff, 1997) at xviii; and James C. Hathaway and Alexander Neve, "Making International Refugee Law Relevant Again: A Proposal for Collectivized and Solution-Oriented Protection" (1997) 10 Harv. Hum. Rts. L.J. 115.

41 William Rogers Brubaker, *Citizenship and Nationhood in France and Germany* (Cambridge, MA: Harvard University Press, 1992) at 182 [emphasis added].

identity of one who is deserving of our grace. Thus, a discourse of humanitarianism contains its own potentials for power.

Acknowledging the liberal humanitarian consensus is vital to interpreting the closed-borders–open-borders debate within liberalism. It is also key to revealing the coherence of migration provisions and the values that underpin them. In a sense, the link between migration law and national identity is hardest to see in the case of humanitarian admissions. It is for this reason, however, that the case of humanitarian admissions is the vital testing ground for the explanatory capacity of this framework for reading migration laws. In the second part of this book, I consider three variations of humanitarian admissions to Australia and Canada. I examine refugee admissions in accordance with international legal provisions, humanitarian admissions as legal exceptions, and the contest between humanitarian arguments and rights arguments in the highest courts.

Part 2
Humanitarian Admissions to Australia and Canada

5
Constructing Others: The Refugee Process

This chapter examines how refugees are constructed in Australian and Canadian law and considers what that process reveals about migration law as a site for assembling a picture of national identity and as the effective boundary of the nation. Of all the categories of people admitted under the migration laws to live permanently in these nations, the label "refugee" describes those who, at least theoretically, differ most markedly from the members of the nation. While family and economic migrants are selected because they have something the nation values – family ties or a contribution to economic growth – refugees are accepted because of something they lack – the protection of another state. This key difference means that the law governing refugee admissions and the way it is applied form a good starting point for seeing the principles set out in Part 1 take shape. Identity construction proceeds through a process of constructing boundaries and of portraying the other as like "us." It is often easiest to see first how the outsider or the absent other is constructed, and to search within this construction for reflected images of self. As well, images of self and other are often best seen in areas of sharp contrast. Both of these conditions are met in the case of refugee admissions.

Refugees are not selected because of their family ties or economic potential, and for this reason they are simultaneously the most unknown of migrant categories and the group that represents the sharpest contrast with existing national values. Using identity as the fulcrum of analysis enables us to observe that the refugee is constructed as the ultimate other to the nation in order to be permitted entry. Refugees are the most unlike us, as well as the most unknown, facilitating our imaginative construction of their identity. This process in turn creates a reflected image of how Australia and Canada, as nations, identify themselves.

Examining refugee law also allows me to begin drawing out two other aspects of the Part 1 framework. First, as refugee admissions are one type of humanitarian admission, this area of the law provides examples of how liberal humanitarianism takes shape in the law and influences the shape that law takes. This theme is taken up further in Chapter 6, which analyzes humanitarian admissions outside the refugee stream. Second, refugee law provides a clear way of focusing on the importance of sovereignty to migration law, as refugee admission is the only aspect of migration law that contains a potential challenge to national sovereignty.

To demonstrate how refugee law constructs the refugee as the ultimate other to the nation and how this process in turn reveals elements of national identity, I begin by describing the international legal regime that generates the legal standards that both Australia and Canada apply in their refugee law. This starting point also allows me to anchor my analysis by examining the interrelationship of sovereignty and international legal standards and demonstrating the place of identity in the refugee definition itself. This highlights key features of the legal framework that are a necessary precedent to considering how it is applied. I then compare the Australian and Canadian refugee admission processes, with particular emphasis on the decision-making processes in the refugee tribunals, and key roles played by identity and credibility in refugee determinations. This refugee determination process raises salient questions engaging identity by bringing the potential refugee face to face with the nation in a setting dominated by legal reasoning and processes despite efforts to temper this influence. In this setting, the importance of background norms and silences – two factors that the identity-based critique of law highlights – are vital. The next section analyzes the emerging refugee identities in each country, including how these identities interact with those of other actors in the refugee process. The final section considers how refugee admissions fit into the broader migration schemes in each country and what insights can be drawn about migration from examining the othering process taking place in the refugee realm. It also takes up the challenge described in Part 1 of testing linkages between legal and popular discourses about refugees.

Refugee as an International Legal Standard

The Internationally Accepted Definition of a Refugee
The relationship between the refugee and the nation is complicated at the outset by the dissonance between the meanings that are commonly associated with the word "refugee" and the legal definition of the term. The images that we associate with refugees may include those fleeing famines in Ethiopia, residents of Sarajevo whose homes were destroyed in the war that rendered Yugoslavia "former," Chinese dissident defectors, and "boat people" from China or the Middle East. The *Oxford English Dictionary* defines "refugee" in a way that fits with these visions: "A person driven from his or her

home to seek refuge, esp. in a foreign country, from war, religious persecution, political troubles, natural disaster, etc."[1] But the legal definition is much narrower.

Both Australia and Canada have adopted the international definition of a refugee for use in their domestic law.[2] This definition was agreed upon in 1951 as part of the international response to the horror of the Holocaust and the vast number of displaced persons in Europe following the Second World War. The definition built on a number of international agreements about refugees in the interwar period.[3] A refugee was defined as any person who:

As a result of events occurring before 1 January 1951 and owing to a well-founded fear of being persecuted for reasons of race, religion, nationality, membership of a particular social group or political opinion, is outside the country of his nationality and is unable or, owing to such fear, is unwilling to avail himself of the protection of that country; or who, not having a nationality and being outside the country of his former habitual residence as a result of such events, is unable or, owing to such fear, is unwilling to return to it.[4]

In 1967, the temporal limitation in the definition was removed, as was the option of interpreting the definition to refer only to events that had occurred in Europe.[5] In 2001, Australia qualified its use of the international standard by legislating definitions of the key terms "persecution" and "particular social group."[6] The components of the definition are: (1) being outside one's

1 *Shorter Oxford English Dictionary,* 5th ed., vol. 2 (Oxford: Oxford University Press, 2002). The alternatives offered are "a displaced person" and "a runaway; a fugitive."
2 The Australian *Migration Act,* s. 36(2) states: "A criterion for a protection visa is that the applicant for the visa is (a) a non-citizen of Australia to whom Australia has protection obligations under the Refugees Convention as amended by the Refugees Protocol; or (b) a non-citizen in Australia who is the spouse or a dependant of a non-citizen who: (i) is mentioned in paragraph (a); and (ii) holds a protection visa." The Canadian *Immigration and Refugee Protection Act* writes the *Refugee Convention* definition directly into Canadian law in ss. 96 and 98.
3 It is notable that the post–First World War rise of refugee movements coincides with the widespread introduction of passports and immigration restrictions: A. Dummett and A. Nicol, *Subjects, Citizens, Aliens and Others: Nationality and Immigration Law* (London: Weidenfeld and Nicolson, 1990) at 145.
4 *Convention Relating to the Status of Refugees,* 1951, 189 U.N.T.S. 150 (entered into force 22 April 1954) [*Refugee Convention*], Article 1(A)(2). Original signatories had the option of reading "events occurring before 1 January 1951" as "events occurring in Europe before 1 January 1951": Article 1(B)(1).
5 *Protocol Relating to the Status of Refugees,* 1967, 606 U.N.T.S. 267 (entered into force 4 October 1967) [*Refugee Protocol*], Article 1.
6 These changes are now found in ss. 91R, 91S, 91T, and 91U of the *Migration Act,* and were introduced by *Migration Legislation Amendment Act, (No. 6) 2001* (Cth.). The provisions also define serious and non-political crimes. These changes curtail judicial interpretation

country and not able or willing to return there; (2) having a well-founded fear of persecution; and (3) that the fear of persecution be on the basis of certain characteristics or "grounds." People who are starving or whose lives are fractured by civil war are not refugees under this definition. Anyone who has not crossed an international border is not a refugee. Of those people imagined above, the only group almost certain to be considered refugees are the Chinese defectors.

This points to two of the most significant ways in which the international legal definition of a refugee is limited. First, the Western powers who dominated the initial norm-building process ensured that their ideological tradition of granting asylum to those fleeing the emerging Eastern bloc would be enshrined in the international agreement. This Western bias is at the root of making persecution a key factor in the definition and in the original time and place limitations, which operated to facilitate an understanding of the refugee as someone who came from Europe but for whom the world community bore some responsibility.[7] Second, the refugee definition is individualistic. It is impossible to say categorically that homeless Afghans, starving Ethiopians, or Indochinese boat people are not refugees. Their individual circumstances may indeed bring them within the definition, and the inquiry is legally located at an individual level, but the labels I have given these groups do not refer to characteristics that, alone, would bring them within the refugee definition. The label "Chinese dissident defector" does, as "dissident" describes directly a political opinion directed at a state opposed to free speech and a defector has already left their country of origin.

The stringency and bias of the refugee definition have met with thorough and detailed criticism from many quarters.[8] Responses to address these concerns have included broadening the mandate of the United Nations High Commissioner for Refugees (UNHCR) to include responsibility for "persons

---

but alone are probably not enough to constitute a breach of the *Refugee Convention*, although they do depart from accepted international law interpretive principles.

7   James C. Hathaway, *The Law of Refugee Status* (Toronto: Butterworths, 1991) at 6-10.

8   Some examples include Melanie Randall, "Refugee Law and State Accountability for Violence against Women: A Comparative Analysis of Legal Approaches to Asylum Claims Based on Gender Persecution" (2002) 25 Harv. Women's L.J. 281; Pene Mathew, "Conformity or Persecution: China's One Child Policy and Refugee Status" (2000) 23 U.N.S.W.L.J. 103; Patricia Tuitt, *False Images: Law's Construction of the Refugee* (London and East Haven, CT: Pluto Press, 1996); James C. Hathaway, ed., *Reconceiving International Refugee Law* (The Hague and Boston: M. Nijhoff, 1997); Guy Goodwin-Gill, "Refugees: The Functions and Limits of the Existing Protection System" in A. Nash, ed., *Human Rights and the Protection of Refugees Under International Law* (Montreal: The Canadian Human Rights Foundation, 1988); James C. Hathaway and Alexander Neve, "Making International Refugee Law Relevant Again: A Proposal for Collectivised and Solution-Oriented Protection" (1997) 10 Harv. Hum. Rts. J. 115; Patricia Hyndman, "Refugees under International Law with a Reference to the Concept of Asylum" (1986) 60 Australian L.J. 148; Goran Melandes, "The Protection of Refugees" (1974) 18 Scand. Stud. L. 153.

of concern"[9] and the emergence of several regional norms defining refugees more broadly.[10] Australia and Canada both incorporate some humanitarian admissions into their migration programs that extend beyond the formal refugee program, in recognition of the fact that many individuals seeking resettlement do not come within the refugee definition. Hathaway argues that while in the immediate postwar period a reasonable fit existed between national self-interest and the refugee definition, this convergence has diminished in recent years. That, in combination with a rising number of involuntary migrants whose circumstances fall outside the definition, means that "refugee law serves fewer and fewer people, less and less well, as time goes on."[11]

In combination, these factors – a narrow definition of refugee, a dissonance between the legal and popular definitions, and reliance on international legal norms in this area – reveal key observations about how refugee law operates *within* nations. The international legal regime enshrines national sovereignty. It is a long-established tenet of international law that nations have complete control over their own naturalization and citizenship law, that is, over their own borders and membership.[12] While there are now some international legal norms that transcend sovereignty either because they apply directly to individuals (such as some human rights provisions or war crimes prohibitions) or because a nation may be bound by them without specifically consenting to them (such as the prohibition against genocide), refugee law is not one of these. The 1951 *Convention Relating to the Status of Refugees* (hereinafter *Refugee Convention*) reads as a

9 The mission statement of the UNHCR says in part: "UNHCR's Executive Committee and the UN General Assembly have also authorized the organization's involvement with other groups. These include people who are stateless or whose nationality is disputed and, in certain circumstances, internally displaced persons": "Basic Information about the UNHCR: Mission Statement," online: <www.unhcr.ch/cgi-bin/texis/vtx/basic>. In its 2002 edition of *Statistics on Asylum Seekers, Refugees and Others of Concern to the UNHCR,* there were 6,727,833 "others of concern" (i.e., who were not refugees or asylum seekers) in a total population of concern of 20,556,781. This information is also available at <www.unhcr.ch>.

10 These are the Organization of African Unity *Convention Governing the Specific Aspects of Refugee Problems in Africa,* 1000 U.N.T.S. 46 (entered into force 20 June 1974); and the *Cartagena Declaration* (entered into by ten Latin American states in 1984), OR OEA/Ser.L/V/II.66/Doc. 10, rev.1 (1984) at 190-93. The Council of Europe has also recognized the existence of de facto refugees but has not formalized this recognition: Council of Europe, Parliamentary Assembly Recommendation 773 (1976).

11 James C. Hathaway, "Preface" in Hathaway, *supra* note 8 at xxv.

12 Confirmed by the International Court of Justice in the *Nottebohm Case (Liechtenstein v. Guatemala)* [1955] I.C.J. Reports 4. Nations have devised two basic regimes governing citizenship or membership: *jus soli* and *jus sanguinis,* belonging by being born there or belonging by being the child of a member. Variations and limitations on these two regimes explain most citizenship laws. Migration laws are not so easily categorized, but do relate directly to citizenship laws as citizens are automatically allowed entry into their nation of citizenship.

constraint on sovereignty in that it obligates states not to return people to places where they are at risk of being persecuted.[13] This amounts to requiring states to keep the refugee within their borders in many instances, because international legal norms limit deportation options by only requiring states to admit their own nationals. In addition to this protection against refoulement, the *Refugee Convention* reads like a rights document, guaranteeing various rights to refugees while in protection-granting states. The convention is therefore similar in tone and form to many of the human rights instruments that are now considered to constrain national sovereignty at some level.

In practice, however, the convention operates as, at most, a minimal constraint on sovereignty, especially in prosperous Western nations remote from most situations that produce refugees. In Australia and Canada, admission of refugees is guided by quotas or target numbers set by the government on a yearly basis. Since refugees are not actually crossing the borders in overwhelming numbers, as may be the case in Pakistan or Macedonia, the number of refugees to be accepted is not determined by an international legal obligation but by internal political wrangling. Any obligation to accept refugees from afar is rooted in moral or political suasion rather than legal requisite. While some international human rights conventions contain provisions allowing at least the option of an international forum to bring complaints to, there is no such forum for breaches of the *Refugee Convention*. In Hathaway's view, "international refugee law rarely determines how governments respond to involuntary migration. States pay lip service to the importance of honouring the right to seek asylum, but in practice devote significant resources to keep refugees away from their borders. Although the advocacy community invokes formal protection principles, it knows that governments are unlikely to live up to these supposedly minimum standards."[14] While the *Refugee Convention* is not treated by states as a significant constraint on sovereignty – and therefore is not one – incorporating its language into domestic law allows governments to maintain that they are meeting their international obligations in this area. The narrowness of the legal definition of refugee, and in particular the requirement that a refugee be outside their own country to fall within this definition, means that even if a nation chose to treat the *Refugee Convention* as a robust constraint on sovereignty, the extent of this constraint in the case of nations distant from refugee-producing situations would be slight. Instead, refugee

---

13 Formally, this protection is provided by the provision against "refoulement" in Article 33 of the *Convention*: "1. No Contracting State shall expel or return ('refouler') a refugee in any manner whatsoever to the frontiers of territories where his life or freedom would be threatened on account of his race, religion, nationality, membership of a particular social group or political opinion."

14 Hathaway, *supra* note 8 at xvii.

law interpretation becomes a site of assertions of sovereignty, for expressions of the identity of the nation as nation. Deciding which refugees to admit and when becomes another potential tool in the construction of the national community.

The Role of Identity in the Refugee Definition

Using the term "identity" to explore the refugee definition is important in two ways, first because identity is a central component of that definition and second because "refugee" emerges as an identity in and of itself. These two aspects facilitate the use of "refugee" as a legal category that incorporates particular background norms and unstated perspectives, building an image of the nation that resembles a photographic negative. I take up the first aspect here and consider the second later in this chapter. While the legal inquiry into whether one meets the refugee definition is individualistic, the permissible grounds on which persecution may be feared are largely group-identity based. This narrows the definition, of course, as a fear of persecution is not the only element. It also parallels a familiar trick of liberal legalism: the focus is on the individual but the labelling of individuals creates a group identity and regulates the boundary of that identity. This feature of legally constructed identities fits within psychological descriptions of how identity is experienced at both group and individual levels.

A refugee fears persecution on the basis of race, religion, nationality, or membership of a particular social group or political opinion. The first four of these grounds can be viewed directly as components of identity. Identity also sheds important light on political opinion, which I discuss separately. While an individual may not identify as a member of a particular race, religion, nationality, or social group in all or even any circumstances, in an atmosphere of persecution this identity will become important whether or not an individual subjectively accepts it as important to them. The Nazi persecution of those with Jewish ancestry who did not view themselves as Jewish is an example that was easily available to the definition's drafters. Claiming refugee status on one of these grounds depends on membership in an identity-based group. The process of asserting this claim will necessarily make this aspect of one's identity come to the fore. The law, therefore, shapes an individual's self-identification in this sense.

The importance of identity to the refugee definition is highlighted by the problematic jurisprudence interpreting the ground "membership of a particular social group."[15] In Australia and Canada, as elsewhere, the courts

15 See the discussion in Krista Daley and Ninette Kelley, "Particular Social Group: A Human Rights Based Approach to Canadian Jurisprudence" (2000) 12 Int'l J. Refugee L. 148; Maryellen Fullerton, "A Comparative Look at Refugee Status Based on Persecution Due to Membership in a Particular Social Group" (1993) 26 Cornell Int'l L.J. 505; Maureen Graves, "From Definition to Exploration: Social Groups and Political Asylum

have been unsuccessful in providing a clear understanding of what will count as a particular social group. The leading Canadian case, which has become internationally influential, *Canada (Attorney-General) v. Ward*,[16] draws a highly problematic distinction between groups based on "what one is" and those based on "what one does," the former meeting the definition and the latter not. The key Australian High Court decision, also referred to internationally, emphasizes that particular social groups must be more than "merely demographic."[17] In each case, the court is grasping at a definition of "particular social group" that articulates a sense of belonging or identity. The Australian court relies on whether the group in question is *identifiable* in society.[18] It seems that in each country any group whose claims are familiar in identity politics debates would qualify as a particular social group. Identity politics can be viewed as having "preconstructed" those groups outside the law, thus making them identifiable in the legal inquiry. This is one example of why the essentialist–constructivist debate is sidelined in law and identity literature. It is not incongruous to accept both that the law has a role in constructing identity (e.g., "refugee") and that identities exist outside the law. This line of reasoning bypasses the question of whether identities exist outside *all* social settings. The identity politics links with these claims also show the cultural bias of the law: groups that the receiving country has no experience of will be much less likely to be deemed "identifiable" and thus viewed as "particular social groups."

The inquiry into whether a group is a particular social group is about one's sense of self and about societal perceptions of selves, and about assertions of belonging (because voluntarily associated groups are captured by this ground). Persons claiming refugee status on this ground fear persecution because of some aspect of their identity that is shared with others, rather than because of some individual characteristic. The jurisprudence can be viewed as aiming to draw parallels between "particular social groups" and races, religions, and nationalities. The crux of each of these four grounds of potential persecution is that while the legal inquiry relates to the individual, the persecution must be directed at an individual *because of* their status as a group member.

Membership in a particular social group is also the main ground that has been used as the legal support for implementation of the UNHCR's Women

Eligibility" (1989) 26 San Diego L.R. 740; Audrey Macklin, *"Canada (Attorney-General) v. Ward:* A Review Essay" (1994) 6 Int'l J. Refugee L. 362; Catherine Dauvergne and Jenni Millbank, "Before the High Court: Applicants S396/2002 and S395/2002, a Gay Refugee Couple from Bangladesh" (2003) 25 Sydney L. Rev. 97 ["Before the High Court"].

16 *Canada (Attorney-General) v. Ward*, [1993] 103 D.L.R. (4th) 1 (SCC) [*Ward*].

17 *Applicant A and Another v. Minister for Immigration and Ethnic Affairs and Another* (1997), 142 A.L.R. 331 [*Applicant A*].

18 I consider this jurisprudence in detail in "Chinese Fleeing Sterilization: Australia's Response against a Canadian Backdrop" (1998) 10 Int'l J. Refugee L. 77.

at Risk initiative in Canada.[19] The legal inquiry therefore becomes: "In what circumstances does being a woman make one a member of a particular social group?"[20] Both Canada and Australia have implemented responses to address the plight of women refugees that the UNHCR worked for over a decade to publicize[21] – namely, that while an overwhelming number of those awaiting resettlement elsewhere are women and children, prosperous countries often accept more male than female refugees because men are more likely to be well educated or English speaking.[22] The guiding principle behind the Canadian approach is to encourage interpretations of the refugee definition that recognize that sometimes women are persecuted *because they are women,* and so they should be recognized as refugees. The Australian program takes a different focus, aiming to assist women in their particular circumstances even though they are not necessarily refugees. Under the Australian program, some Women at Risk visas are taken from the refugee target number within the overseas program, but do not include an explicit determination that a woman is a refugee. The key difference is that Canada *expands* the refugee definition while Australia keeps tight control over it. These various initiatives call attention to difficulties in meshing female identity with the refugee definition: first, by highlighting the definition's bias towards political and therefore male-dominated experience, and second, by underscoring the difficulties of treating "women" as a social group. That is, this experience forms the background norm for the refugee definition. Observing identity function in the law is one way of highlighting this. Finally,

19 See "Guidelines Issued by the Chairperson Pursuant to Section 65(3) of the *Immigration Act:* Women Refugee Claimants Fearing Gender-Related Persecution," Immigration and Refugee Board, Canada, 9 March 1993, updated 1996.

20 Nurjehan Mawani, "Introduction to the Immigration and Refugee Board Guidelines on Gender-Related Persecution" (1993) 5 Int'l J. Refugee L. 240; Department of Immigration and Multicultural Affairs (Refugee and Humanitarian Division) One-Pager entitled "Australia's Women at Risk Program"; see also Australia's *Migration Regulations,* subclass 204: Women at Risk Visa.

21 UNHCR, *1999 Global Appeal: Refugee Women* (1999), online: <www.unhcr.ch/fdrs/ga99/women.htm> (copy on file with the author).

22 Canada has been criticized for this behaviour by European nations; reported in interviews with CIC officials, Ottawa, June 1997. Australia's Women at Risk program makes a small contribution to addressing this disparity. While the program has now been operating for more than a decade, male refugees still outnumber female overall (primary applicants statistics from the Department of Immigration and Multicultural Affairs show the following: 1997-98, 711 men, 428 women; 1996-97, 850 men, 392 women; 1995-96, 1,035 men, 510 women). The target number of Women at Risk visas has stayed at 420 for about a decade. In program year 2002-3, the number of Women at Risk visas granted was 504, the highest to date. (See *Department of Immigration and Indigenous and Multicultural Affairs Annual Report 2002-2003,* online: <http://www.immi.gov.au/annual_report/annrep03/report27.htm>.) See also Monica Boyd, "Gender Concealed, Gender Revealed: The Demography of Canada's Refugee Flows" in *Gender Issues and Refugees: Development and Implications, Conference Proceedings* (York University, 9-11 May 1993) at 172, cited in Audrey Macklin, "Refugee Women and the Imperative of Categories" (1995) 17 Hum. Rts. Q. 213 at 219.

these initiatives expose the control imperative of the refugee definition that is threatened by the potential acknowledgment of half of some populations as "social groups."[23]

The fifth ground of eligible persecution in the refugee definition, political opinion, is not so obviously an identity label but nonetheless merges with identity-based analysis as political opinion can be imputed by the prosecuting authority, in which case it functions in the same way as identity stereotyping.[24] In a twist on the Supreme Court of Canada's *Ward* reasoning, being a refugee is who you are. The insights of identity call attention to the integral distinction between those who choose identities and those who are consigned to them. The refugee standard is highly personalized both at this definitional level and in its individualized application. Using the analytic tool of identity to examine the law and its application draws attention to the strictures of this definition, the background norms it embeds, the incentives it creates for individuals to choose some identities over others, and the role of both persecuting states and receiving states in consigning individuals to identity boxes.

Political opinion has been elaborated jurisprudentially in part through reliance on a strong sense of selves and of consciences.[25] This reflects the Cold War backdrop to the negotiations leading to the *Refugee Convention,* where the Western nations sought to protect their tradition of granting asylum to Eastern bloc defectors. The case law supports this tradition by viewing political opinion as a belief that one ought not be forced to relinquish because of its importance to one's sense of self. The Supreme Court of Canada ruled that Ward, "who believes that the killing of innocent people to achieve political change is unacceptable,"[26] was persecuted by a paramilitary organization because his conscience could not allow him to depart from this view, and implicitly that the *Refugee Convention* protects politically linked expressions of conscience. This very personalized interpretation of political opinion links political and self-identity very closely, drawing the ground of persecution because of political opinion parallel to the other identity-based grounds. The approach implicitly divides political opinions into those that are linked to a sense of self, and therefore that could ground

23 This concern is addressed head-on and rejected by the House of Lords in *Reg. v. I.A.T. ex p Shah,* [1999] 2 A.C. 629 (H.L.), a case that has also attracted international attention, for example, by the Australian High Court in *Minister for Immigration and Multicultural Affairs v. Khawar,* [2002] H.C.A. 14.

24 Imputed political opinion was confirmed by the Supreme Court of Canada in *Ward, supra* note 16, and by the High Court of Australia in *Minister for Immigration and Ethnic Affairs v. Guo Wei Rong,* [1997] 144 A.L.R. 567 at 575.

25 The range of views on whether a conscientious objection to military service can be grounds for refugee status provides an example. See the discussion in Goodwin-Gill, *supra* note 8 at 54-59.

26 *Ward, supra* note 16 at 40.

status as a refugee, and those that we would expect people to relinquish, such as a preference for voting Liberal to gain a personal tax advantage.

The refugee definition fits squarely into the role for migration law in the liberal nation that I described in Part 1. It could theoretically impinge on sovereignty but does not do so in a significant way in practice and thus becomes another mechanism for the nation to meet its needs and to constitute its community. Although it is written in the language of group membership and sense of belonging, it is honed by liberal legalism's commitment to analysis at the level of the individual. As it is taken up by sovereign nations, it becomes imprinted with their sovereign identity. Simultaneously, it is a key element in the construction of refugee as an identity category with a precise relationship to that nation. Looking at the refugee admission processes in Australia and Canada provides a basis for deepening my analysis of the refugee standard and of illustrating the importance of identity to that standard and to the nation.

Refugee Admissions to Australia and Canada

Legislative Frameworks

Australia and Canada each have two ways of allowing people who meet the international definition of refugee to become permanent members of the community. Refugees are selected abroad, and some of the people who arrive on their own are determined to be refugees and are allowed to stay on that basis. The two procedures are distinct. When refugees are selected abroad, no international legal obligation is triggered, although the international definition of a refugee may be used. By all existing legal standards, a nation is free to take in refugees in this way or not. There may be some pressure in the international community to do this,[27] and there may from time to time be international agreements to facilitate this,[28] but there is nothing more. On the other hand, when a person has made it to Canada or Australia[29] and then claims to be a refugee, the obligation under the *Refugee*

---

27 The United Nations High Commissioner for Refugees, for example, tries to exert pressure on states to take in refugees and quasi-refugees from abroad.

28 For example, the Comprehensive Plan of Action relating to Indo-Chinese refugees initiated in 1989, under which participating governments made specific commitments regarding issues such as resettlement, deterring clandestine departures, repatriations, and regular communications. See "Statement of the Steering Committee: Reaffirmation of the Comprehensive Plan of Action" (1991) 3 Int'l J. Refugee L. 367. This agreement was as much about limiting resettlement of refugees abroad as it was about facilitating it.

29 By this I mean those who have physically reached the country, including those who make a refugee claim at a port of entry and therefore could be considered not to have entered the country legally. For a time in the 1980s, Australia made much of this legal distinction as a way of limiting refugee claims. See James Crawford and Patricia Hyndman, "Three Heresies in the Application of the *Refugee Convention*" (1989) 1 Int'l

Convention not to return a person to a place where they may be persecuted is triggered.[30] My principal interest in this chapter is to consider how Australia and Canada respond to this international obligation – that is, how they respond to those who are already within the borders of the nation.

While offshore programs do not trigger an obligation in international law and therefore do not raise the intersection of sovereignty and rights claims, both Australian and Canadian offshore programs have notable features for my analysis. In Australia, the offshore program makes up the larger portion of refugees admitted and is treated by the government as being the neediest group.[31] As the Australian programs are formally linked, the offshore intake is reduced when onshore claimants increase. The effect of these provisions is to ensure a very high level of control over refugees admitted, as most are preselected before arrival in Australia, and to ensure tight control over the total number admitted, as any unanticipated increase in successful onshore claims can be absorbed without increasing total numbers. The minister responsible uses the policy link between the two programs in anti-refugee rhetoric, claiming that those who gain admittance within Australia are stealing the places of the others.[32] This ostensible result of the current system could easily be altered by the government, but not without sacrificing some degree of control.

J. Refugee L. 152. More recently, Australia has legislated to excise parts of its sovereign territory from its "migration zone," with the effect that "arriving" does not count for purposes of making a refugee claim. See *Migration Amendment (Excision from Migration Zone) Act 2001* (No. 127, 2001).

30 Article 33.

31 The target numbers remained constant from the election of the Howard government in 1996 until 2004. The overall target for Humanitarian Admissions was 12,000, with approximately half the places for refugees: notionally, 4,000 refugees from offshore and 2,000 from onshore. As the two numbers are linked, when onshore claims dropped sharply in 2002-3, refugees brought from overseas increased, but only to 4,376. The Howard government has consistently taken the position that offshore refugees are needier. For an early statement, see Honourable Philip Ruddock, Minister for Immigration, Address [Conference on Immigrant Justice, Sydney, 6 June 1997]. This was also included in election campaign material in 2001 (Liberal Party of Australia, *Immigration Building on Integrity and Compassion*, online: <www.liberal.org.au>, copy on file with author).

32 The government expresses this concern as follows in its 2004 description of its "new humanitarian visa system": "The system provides for a hierarchy of benefits depending on where they have made their application and whether a person has moved from a country of first asylum ... This is done in order to create further disincentives to a person who abandons effective protection opportunities in a country of first asylum and travels to another country or seeks unauthorised arrival in Australia by using people smugglers with the aim of gaining a resettlement place they may well not need – a place taken from refugees with no other options available to them": online: <www.immi.gov.au/facts/65humanitarian.htm>. See also Philip Ruddock, *supra* note 31, and Paul Ruddock, Address (Australian Institute for Administrative Law Twilight Seminar, Canberra, 30 October 1997).

The overseas program in Canada is considerably smaller than the domestic program.[33] The Canadian government has been criticized for using its offshore program as an adjunct of its independent migration program, that is, for choosing offshore refugees who are well educated and able-bodied and therefore likely to quickly become contributors to the Canadian economy.[34] This demonstrates that even in admitting the very needy, the usual logic of immigration – that the national interest is paramount – is not far from view. Educated, able-bodied refugees are most like the "us" group and most able to fit into the community quickly.

The most interesting feature of the Canadian program is the opportunities for private sponsorship. Following very successful private sponsorship programs during the Indochinese refugee influx of the 1980s, the Canadian government has now formalized opportunities for Canadians to increase the total annual number of refugees admitted through private sponsorships.[35] Private sponsorship both allows the government an easy response to domestic pressure to act more humanely and allows it to withdraw from direct responsibility for admission totals. It also underscores Don Galloway's point about the moral duty of the liberal nation that I considered in Chapter 4. That is, a nation must allow its individual members to help needy others if they choose to, but the nation itself does not have this duty. In this account of humanitarianism, the obligation is privatized and thus the responsibility of the nation is drastically reduced.

Refugee admission in both countries is part of their respective immigration programs. While refugee determination is set aside from economic and family migration, it is provided for in the same legislation and administered by the same department. Also, while the *Refugee Convention* would suggest that only temporary protection need be afforded to refugees,[36] those who are determined to be refugees have typically been given the right to remain permanently, although changes to Australian law in late 1999 created a new temporary visa for refugees arriving by unauthorized boat.[37] The

33 Although still slightly larger than the Australian program in raw numbers. In the 2002 fiscal year, ending in March 2003, the planning level for refugees brought by the government from abroad was 7,500, and 7,504 actually arrived; online: <www.cic.gc.ca/english/pub/facts2002/immigration/immigration_2.html>.

34 This criticism was reported in two separate interviews with officials at CIC in June 1997. European nations are especially critical, arguing that Canada takes the "cream" of the refugee crop and leaves the nations who are closer to the crisis regions to grapple with the remaining refugees.

35 2,800 to 4,000 privately sponsored refugees were targeted to be admitted in 2001-2; 2,900 to 4,200 were targeted for 2002-3, and 3,044 were actually admitted (*supra* note 33). A number of community groups are now concerned about the difficulty of making private sponsorships happen.

36 Making temporary protection the norm is a central aspect of Hathaway and Neve's plan for revitalizing international refugee law: *supra* note 8 at 156-69.

37 In Canada the result of a successful refugee determination is the right to remain in Canada and the right to apply for permanent residency. In Australia, those determined

internationally agreed definition of refugee has been written into the Canadian law since the immigration legislation was rewritten in 1978.[38] It has been specifically referenced in the Australian law since 1980.[39] Thus, there is no difference in the refugee definition between the two countries, save Australia's legislative shaping of some terms in 2001, which has not yet had a strong impact. Significantly, however, the definition has been written directly into the Canadian legislation, whereas the Australian *Migration Act* makes reference to the *Refugee Convention*. This provides one way for the nation to imprint its identity on the law, even when the text of the law is identical. Incorporating the definition into domestic law directly strengthens its status because domestic law generally has higher status than international law in national legal systems.

Both Australia and Canada set annual targets for the number of refugees who will be admitted through the domestic determination process.[40] The Canadian target is a soft one as a range is specified (e.g., 10,500 to 15,600 for 2002-3) and compliance with it is not rigorously required. The Australian policy of reducing overseas refugee numbers to accommodate the domestic target makes the target much firmer in Australia. The targets tell us two things: (1) Canada is admitting approximately twelve times as many refugees as Australia when domestic landings are compared,[41] in the context of a much larger overall immigration program;[42] and (2) domestic refugee claims are not treated solely as rights claims by either nation. The logic of a target is antithetical to that of a rights claim. While both programs do

to be refugees are given a "protection" visa, which carries the same rights and privileges as other categories of permanent resident visas, including the right to apply for citizenship after two years in the country. In November 1999, the Australian government created a new visa with reduced rights for refugees who arrive by boat. Holders of this three-year temporary entry visa (subclass 785) also have reduced entitlements to medical insurance and social security, and no entitlement to family reunion.

38 This is the year the former *Immigration Act* was proclaimed. Under the new *Immigration and Refugee Protection Act,* the refugee determination system is somewhat modified but the basic model is retained.

39 The *Migration Act* first referred to the *Refugee Convention* in s. 6A(1)(c), which was introduced into the act in 1980.

40 This is a legislative requirement in Canada. In Australia the targets are part of a well-established process but are not legally required.

41 The overseas intake programs are much more comparable, with Australia taking in 4,000 refugees and 6,000 "other humanitarian" migrants from overseas over the past few years. The Canadian figure for 2002-3 was 7,504 government-sponsored and an additional 3,044 privately sponsored. As in Australia, these figures are similar to those for the past decade or so. This is strong evidence for Mary Crock's conclusion that "Australia has had a substantial overseas program for many years, upon which it has founded its international reputation as a caring and generous country": Mary Crock, *Immigration and Refugee Law in Australia* (Sydney: Federation Press, 1998) at 124.

42 For some time, the annual immigration intake in Canada has been set at roughly 1 percent of the population, whereas in Australia over the same period it has been approximately 0.3 percent of the population.

partially reflect a right on behalf of a successful claimant not to be returned to danger because the targets can be expanded, this is countered both by measures ensuring that it is difficult to get to the country in the first place[43] and by rhetoric that equates refugee admission with the generosity of the nation rather than with its legal commitments.

In Australia, a refugee claim is first assessed by the Department of Immigration and Multicultural and Indigenous Affairs, Refugee and Humanitarian Division. The applicant submits a written account of their story and is interviewed in about 10 percent of cases.[44] Approximately 12 percent of claims are successful at this stage.[45] Unsuccessful claimants can seek a merit review before the Refugee Review Tribunal (RRT).[46] The RRT alters the department's determination in approximately 12 percent of cases.[47] Judicial review of RRT decisions was formerly possible before the Federal Court and the High Court. Migration cases comprised approximately 65 percent of the Federal Court's administrative law caseload in the late 1990s, which prompted first a reduction in the available grounds of review, followed by the introduction of a privative clause in 2001.[48] In 2003, the High Court ruled that while the privative clause is valid, it cannot oust review for jurisdictional error.[49] In addition, the minister can, as a matter of discretion,

43 Both countries use carrier sanctions to penalize transport companies who bring in people without a prearranged right to stay. Australia also employs a universal visa system and makes the living circumstances of those awaiting refugee determination miserable (many claimants are denied work rights, access to state support was reduced in 1998, and some are put in detention) in a high-profile effort to discourage refugee claimants. These measures all work to reduce the number of people who are in a position to assert this rights claim.

44 This figure does not appear in annual reports of the department or of the Refugee Review Tribunal. The department would not confirm, and advised me to file a Freedom of Information request. I have generously estimated the rate based on conversations with refugee law practitioners in Sydney over the course of 1999.

45 Department of Immigration and Multicultural Affairs, *Annual Reports 1998-99, 1999-00, 2000-01, 2001-02,* and *2002-03.* The most recent two years are anomalous, with a success rate of 25 percent at this stage in 2001-2 and of 4 percent for 2002-3.

46 This Tribunal has been in operation since 1993. Its operation is outlined in Pt. 7 of the Australian *Migration Act.*

47 This number also saw a marked drop in 2002-3, when only 6.6 percent of decisions were set aside (359 of 5,388). In 2001-2, the figure was 15.5 percent (710 of 4,647; in 2000-1 it was 12.7 percent (620 of 4,858). The percentages set aside were 8.2 percent in 1998-99, 8.9 percent 1997-98, 14.7 percent in 1996-97, and 16.3 percent in 1995-96. See RRT *Annual Reports,* online: <www.rrt.gov.au/publications>.

48 *Migration Legislation (Judicial Review) Act,* 2001 (Cth.). This clause was opposed by the principal opposition party for several years until the *Tampa* affair in 2001, after which opposition parties cooperated in passing a series of stringent migration law amendments. The principal concern animating this reform was that people who were not bona fide refugees engage in pointless judicial review and further appeals to prolong their stay in Australia. Philip Ruddock, "Narrowing of Judicial Review in the Migration Context" (1997) 15 Australian Institute of Administrative Law Forum 13 at 16.

49 *Plaintiff S157/2002 v. Commonwealth of Australia,* [2003] H.C.A. 2. This is discussed further in Chapter 7.

replace a negative decision of the RRT with a favourable determination, a procedure I discuss in detail in Chapter 6. Very few RRT decisions are reversed by the courts.[50]

In Canada, a refugee claim is considered in the first instance by the Refugee Protection Division of the Immigration and Refugee Board (IRB),[51] on referral by Citizenship and Immigration Canada (CIC). The 2002 legislation also provides for a Refugee Appeal Division, but implementation of this division has been indefinitely delayed. Claimants who are unsuccessful at the IRB may seek leave to appeal to the Federal Court, although this is rarely granted, with the result that IRB refugee decisions were set aside in only 1 percent of cases between 1995 and 2002.[52] The minister may also seek leave from the Federal Court. If a special question is certified and leave is granted, the Federal Court of Appeal and the Supreme Court of Canada are also available. An unsuccessful claimant may also seek a pre-removal risk assessment,[53] which can result in protected status or a stay of removal. Failed refugee claimants may also seek humanitarian and compassionate exceptions to the law to allow them to remain in Canada.[54] This is discussed in Chapter 6.

The next section considers the refugee hearing process in Australia and Canada as the key site of refugee identity construction. While the RRT and the IRB are not identically placed in the respective refugee determination processes, their roles are highly comparable. Each tribunal is responsible for the majority of successful refugee determinations in the country, and each tribunal provides the opportunity for face-to-face contact between the individual claimant and the state.[55] The tribunals are also similarly situated as

50 In 2002-3, 6 percent of cases proceeding to the Federal Court were remitted to the RRT for reconsideration, amounting to 1 percent of all RRT decisions that year. The number was 15 percent in 2001-2 and 18 percent in 2000-1. RRT *Annual Report 2002-03*, online: <www.rrt.gov.au/publications/annrpts/0203/part3/3_performance_outcome.html>.

51 This was known as the Convention Refugee Determination Division until mid-2002, under the former Immigration Act.

52 As reported in the IRB *Performance Report 2001-02*, available from the IRB website at <www.irb-cisr.gc.ca/en/researchpub/pub/index_e>. The IRB has been reporting this rate as less than 1 percent for the last several years since at least 1997. The requirement to seek leave was introduced in 1989 and applies to all IRB decisions, not just refugee decisions. No reasons for refusing leave are given by the Federal Court. This provision obviously limits the number of immigration cases reaching the Court and curbs the Court's influence over the IRB, as few decisions are handed down.

53 *Immigration and Refugee Protection Act*, S.C. 2001, c. 27, Pt. 2, Div. 3.

54 This is provided for under s. 25 of the *Immigration and Refugee Protection Act* and was formerly allowed under s. 114(2) of the old *Immigration Act*. Rejected applicants could also formerly seek to have their circumstances assessed against the criteria of the Post-Determination Refugee Claimants in Canada class, which provided permanent residency for some people in refugee-like situations under s. 11.4 of the former regulations.

55 A small number of cases that go before the Australian RRT are resolved "on the papers." In 1996-97, 191 of 15,139 cases, or 1.3 percent, were decided on the papers. A further 25 percent of RRT cases are settled when the claimant fails to attend the hearing. No

being at arm's length from the government. This is more prominent in Canada, where the IRB is a quasi-judicial body with the status of a superior court of record. In Australia, the constitutional separation-of-powers doctrine ensures that the tribunal remains part of the executive branch of government. This removes the ideology of judicial independence from the tribunal setting. The tribunals have similar legal staffs and information-gathering apparatuses. Finally, the Canadian model was in place when the Australian model was established, and undoubtedly served as an example, if only of what not to emulate.

The Other in the Refugee Tribunals

Any comparison between the refugee tribunals in Australia and Canada will highlight differences between the two forums. While these differences draw attention to key facets of the process, I aim to also retain a focus on parallels between the two tribunals. This central site for the construction and dissection of the refugee as other has important similarities in both nations. These similarities show how this stream of migration law fits within the framework of liberal migration laws I have described. By looking at similarities, along with some of the divergences, I outline how these tribunals carry out an othering function that is at the core of refugee identities. I look in particular at how identity and credibility are intertwined in the process, and at what counts as proof in these settings. To conclude the analysis, I step back from the similarities and consider what refugee othering contributes to an understanding of Australia and Canada as nations.

The Elements of a Refugee Hearing

A refugee hearing is intensely personal and the stakes are dramatic. The claimant tells a story and the ensuing decision determines whether they will be allowed to live the rest of their lives in a new and very different place. In observing the hearings, the most challenging task was to remain an observer and evaluator rather than become completely immersed in the story.[56] The first tribunal I saw concluded oral reasons by tritely saying, "Welcome to Canada and best wishes for your life here." The burly, confrontational claimant and I were equally surprised to find ourselves weeping. I found that this initial reaction soon wore thin for me under the weight of mundane and repetitive process aspects. It remains vital, however, to

---

figures for "on the papers" decisions are available in the 2002-3 RRT *Annual Report*. In Canada, when a claimant does not attend the hearing, the claim is deemed abandoned and no decision is made.

56 In the early stages of my research, I observed RRT and IRB hearings in 1997, 1998, and 1999. I saw the IRB in Ottawa, Toronto, and Vancouver, and the RRT in Sydney. I also interviewed tribunal members presiding in the hearings and, in Canada, the claimants' lawyers.

retain a sense of the enormity of the process for those who encounter it only once.

Both Australian and Canadian refugee hearings are symbolically charged: the nation is on display. The Canadian flag and the kangaroo and emu crest are displayed. Claimants, and the occasional witness, must swear or affirm that they will tell the truth, even though this ritual is evidently the barest of formalities as they are frequently disbelieved. The hearings are closed to the public, adding to the sense of intimacy, and the rooms are smaller than most courtrooms in either country. At the RRT hearing rooms in Sydney, the doors have no handles on the public side. Those waiting to enter and tell their stories see only a keyhole. Even when their name is called, they cannot enter the room without an escort. The symbolic passage to the nation is complete in this one detail.

In camera hearings accommodate the personal stories and the vulnerabilities of genuine claimants. For this reason, they are immunized from the ideological need for justice to be seen to be done. One result is to remove claimants from the procedural protections that visibility provides and to protect the hearing from scrutiny, which is therefore reserved for the written reasons. The crucial process for construction of refugee identity is hidden from view. While the goals this achieves are vital, and to conduct hearings in public would lose more than it would gain, it does foster public misunderstanding of the process and provide scope for imaginative speculation about the content and meaning of refugee identity. It ensures that the other remains unknown.

The hearing is in both instances designed to be non-adversarial. In Canada, this aim is reflected in the roles assigned to people in the room; the Refugee Protection Officer does not "prosecute" the case but assists the tribunal by selecting issues to be explored and questioning the claimant.[57] At its outset in 1989, the IRB had three-member panels. For most of its existence, it has been constituted by two members and the claimant need only convince one. Under the 2002 legislation, one member constitutes the tribunal, providing legislative recognition of the direction that practice had often followed, by claimant consent, since the late 1990s. Most claimants are represented by legal counsel.[58] Until late 2003, counsel typically took the

57 The role and behaviour of Refugee Hearing Officers is one of the principal topics of James C. Hathaway's "Rebuilding Trust: Report of the Review of Fundamental Justice in Information Gathering and Dissemination at the Immigration and Refugee Board of Canada," submitted to the Chair of the IRB, Ottawa, December 1993. The report was commissioned to address concerns of inappropriate behaviour of Refugee Hearing Officers (now called Refugee Protection Officers) and information-gathering practices at the IRB. While many changes have been made in the ensuing decade, discussions at the March 2004 University of Ottawa Human Rights Centre Roundtable on Refugee Determination suggest that the Refugee Protection Officer role is still problematic.

58 Cuts in legal aid funding have had an effect on the number of claimants who are represented. As of early 2004, however, most claimants in Canada still had lawyers.

lead in hearings. In the name of efficiency, however, the IRB began having the Refugee Protection Officer take the lead. In theory, the hearing is not conducted as though the claimant has a case to meet. Most tribunal members play an active role in the hearings through establishing an agenda in a pre-hearing conference and through active questioning during the hearing. These efforts to move away from the adversarial model, to reflect both the informality and efficiency values of the tribunal and the fact that the claimant is not on trial, are only moderately successful in meeting that goal. Since lawyers represent most claimants, and many tribunal members are legally trained, implicit norms of the adversarial system do tend to dominate the proceedings.[59] The new *Immigration* and *Refugee Protection Act* provision allowing the minister the option of attending refugee hearings adds a more adversarial element.[60]

The Australian hearings have moved further from the adversarial model. The tribunal is constituted by one member, and the hearing proceeds with the member putting questions to the claimant. Even when the claimant has a legal representative,[61] that person has no formal role in the hearing and can address the tribunal only if invited to do so. Most hearings proceed with only three voices in the room, those of the sitting member, the claimant, and the interpreter. The Hearing Officer is a member of the administrative staff who starts the tape recorder and administers the oath, then leaves the room. The Hearing Officer's role is in no way parallel to that of the Canadian Refugee Protection Officer. As with the IRB, some RRT members have legal training and others do not. The hearing is a very private setting and the personal style of the member greatly influences how the event proceeds. Accordingly, whether that person is legally trained or not is likely the biggest factor in determining the extent to which the values of the adversarial system influence the hearing. Australian tribunal members receive far less initial and ongoing training than their Canadian counterparts, and never work as a team in the hearing room.[62] The Australian hearing is designed to follow an inquisitorial process, but even those who are legally trained would

59 In "Rebuilding Trust," *supra* note 57, James Hathaway argues that refugee hearings achieve a non-adversarial format. I agree that the potential for this is provided, but in the hearings I observed that it was achieved only occasionally.

60 Section 170.

61 In 1996-97, 58.79 percent of claimants before the RRT had an "advisor" on the record (statistic generated at my request from the RRT database, not publicly available past this date). At the RRT, the term "advisor" can mean anyone, even a friend, who is assisting with the application. No statistics are kept on how many advisors actually attend the hearings, but tribunal members and refugee lawyers suggested in interviews that often the advisor would not attend the hearing, as it was time consuming and therefore expensive for the client and their potential role in the hearing process was minimal.

62 When new members join the RRT, they undergo a five-day training period. This training includes an introduction to the tribunal's role and function, an introduction to

not likely have training in the procedural values and mechanisms of the inquisitorial process beyond that provided by the tribunal.

One reason for moving away from the adversarial format is to make the hearing less onerous for the applicant.[63] Hathaway points out that when the purpose of the hearing is conceived as being to assist the nation in meeting its legal obligations, there are no adversaries.[64] The hearing could be conceived in this way in Canada but often seems not to be, especially now that the minister can be a party. In Australia, the RRT is a review tribunal. Accordingly, the refugee claimant is confronting the state that has already rejected them. This adversarial structure element is tempered, however, by the fact that the state does not send a representative to the hearing, only the reasons for the earlier decision. Concerns over abuse of the refugee process are widespread in the popular discourse of both nations, belying the non-adversarial vision. While a classic adversarial process is impossible in the tribunal setting, it is difficult to jettison. The extent to which a non-adversarial process is achieved depends in part on the tone set by the individuals in the room, rather than on any difference in the Australian and Canadian formats. While the Australian system is formally less adversarial because it takes the form of a conversation between tribunal member and claimant, it is not necessarily less of an ordeal for the claimant.

Moving away from the adversarial format is problematic when the hearing is set within a legal paradigm that relies on the adversarial system to protect the interests of the individual and to ensure fair process. While the adversarial system is not the only measure of fairness,[65] Australian and Canadian notions of what constitutes a fair hearing and of the extent to which an adjudicator is responsible for assisting someone appearing before them

---

administrative arrangements, a session on different aspects of the refugee definition, and instructions on managing caseload and writing reasons. New members also observe two or three hearings before beginning their own. They receive regular written updates on legal developments and meet to discuss important cases from the Federal Court or the High Court. New members of the Refugee Protection Division (RPD) of the IRB begin with a two-week training period covering similar topics; in addition, they complete sessions on job-specific topics such as "weighing the evidence" and "assessing credibility" (copies of these training modules are on file with the author). Under the old legislation, they sat as the second member in their hearings for the first six months of their tenure. They also receive regular updates on legal developments. The IRB has a training department and offers ongoing training modules for all tribunal members. A proportion of these sessions are tailored for RPD members.

63 Although it is notable that many tribunals not concerned with refugee claims have abandoned aspects of the formal adversarial process, such as the rules of evidence, in the name of cost and time efficiency.

64 Hathaway, "Rebuilding Trust," *supra* note 57 at 6.

65 In both Australia and Canada, the courts have explicitly held that fairness will vary with each setting: *Mobil Oil Pty Ltd v. Federal Commissioner of Taxation* (1963) 113 C.L.R. 475; *Baker v. Canada (Minister of Citizenship and Immigration)*, [1999] 2 S.C.R. 817.

have been honed in a system presuming professional representation. Thus, the federal courts' decisions that build the parameters for the tribunals' actions assume adversarial norms. Judges in a civil law system receive specialist training for their inquisitorial role, but the common law norm is that good advocates become good judges because the truth of any matter emerges through the clash of informed adversaries. When this norm is taken away, as in the refugee hearings, the values and norms of the inquisitorial system do not simply flow in to take its place. The adversarial system remains the operating background norm. The respective federal courts, through judicial review, have had some role in infusing adversarial values into tribunal procedure.

The central role of the tribunal member in setting the tone for the hearing, especially in Australia, draws attention to another way in which identity is constructed and played out in the hearing room. The member's identity is also constructed in this setting, although, significantly, this identity is a privileged choice rather than an identity assigned by others or as a desperate last resort. Those who comprise the tribunals are very similar in both countries. Members are selected from among lawyers, bureaucrats, and nongovernmental organization (NGO) members who have experience with refugees and refugee issues.[66] Most tribunal members come to the job with a high degree of personal commitment to refugees.[67] The identity of the tribunal member emerges through the matrix of personal and role expectations in the setting. What tribunal members believe about their role in this setting influences their approach to the hearing and, ultimately, their ruling. These factors mean that there are important differences in the way self-identifications of tribunal members affect Australian and Canadian processes.

There is less variation in the self-perception of roles by IRB members because of their greater level of training and because of the greater number of people in the room. Norms of behaviour are constructed and reinforced by working side by side with a colleague (as present members did under the training regime made possible by the old act) and by conducting a hearing with a Refugee Protection Officer and a lawyer representing the claimant. These two factors mean that norms of behaviour and of self-identification

66 IRB members are appointed by the Governor-in-Council under s. 153 of the *Immigration and Refugee Protection Act*. An independent Ministerial Advisory Committee (composed of members of the NGO and legal communities) was created in 1995 to advise on appointments. RRT members are appointed by the Governor-General under s. 459 of the *Migration Act*. In practice, they are selected by a committee including the minister for immigration.
67 In Canada, a persistent minority of IRB members can be characterized as purely political appointments with no backgrounds in refugee or immigration issues. The minister of citizenship and immigration announced plans to end such appointments in March 2004, but the basic components of the selection process are the same.

are likely to vary less in Canada, which fits with my observations.[68] Having tribunal members do the same things in the same way promotes one view of fairness. While fairness is not the only value of importance in the tribunals, and sameness is not the only path to achieving it, fairness is a crucial part of the rationale for providing a hearing and sameness is one of the easier fairness indicators to provide. The rationale for attempting to do this in a setting where little else can be standardized is strong.

The multiple players in the Canadian hearings mean that the identities at play can be divided into professional and claimant, insiders and outsiders, nation and other. For the tribunal members, the Refugee Protection Officers, and the lawyers,[69] the hearing is a professional pursuit. It is one hearing among many and their personal stake in it is low. Many of these individuals know each other from earlier hearings and know that their paths will cross again, and of course the tribunal members and the Refugee Protection Officers work in the same office. They chat informally during hearing breaks and have more in common with each other than with the claimant. This is true even for the claimant's lawyer. The collegiality that we could characterize as the sign of a good working relationship makes the demarcation between members and others particularly obvious. The claimant is an outsider to the nation necessarily, and in the hearing room this is underscored by their exclusion from the friendly banter and the professional courtesies. This insider–outsider demarcation is enhanced by the informality of the hearing room and the non-adversarial features, which allow the common interests and common enterprise of the professionals to be evident, as opposed to a court, where formality fixes roles. What the tribunal hears of the claimant is mediated not only by interpretation[70] but also by the questions and analyses of the Refugee Protection Officer and the lawyer. These actors, therefore, influence how the individual claimant's identity is constructed and to what purpose.

The structuring of the story by professionals is not so apparent in the Australian hearings. In the RRT, the contact between tribunal and claimant is more intimate, mediated only by translation. While tribunal members are part of a professional team within their working environment, in the hearing room they, like claimants, are alone. Opportunities for familiarity and collegiality are minimized. These factors contribute to the heightened

68 This will probably change as the IRB moves to single-member hearings as the official norm.

69 Interpreters are not involved in this group to the same extent. This could be because they are often seen by the others as an extension of the claimant. Interpreters are often members of the same cultural community as the claimant, which may account for this difference to some degree. Also, interpreters share a level of communication with claimants that is impossible for the others. During breaks in the hearings, I often saw interpreters talking with the claimants.

70 Not all claimants use interpreters, but most do.

intimacy of the Australian hearing process. The hearing unfolds as a long conversation between tribunal member and claimant. The distancing devices, such as questions and directions of others, which map out the boundary between the two identities, are minimal. This, in combination with the other factors making the RRT member's identity more flexible, means that the Australian process is more open to an intertwining of identities, which can potentially produce either empathy or bias. The boundary between the nation's representative and the outsider is more malleable in this model. There are more opportunities for renegotiation of identities by both parties. The othering of the claimant is less obvious in the hearing room, as there are fewer interventions guiding the story and the hearing proceeds often seamlessly, without the law's procedural interruptions. There is strong potential in this setting to move beyond an insider–outsider formulation and to escape the legal strictures that many argue are inappropriate in refugee hearings. However, this is largely untapped because of other factors shaping tribunal members' identity, because the process operates within a legal framework, and because of the influence of review by the Federal Court.

The most significant influence on the identity of RRT members is that of the institutional culture. The Principal Member remarked that he would have absolutely no way to influence the decisions made by individual members because of their uniformly high level of independence.[71] This independence and personal commitment is part of the institutional culture, as is the knowledge that each claim under review has already been rejected by the department and various pressures to keep the set-aside rate down.[72] Tribunal members work in a setting where close to 90 percent of the claims they hear are determined to be invalid. This rate alone contributes to a view of the tribunal member as a gatekeeper who must work to ensure that the correct determinations are made so that the system is not ground to a political halt. The RRT member's self-perception, shaped by these factors, is in turn the greatest influence on the tenor and outcome of the hearing in a system where there are so few players in the hearing room and such minimal training for members.

Attention to the identities in the hearing room demonstrates how many of the differences between the two systems can be explained by considering the construction of the tribunal member's identity. This identity is key to

---

71 Interview with former Principal Member Shun Chetty, January 1998.
72 Some pressure on the tribunal comes from the current climate of hostility towards refugee claimants and concern over rising levels of claims, which are now frequently reported in the mainstream press. Some pressure is also generated directly by the current minister's hostility towards inland claimants (see *supra* notes 40 and 41). In 1997, the minister publicly stated that tribunal members who set aside too many of his department's decisions would not have their terms renewed: M. Steketee, "Tribunal Defends Refugees' Status" *Australian* (6 February 1997) at 2. This threat appears to have been carried out, according to my discussions with two former tribunal members.

the process when legal norms are put aside as inappropriate or unworkable and the tribunal member stands in the place of the nation sizing up the other. The informality of the refugee hearing serves to make the identities involved in the hearing more malleable. While identity-based critiques of law point to the malleable and negotiated qualities of all legally constructed identities, these features are particularly important in these settings. The tribunal and the claimant come face to face in the hearing room and their interaction creates an image of the boundary of the nation. This construction is aided by the strong symbolism of the hearing context and the way the adversarial system becomes a hidden background norm to the process. In this setting, the identity of the individual is tested against that of the refugee category.

The Central Issues: Identity and Credibility
In a refugee determination hearing, there are two central issues: identity and credibility. They are necessarily intertwined. By the time claimants get to a hearing, they are usually telling a story that fits broadly within the refugee definition, because in Canada claimants likely have a lawyer and in Australia they have already been through the departmental process. Tribunals are then faced with determining whether people are who they say they are and whether their stories are true. Is this person a Kenyan posing as a Somali? Was he really a member of the Mujahadeen? How are divorced women treated in Liberia? What needs to be proven and how it may be proven are markedly different in a refugee determination tribunal and in a courtroom setting. Proving identity and assessing credibility raise problems that deepen our understanding of the role of identity in refugee hearings and offer further insights into the encounter of the refugee claimant with the background norms of the nation and with the fitted form of the refugee definition.

The basic issue of identifying oneself is the starting point of a successful refugee claim. For most of us, proving our identities is done through documents: passports, birth certificates, driver's licences. Our identity is genuine because it is certified and enumerated by the state. These foundations for identity are destabilized in a refugee claim in several ways. Many people arrive to seek refuge without documentation and are then faced with establishing their identity in other ways. One's own account of self is not sufficient – a truth that most of us are spared from confronting. Personal identity in this border crossing scenario is about ties to a particular state, about membership in a given community, about belonging somewhere. As my framework of analysis suggests, these border crossing scenarios are where the identity brought to the fore is national identity. Without documentation, an individual's account of their identity is left to be assessed along with all other aspects of the story. The problem of undocumented arrivals is extensive[73] and both Canada and Australia have introduced provisions to penalize those who do not cooperate in efforts to document their identities.[74]

Even when claimants arrive with some documentary evidence of their identity, it is often not the piece of paper that we as Australians or Canadians are expecting. Claimants arrive with military service records or baptismal certificates, which are sometimes impossible to authenticate. A considerable number of claimants arrive with admittedly false documents, in part because of almost universal carrier sanctions and the prevalence of smugglers. The array of documents from around the world that may be presented as proof of identity in the refugee process jars against the standard practices of legal systems that generally operate on the basis of narrowly defined rules about what kinds of documents, under what sorts of circumstances, will be viewed as authoritative.

The question of what oral evidence we can give of ourselves has been addressed in various ways in the tribunals. I have seen tribunals set up language tests to differentiate ethnic Albanians from Kosovar Serbs and quiz Somali claimants about the founding myths of their people. Claimants who assert identity with a particular religion are often asked about articles of their faith.[75] To begin the process, a claimant must have a known and stable identity, a starting point label, as without this the other issues do not matter. The stakes are high in the refugee hearing, as are the incentives to lie.[76]

---

73 "More than half of refugee claimants do not present a passport or other legitimate travel document at the time they claim status. The majority of these claimants do not have any other identification": *Building on a Strong Foundation for the 21st Century: New Directions for Immigration and Refugee Policy and Legislation* (Hull, QC: Supply and Services Canada, 1999), c. 11. Given Australia's universal visa requirement, the problem is transformed into one of false documents or documents destroyed en route.

74 In Canada, this is found in s. 106 and in Australia in s. 91W. These provisions were introduced in 2002 and 2001, respectively.

75 One Jewish lawyer who had represented many Jewish claimants from the former Soviet bloc stated that he always tested his client's bona fides and was most suspicious of those who knew all the answers, as if they were making a studied presentation. This observation underscores that credibility is a fine line in all these sorts of "identity tests."

76 There are a large number of people who may simply be said to "feel they are refugees." They want to escape situations where they are impoverished, oppressed, or threatened by violence. They know that rich nations like Australia and Canada sometimes help people in misery. They see that life in one of these places is much easier than the life they have come from, and so they claim refugee status. The dissonance between the popular understanding of "refugee" and the formal legal definition may account for what politicians refer to an abuse of the system. Most people seeking refuge from horrible life circumstances are not, legally, refugees, but may genuinely identify as refugees. Patricia Tuitt takes the provocative approach of considering all who seek refuge in a wide variety of circumstances as refugees, and begins her analysis of refugee law by considering the vast number of refugees whose lives the law does not affect. From this starting point, she inevitably concludes that "refugee law is at the margin of most refugees' lives": *supra* note 8 at 23.

This identity is a prerequisite to refugee identity. Those with identity documents that are suspect are asked to give an account of how they obtained the documents and why the state would agree to provide them. Letters addressed to the claimant at the address they are fleeing are useful evidence, particularly if they are written in the "correct" language.

Proving identity often places the refugee claimant in an unresolvable dilemma. For many claimants, obtaining identity documents from the state they are leaving is difficult or impossible. On the other hand, to travel to somewhere as distant as Australia or Canada, some sort of documentation is necessary. The incentives for genuine refugees to use falsified documents are high. In order to get into the position to make a refugee claim based on truthful evidence, one must tell some sort of lie along the way. To give a coherent account of one's identity, that lie must be revealed, in a story that gives a full account of the lie. The false and the true identities are both an essential part of the refugee identity. The challenge for both the claimant and the decision maker is not to trip over the lines between the two.[77] Both false and true identities, however, are intertwined in the "genuine refugee" identity, as the need for a false identity enhances the likelihood of meeting the refugee identity threshold. The *Refugee Convention* recognizes this dilemma with its requirement that claimants not be penalized for entering a receiving country illegally.[78]

The story of identity in the refugee hearing is one part of the broader analysis of how the tribunals decide whether to believe a claimant. The common law's ways of knowing are foreign to this setting. There are usually no witnesses to the story being told. The claimant's narrative is the key to the outcome. The formal rules of evidence are obviously unworkable in these settings and are inapplicable.[79] It remains important, however, to consider the values these rules represent, what is traded away for that necessary efficiency, and how the hearings are overshadowed by the absent evidence rules. However idiosyncratic those rules may be, they do represent an agreed-upon code for accepting that certain things are true or known.

---

77   In one hearing that I observed, the tribunal was troubled by the Swedish passport that the Iranian claimant had used to come to Canada. For over an hour, discussion turned on the extent of the claimant's ability to speak Swedish because the gate agent (under the incentive of carrier sanctions) had signed an affidavit saying that the claimant was Swedish-speaking. The claimant stated that he was Iranian and had merely memorized a few phrases to go with his fake passport. No one in the hearing room could speak Swedish and the claimant's lawyer asked that the gate agent be made available for questioning about their own Swedish skills and the extent of the interview. While the tribunal refused and asserted that nothing turned on this point, the extent of questioning belied that.

78   Article 31.

79   This is provided for in the Australian *Migration Act,* s. 420(2), and the Canadian *Immigration and Refugee Protection Act,* s. 170.

Part of the evidence code involves asking anyone giving testimony to swear an oath to tell the truth. This ritual is striking, as each hearing room contains an assortment of holy books so that one may swear on the culturally appropriate symbol. Alternatively claimants and witnesses may simply swear to tell the truth. The contents of the oath in Australia do not change with the religion chosen, and no one I spoke to at the RRT could confirm that this form of oath swearing plays the same role in Muslim or Jewish cultures as it does in Christian ones. The assumption that a religious oath has the same function in any religion requires a more thorough examination. This serves as a marker of how inadequate our interpretations of the other are in this setting. It also demonstrates how the evidence code – including belief that we are bound to tell the truth because we have sworn an oath – injects values into the process even though rules of evidence need not be followed.[80]

Much of the logic of the common law approach to evidence cannot be applied in a setting where the adversarial format has been set aside and the only witness is the claimant. The ideological foundation of the adversarial system – that the best way to the truth is through equal adversaries arguing from positions of self-interest – is absent in this setting. While the flaws in that ideology are easy to point to, no equally persuasive account of the pursuit of truth in legal settings has yet captured the common law imagination. The crucible of cross-examination, while available in modified form in refugee hearings, is inappropriate for those who have been persecuted and sometimes tortured and interrogated by states with little respect for human rights. Credibility assessments are further complicated by the use of interpreters and by cross-cultural communication.

Given this setting, particular techniques of proof have evolved for the refugee hearing. Dominant among these is extensive reliance on independently gathered documentary evidence of conditions in the countries that refugees are fleeing. The RRT maintains a library of selected documents and has a small staff who prepare country reports and respond to tribunal members' queries. The Immigration and Refugee Board's Documentation and Information Research Centre is considerably more sophisticated. There are up to twenty-five full-time staff involved in the research program in the Ottawa headquarters, and an additional ten to fifteen positions spread among the other offices. The centre works to an annual research agenda, which is fine-tuned at monthly meetings, and also deals with specific members' requests. Both tribunals rely on information gathered by newspapers,

---

80 See further Catherine Dauvergne and Jenni Millbank, "Burdened by Proof: How the Australian Refugee Review Tribunal Has Failed Lesbian and Gay Asylum Seekers" (2003) 31 Federal L. Rev. 299 ["Burdened by Proof"], arguing that important values at the core of the law of evidence ought not to be jettisoned when the technicalities of the rules of evidence are.

by NGOs – especially those concerned with human rights issues, such as Amnesty International – by their own government's diplomats, and by other governmental sources, such as the annual reports of the United States State Department.[81] The Australian tribunal also draws on the IRB's resources. While much of this evidence would not be accepted as proof of fact in an Australian or Canadian court, it has authoritative weight in the refugee hearing.[82] The principal technique of proof is to assess the claimant's narrative against the situation described in the documents. Do the police really refuse to help women? Have ethnic Chinese shopkeepers been harassed in this way? They provide an alternative avenue to truth that a tribunal member can then try to fit with the claimant's story.

In the context of a refugee hearing where oral evidence, even when it is delivered in a way that fits with Western stereotypes of reliability, describes situations that are literally unimaginable, recourse to anything at all that is published takes on heightened importance.[83] While IRB members in particular are given considerable training in weighing evidence from diverse sources,[84] there is often only one source available and so this balancing act cannot be performed. The RRT has little or no training in this area and is demonstrably worse at weighing competing sources.[85] The context is such that there will almost always be holes in the evidence and a decision about credibility will frequently involve a leap of faith that cannot be filled with newspaper reports of human rights abuses.[86] Among documentary evidence,

81 In my study with Jenni Millbank of 331 tribunal decisions concerning lesbians and gay men in both countries, our data showed that the most commonly used information sources were international commercial and mainstream media reports, which are referred to in 36 percent of cases; international human rights organizations such as Amnesty International and Human Rights Watch, whose reports were referred to in 29 percent of cases; United States State Department country reports, which were used in 28 percent; published academic papers, which were referred to in 18 percent; and reports prepared by queer activist groups, which were used in 14 percent of cases: *ibid.* at 309.

82 Hathaway noted in 1993 that in the IRB "nearly any piece of documentary evidence adduced has been received" (*supra* note 57 at 22), despite the tribunal's discretion to exclude documents if they are not deemed to be credible or trustworthy.

83 This technique of credibility assessment by document analysis is strengthened by the practice in both tribunals of having members specialize in claims from a given country or region. This allows a member to become familiar with the types of issues raised, with the range of documentary evidence available, and with the demeanour of claimants from that region giving evidence. All these factors can assist in overcoming the problems posed in assessing credibility.

84 Weighing evidence and assessing credibility are identified as separate training issues for the initial training of members. The Legal Services Branch of the IRB has produced separate reports on "Assessment of Credibility in the Context of CRDD Hearings" (39 pages), "Weighing Evidence" (50 pages), and "Commentary on Undocumented and Improperly Documented Claimants: Assessing the Evidence, Enhancing Procedures" (30 pages) to be used in initial and ongoing training.

85 See Dauvergne and Millbank, "Burdened by Proof," *supra* note 80.

some sources are more reliable than others. In a review of approximately 280 RRT decisions, Jenni Millbank and I found extensive reliance by the RRT on cables from Australia's Department of Foreign Affairs and Trade (DFAT). While these are convenient and easily obtained, their contents are often idiosyncratic and anecdotal rather than research-based.[87] The RRT often prefers evidence from DFAT to that from other sources, regardless of its level of detail or its verifiability, both of which are often weak. The Canadian counterpart is not used as a source of evidence. A further Australian issue in the information stakes is that the RRT's information-gathering resources are not available to the public. While claimants in Canada can access the resources of the Documentation and Information Research Centre,[88] this is not the case in Australia, and pre-hearing disclosure of information obtained varies from member to member.[89] Adverse information must be put to the claimant at the hearing, but the inaccessibility of the documents gathered by the RRT means that claimants must discover documents on their own if they wish to present them.

The review of the courts ensures that the rules of evidence cast a long shadow over tribunal procedures. While the evidence rules are banished, their discourse (credibility, trustworthiness, probative value) and their results (found facts) are not.[90] While cross-examination is officially removed, its allure is irresistible. The law needs stable identities and known facts. These characteristics are key to the hearing as identity construction process. By believing an individual's account of their identity, the tribunal makes that identity exist as a legal fact. By rejecting that account, the tribunal rejects the individual's identity, along with the individual's aspiration to a refugee identity. The role of documentary evidence in the process of proving a refugee identity emphasizes the place of the refugee as the ultimate other to the nation. We understand and believe the refugee on the basis of

---

86 In the recent high-profile Australian case of *Minister for Immigration and Multicultural Affairs v. Eshetu*, [1999] H.C.A. 21, the RRT rejected the claimant's account of political persecution in part because there was no available newspaper account of a key event he described.

87 Dauvergne and Millbank, "Burdened by Proof," *supra* note 80 at 313-17. My examination of the High Court files in the *Applicant A* case confirm that this source is highly regarded. The stack of documents concerning the application of the one-child policy in China was approximately 30 cm high and included reports from academics and NGOs. The DFAT information totalled approximately 10 pages, but it was the DFAT version of the policy that was taken up by the RRT and hence by the High Court.

88 Unlike members, claimants cannot lodge specific requests for information.

89 Susan Kneebone, "The Refugee Tribunal and the Assessment of Credibility: An Inquisitorial Role" (1998) 5 Australian Journal of Administrative Law 78. An applicant may request that the RRT call certain witnesses, but the tribunal retains discretion to refuse the request (s. 426).

90 In Australia, a number of cases have challenged the inadequacy of tribunal reasons: *Paramanathan v. Minister for Immigration and Multicultural Affairs*, [1998] 160 A.L.R. 24; *Mulalidharan v. Minister for Immigration and Multicultural Affairs*, [1996] 62 F.C.R. 402.

information gathered in foreign lands. The stories of refugees are so un-imaginable to us, so unknown and unknowable, that our usual methods of proof are unreliable or impossible. To make a refugee determination, the tribunal must imagine that other place and situate the claimant within it.[91] This provides another way of distinguishing refugees from other migrants: we allow refugees to stay on the basis of their "otherness," on the basis of knowing things we cannot imagine. Family and economic migrants are al-lowed to stay on the basis of knowledge that they share with us: knowing family, language, skills, professional standards, economic trends. We mea-sure them against the known and refugees against the unknown.

The Final Product: Tribunal Decisions

The way in which identity and credibility dominate the hearing process is, of course, reflected in the reasons of the tribunals, but in significantly dif-ferent ways in each country. Reasons of the Australian tribunal make stultifyingly dull reading. The RRT is required to provide written reasons in each case, even where the case is so compelling that a positive decision is made on the papers or in cases where the applicant does not attend the hearing. RRT reasons reflect a formula that includes a canvass of all the principal cases of the High Court and Federal Court on the contours of the refugee definition and often involves extensive and detailed citation of docu-mentary sources. The decisions contain a number of boilerplate paragraphs, a practice that has been approved by the courts.[92] As credibility assessment is crucial almost all of the time, the reasons contain statements such as, "The applicant varied and enlarged progressively over time the reasons for the demonstration,"[93] and "The Tribunal is not satisfied that the Applicant has provided completely accurate information."[94] The most important parts of any account are those that can be compared with the other sources of information in the credibility assessment process.

The IRB reasons are more compelling because they usually focus narrowly on the issues that concerned the tribunal. While the RRT discusses evidence in a general way, the IRB, instructed by the Canadian Federal Court, isolates precisely contradictions in evidence and makes its reasoning about credibil-ity explicit. IRB decisions are much shorter, do not contain boilerplate, and deal primarily with fact rather than law. There are several reasons for this. First, the IRB does not provide written reasons in every case, and is obliged

---

91 One way of testing credibility that I observed in both tribunals is by using maps and asking the claimant to describe from memory the distances and travel times between places while the tribunal member looks at the map. Here the spatial dimensions of the nation are paramount.

92 *Muin v. Refugee Review Tribunal; Lie v. Refugee Review Tribunal,* [2002] 190 A.L.R. 601, [2002] H.C.A. 30.

93 RRT Ref. No. V98/09074 at 6 (of electronic version).

94 RRT Ref. No. V96/05071 at 8 (of electronic version).

to provide reasons only in cases where claims are rejected after a full hearing.[95] Second, the IRB has the benefit of a longer and more established jurisprudence and the use of pre-hearing negotiations to narrow the issues to be discussed. In part, therefore, a narrow focus on facts and credibility represents a type of maturity of the refugee determination process.[96] Finally, the fact that almost all claimants tell stories that fit easily within the definition undoubtedly reflects the greater involvement of lawyers in the Canadian process. Like the reasons of the RRT, the IRB reasons demonstrate the crucial importance of documentary evidence as a test of the story.

It is tempting to assert, on reviewing the cases, that the IRB is more likely to believe a story than is the RRT.[97] But this type of conclusion is difficult precisely because of the role of credibility in the process and the importance of assessing differences in the stories carefully, of considering how evidence is delivered and the effects of interpretation, trauma, and culture in this process. In addition, the hearing processes are remarkably different, making it very hard to compare the conclusions. The written reasons, in whichever format, do little to convey the atmosphere of the hearing room and the subtleties of the process through which refugee identity is constructed. Both process and written reasons confirm that refugee determination decision making occupies a space at the very limit of our system of legal decisions.

To give some sense of the tribunals' differing approaches to identity and credibility, I draw on a larger comparative study of refugee claims on the basis of sexual orientation.[98] These claims provide a powerful example of

95 Section 169. Reasons for positive findings are written in a number of cases at the request of the chair of the IRB. For example, reasons may be requested where there appears to be a divergence in practice between RPD locations or where a newly arising type of claim is being considered. If the minister seeks judicial review of a positive decision, written reasons will be provided.

96 The tribunal itself reflected on the character of its decisions in a 1998 ruling: "Decisions of claims to Convention Refugee status have become increasingly difficult. The majority of claimants present a Personal Information Form [original application] including a narrative which, if credible, gives rise to a well-founded fear of persecution. Few claims are decided on definitional grounds, for example, whether there is a nexus to the definition. This is quite different than in the early years of the Refugee Division when many cases were decided on legal issues, for example that the claimant feared persecution by a non-state agent": *Re S.S.W.*, [1998] C.R.D.D. 104 (No. U96-05945) at para. 43.

97 This must be considered too against the backdrop of the guiding courts' decisions in each country. For example, the IRB will consider that someone fleeing compulsory or forced sterilization under China's one-child policy may be a refugee, whereas the RRT will not. A separate difference is reflected in the documents to be relied upon. The RRT generally finds that Christians in China are not persecuted; the IRB is still finding persecution in some cases. Both tribunals note that religious persecution in China has been declining, but rely on differing documentary sources in their decision making.

98 The larger study is a joint project with Jenni Millbank at the University of Sydney. We began this work in 2001 with a database of 331 Australian and Canadian tribunal and

the role of identity in refugee claims because they rely for the most part[99] on the "particular social group" ground of persecution and because sexual orientation as identity has had a prominent place in the evolving identity politics of both Australia and Canada. The construction of identity in these decisions highlights pronounced differences in the way the two countries approach both identity and credibility. Both Canada and Australia accepted that sexualized minorities would fit within the "particular social group" ground in the early 1990s.[100]

The Australian decisions first confront identity in these claims in their concern over whether the claimant is gay or lesbian.[101] Predictably, given the extent to which individual tribunal members control the hearing process, the reasons vary enormously. The tribunal's approach to this question reveals a view of the essence of identity as gay or lesbian. For some RRT members, sexual orientation is about particular sexual acts. For example, in summarizing evidence given about persecution, the tribunal noted that "they had a sexual encounter, although not anal intercourse."[102] In analyzing a claim where the applicant had not initially stated that he was gay, the tribunal considered whether this identity could have been inferred and stated, "I am prepared to concede that it would be a reasonable inference from the fact of sexual abuse by organization X that the applicant had become a homosexual."[103] In analyzing the question of membership in a particular social group, the Federal Court of Australia has stated that "the mere possession of some homosexual feelings might not necessarily be enough."[104]

The tribunal in these cases is clearly relying on conflating sexual orientation with sexual activity, which then generates pressure on the accompany-

---

Federal Court decisions made between 1994 and 2000. We have since extended the work to include cases up to 2002. Our work with these cases and other sexual orientation refugee claims around the world will continue through 2005. This brief discussion draws on a small number of these cases and is sole-authored. Full details of cases in the database are available from the author.

99   Sometimes a claim on the ground of sexual orientation overlaps with a claim on another ground. For RRT examples, see: V95/03527, V96/04324, N98/21948, N98/241116, N98/24718, V97/06971, N98/25216, N99/27818. For IRB examples, see: *Re F.C.B.*, [1999] C.R.D.D. 89 and *Re H.G.P.*, [1999] C.R.D.D. 188. I have not included claims made in the IRB by lesbians that are considered under the guidelines on women refugee claimants in this list.

100 The respective highest appellate courts confirmed this in *Ward, supra* note 16, and in *Applicant A, supra* note 17.

101 In this brief discussion, I consider only claims made by lesbians or gay men. Our database includes a number of claims by people of other sexual minorities, such as transgendered people and transsexual people.

102 N99/27499 at 3.

103 V96/05496 at 5.

104 *F v. Minister for Immigration and Multicultural Affairs*, [1999] F.C.A. 947 at 6.

ing credibility conclusions.[105] One tribunal stated that a claimant's former lawyer "presumably realized that the applicant was homosexual."[106] As the claimant had not disclosed this to his lawyer and was offering an explanation for lodging an earlier claim on different grounds, the tribunal's conclusion must surely reflect discriminatory stereotyping not explained in the reasons. While the tribunal almost invariably states whether it finds the claimant to be gay or lesbian, some members do this without focusing on particular sexual acts, signalling a broader understanding of identity as gay or lesbian: "I am satisfied that the applicant is genuine in his homosexuality. He stated that it was not so much a choice as the way he is."[107] Another tribunal member summarized evidence by stating: "He said that he recognized that he was gay for some time, yet it took several years to admit that it was an integral and permanent feature of himself."[108] Rather than reflecting discriminatory stereotypes, these could be read as reflecting the "particular social group" jurisprudence.

It was rare for the Australian tribunal to consider a claim without making a finding on whether the claimant was gay or lesbian. This was a marked difference from the IRB cases, where the *existence* of sexual orientation is often not treated as an issue in the case. Despite these potential influences, however, subjecting identity as a gay man or lesbian to a credibility assessment in each instance introduces an air of suspicion into the reasons and conveys the judgment that it is too "easy" to claim to be gay or lesbian and thereby gain passage into Australia.[109] Focusing on the question of whether one's identity as gay or lesbian is "genuine," in the RRT atmosphere of little standardization, also ensures that the tribunal reasons are a vehicle for the expression of individual members' own stereotypes and prejudices. As the refugee hearing brings the nation and the other into direct contact and establishes the meaning of the boundary between them, these factors become part of that boundary. Discriminatory stereotyping is reflected as national value, and conforming to stereotype becomes a requirement of entry.

The late 2003 Australian High Court decision *Appellant S395/2002 v. Minister for Immigration and Multicultural Affairs*[110] provides an important illustration of the intersection of gay identity and cultural stereotyping. A gay

105 The IRB also engages in this type of analysis, although less often. In one case, it stated that it accepted that the claimant was lesbian, even though she was not in a relationship with anyone at the time: *Re E.K.B.*, [1999] C.R.D.D. 175.
106 V96/05496 at 5.
107 V96/04143 at 3.
108 V95/03527 at 4.
109 This claim has also had an airing in the Canadian press: Marina Jiminez, "Refuge from the Stones" *The Globe and Mail* (6 December 2003) F6.
110 [2003] H.C.A. 71 (9 December 2003). See also Dauvergne and Millbank, "Before the High Court," *supra* note 15.

couple from Bangladesh had sought refugee status in Australia. The country information from Bangladesh mostly supported the view that young men who held hands in the street or who had occasional gay sex would not be at risk of persecution. On the other hand, older men, and those who wanted to live in monogamous relationships, were at greater risk. The case presented a challenge to the Australian stereotype where the middle-aged gay man in a long-term monogamous relationship fits the "good gay" mould more easily than the twenty-something man having anonymous sex in bars and on beats.

This case was important because it overruled a string of RRT and Federal Court cases holding that gay men and lesbians should conceal the sexual orientation aspects of their identity to avoid persecution, which had been a feature of Australian law for close to a decade. The persistence of this reasoning, despite it being at odds with refugee jurisprudence regarding religion and political opinion, points to unease at the tribunal with sexual orientation as identity and to its difficulty in grappling with criminal sanctions against gay and lesbian sexual and social activities.[111]

Even in cases that reject the argument that a "secret gay life" is an appropriate solution or in keeping with the intention of the *Refugee Convention*, the possibility has been raised. While ultimately finding the claimant to be a refugee, and stating that it would be "unacceptable" to require someone to live a "hidden inconspicuous life," the RRT in V95/03527 stated that "neither heterosexuals or homosexuals have a right to behave indiscreetly" and that "persons should, to the extent that it is possible, co-operate in their own protection."[112] Reasoning of this sort should cease following S395,

---

111 For example, in *Bhattachan* the Tribunal "put it to the applicant that homosexuality had existed in traditional Nepalese society, as it had in all societies, and asked whether he had considered living a secret gay life and perhaps even marrying as many had." This reasoning was rejected in the strongest terms in that instance by the Federal Court: *Bhattachan v. Minister for Immigration and Multicultural Affairs*, [1999] F.C.A. 547. However, in *Gui Ping Gui* the unanimous Federal Court stated that "what precipitated the police action was not Mr. Gui's membership of a particular social group but his conduct in a public place": *Minister for Immigration and Multicultural Affairs v. Gui*, [1999] F.C.A. 1496 at para. 28. Mr. Gui had been detained for three months after having been caught kissing his boyfriend in a public park. In *W.A.B.R. v. Minister for Immigration and Multicultural Affairs* (2002), 121 F.C.R. 196, the Full Federal Court stated: "It was open to the Tribunal to conclude ... that there was no active program for prosecution of homosexuals in Iran, so long as they were discreet and conducted their affairs privately. It was also open to the Tribunal to conclude that it was reasonable to expect that the appellant would accept the constraints that were a consequence of the exercise of that discretion" (at 205).

112 At 7 and 18. Similar comments, also in cases that led to positive findings, include: "My difficulty as a decision-maker, even when armed with the above reports on attitudes towards and treatment of homosexuals, is in deciding what the degree of risk would be for the applicant if he returns to Brazil and no longer hides his sexual orientation. I am of the view that if he were to exercise caution and steer clear of meeting places where homosexuals are likely to be attacked he would minimize the

but the proposition that one's sexual orientation could or should be hidden highlights a particular view of what constitutes identity. Identity here is treated as an optional accoutrement, not something integral to one's being. In presenting identity this way, the reasons construct identity as a gay man or a lesbian as a lesser order of identity, somehow not the same as one's ethnic or racial identity, or even as one's gender. The word "discretion" continues the presentation of gay or lesbian identity as being about sexual activity itself, rather than something about intrinsic self-concept. This version of identity also differs markedly from the treatment of political opinion or religion in the refugee definition, which are treated as nonrelinguishable because they are matters of conscience. The idea of hiding identity in this way also assumes that it is always possible to do so as a matter of choice. This assumption relies on ignoring the reality of "outing" in Australian and Canadian culture, and on assuming a universal knowledge of how lesbian or gay identity may be known.

The Canadian tribunal and Federal Court construct identity based on sexual orientation in a markedly different way from the Australian. In part, this is accomplished by not always treating the question of whether the claimant is gay or lesbian as an issue that requires credibility testing. Even when this issue is tested, the analysis differs from some of the RRT approaches. In *Polyakov v. Canada (Minister of Citizenship and Immigration)*, the Federal Court upheld a positive decision where "aside from two homosexual encounters ... the Board found that the applicant offered no evidence regarding his sexual orientation."[113] In *Tchernilevski v. Canada (Minister of Citizenship and Immigration)*, the applicant's own testimony regarding his gay identity was accepted even though the woman he was married to was pregnant at the time of the incidents he recounted.[114] In *Re EKG*,[115] the testimony of a friend (not a lover) that the claimant was gay was accepted without question.[116] In these cases, the issue of identity as a gay man or lesbian is treated as being explicitly *not* about particular sexual activities. In this analysis, identity is therefore integral to one's being, rather than something that one does occasionally or not at all. This understanding of identity

---

risk to himself" (V96/04324 at 11). And: "Even if one accepts the view that it is not unreasonable for homosexuals in the PRC to exercise discretion in giving expression to their sexuality, this does not end the matter. What does 'discretion' mean in this context? When does the degree of discretion required to avoid the chance of persecution become unreasonable? How discreet must an applicant be? Clearly it cannot mean avoiding all homosexual activity, even adult consensual sexual activity in private, this being covered by the concept of 'privacy' under Article 17 of the ICCPR" (V96/04813).

113 [1996] F.C.J. No. 300 at para. 5.
114 [1995] F.C.J. No. 894 at para. 3.
115 [1999] C.R.D.D. 54.
116 See also *Re N.W.P.*, [1999] C.R.D.D. 3; *Re V.P.C.*, [1999] C.R.D.D. 191.

facilitates fitting these cases within the refugee definition as it presents an understanding of identity based on sexual orientation, which makes it more like the other grounds of persecution.[117]

Few Canadian cases we reviewed considered whether identity as a gay man or a lesbian could be hidden. In contrast, this set of cases contains several where the applicant was involved in gay and lesbian activist politics. The tribunal considered that this participation fell within the ambit of protection from persecution.[118] The IRB has also found that persecution because of dressing in drag was intolerable.[119] Whereas the Australian cases concluded in several instances that criminal provisions outlawing gay and lesbian sexual activities did not in themselves amount to persecution,[120] the Canadian cases, in contrast, contain several examples of positive refugee determinations where homosexuality is not criminalized and other actions alone constitute the persecution.[121]

My objective in this brief analysis is not to present a comprehensive overview but to illustrate the capacity of an identity-based analysis to generate insights into the way the law is operating, and to demonstrate the importance of identity to refugee determinations. These cases also highlight the fact that the differences in tribunal processes in each country contribute to different outcomes by allowing RRT members more influence over shaping how evidence is delivered and how credibility is assessed. The standardization in the IRB mitigates against translating stereotyping directly into law. In a setting that is impervious to what our legal system normally accepts as proof, the identity of a refugee is constructed from pieces of stories told and documents preserved. The ability to detail personal experiences that dovetail with reported instances of human rights abuse become a key to establishing one's identity. The refugee setting is at the coal face of law's work in identity construction; from fragments of "evidence" that other legal processes would discredit and discard, something new is forged. Members prod at a story that has necessarily been recounted many times and that equally necessarily has been lied about at some point. The role of the lawyer in constructing the refugee story is important, first, in the sense that the professional advocate skilled in the pitfalls of legal definitions is best suited to

---

117   This also means that the analysis of whether gay men or lesbians can constitute a particular social group under the refugee definition is not particularly important in these cases. Following the *obiter dicta* of the High Court in *Applicant A, supra* note 17, this also seems settled in Australia.

118   *Re F.C.B.*, [1999] C.R.D.D. 89; *L.J. v. Canada (Minister of Citizenship and Immigration),* [1996] F.C.J. No. 1042; *Re H.F.P.,* [1999] C.R.D.D. 188.

119   *Re E.H.F.,* [1999] C.R.D.D. 142.

120   *F v. Minister for Immigration and Multicultural Affairs,* [1999] F.C.A. 947; *M.M.M. v. Minister for Immigration and Multicultural Affairs,* [1998] 1664 F.C.A.

121   *Muzychka v. Canada (Minister of Citizenship and Immigration),* [1997] F.C.J. No. 279; *Re E.K.B.,* [1999] C.R.D.D. 175; *Re U.O.D.,* [1999] C.R.D.D. 106.

telling the story in the most persuasive way, and second, because a success-ful refugee story is one that is completely other, unknown. Having a lawyer shape the story, like using an interpreter, keeps the refugee at a distance, unknowable, other.

The Lessons of Identity

The process of fitting into the refugee category and thereby gaining permis-sion to remain permanently in Australia or Canada involves the construc-tion of an identity as other and then of an identity as refugee. The claimant must fit into the narrowly defined category that the nation views as most needy in order to be granted the privilege of membership. The prize that is offered is belonging, a new identity within a new nation. This identity shift is poignant in settler societies, where the nation itself is new and all mem-bers can claim varying degrees of attachment to another nation.[122] The na-tional identification of the refugee is reconfigured through this process, which in a parallel movement brings a new identity into the nation itself. The law and identity relationship is displayed at several levels in this process. The refugee definition sets up a category in the migration law hierarchy. This identity is constructed within the text of the law but it then becomes a standard that individuals aim to fit within on the basis of other identity characteristics. Law does not simply construct the identity, but provides a map of which characteristics are important in the legal setting.

The Ultimate Other to the Nation

The importance of establishing identity in the refugee hearing points to the first phase in the nation's absorption of the other. Refugee claimants, many of whom cannot prove their self-identity, who cannot authenticate their membership of a state, are the extreme point of contrast with the nation itself. The claimant appears in the hearing room isolated and atomized. While we accept that all individuals are identified with some nation, our ways of knowing that identity are brought to the forefront here. The iden-tity is proven through legal text: passport, visa, national identity card, mili-tary record. The imprimatur of the state is the chief value here, providing a succinct definition of what the law will accept as national identity. Without that imprimatur, other identifiers can be offered. These provide a map of the constructs of mythological nation – of the collective imagination that is the signifier of belonging. What would we ask an Australian or Canadian in a hypothetical hearing elsewhere? Do you know the words to *O Canada?*

---

122 Indigenous peoples in settler societies also fit into this analysis as they have attach-ments with older nations, nations that have been pushed aside by the settler nation's development. The voices of indigenous peoples are absent from migration narratives. This is part of the mythological power of those narratives – they exist in order to validate an account of the nation that does not recognize the original inhabitants.

What is fair dinkum? Where is Rockhampton? Which is further south, Toronto or Vancouver? Explain the importance of ANZAC Day. Name the smell of the first snow of a prairie winter. Draw the map in red sand with a gum leaf. In the absence of law, we offer these accounts of ourselves. To authenticate the documents, to *prove* they are real, we tell stories learned and relearned in primary school. Through this first phase of the refugee process, we ensure that we know the other *as other*. Not as some trickster who may take advantage of our goodness, but as someone who is genuinely linked to another named nation.

The identity-labelling process also points to how little we know of this other. Their identity is reduced to a pinpoint – a passport printed on the correct type of paper, a number registered in the correct way, a nursery rhyme correctly recalled, the scars of a regime's favourite torture exposed. This pinpoint is what it is to be other: to be reduced to almost nothing, a blank space against which we can imagine otherness. The refugee determination process hidden from view preserves the unknown otherness of the claimants in the collective public imagination – leaves space to imagine, alternately, the horrors they have faced or the lies they are telling. The other is always largely unknown, constructed in opposition to the self in a move that reinforces and affirms the identity of the self. The refugee claimant, whose very identity is so tenuous as to be always at issue in a hearing and that the operation of our law must solidify it by finding it as a fact, plays this role for the new nation. Refugee law is structured to ensure that the refugee is everything, everyone, that we as members of a prosperous nation are not. Above all, refugees are persecuted or left to suffer by their own nation.[123] Their nation itself has treated them in such a way that our nation feels compelled to allow them haven, and allows that compulsion to act as a constraint on sovereignty.[124] We condemn the behaviour of the other nation in a gesture signifying that our standards are better.

The refugee is the ultimate other to the nation in part because their identity is defined so narrowly. When someone applies for admission as an economic or family migrant, that person's identity is closely scrutinized and recorded. Not only are the official state documents a sine qua non for the process but the picture of their identity is filled in considerable detail.

123   Both Australian and Canadian courts have now held that persecution need not be by an organ of the state itself but that the state must at least be connected to the persecution to the extent of being unable or unwilling to end it: *Ward, supra* note 16 and *Minister for Immigration and Multicultural Affairs v. Khawar*, [2002] H.C.A. 14.
124   Refugee law is frequently perceived in these political terms. Accepting refugees from a given state is viewed as a statement against that regime's policies, particularly its human rights records. During the Cold War, the refugee policy of the United States was highly influenced by Cold War lines of allegiance: Mark Gibney and M. Stohl, "Human Rights and US Refugee Policy" in Mark Gibney, ed., *Open Borders? Closed Societies? The Ethical and Political Issues* (New York: Greenwood Books, 1988) at 152.

Police certifications of good behaviour and detailed medical examinations are required. In some categories, bank statements and employment histories are verified. The immigration process creates a concentrated pool of information about identity that for members would be dispersed through the networks of the state. In the refugee category, the nation accepts that the same depth of information may not be available, and may not be susceptible to proof in the same way. While the emphasis on identity is maintained in all migration categories, it is the refugee who most closely fits the idea of other to the nation. Other migrants fit this role to some extent, as part of the identification process ensures that they are labelled and categorized as not one of us and ensures that most of them will not be admitted. But the refugee process does that and more, putting a cipher in the place of the outsider.

Once the identity of the claimant has been established, construction of refugee identity can begin.[125] "Refugee" is a narrow legal category box with specified borders. The claimant must fit within that box to become identified as a refugee, rather than as an "illegal" or a "mere economic migrant," the category labels for the putative abusers of the system. As self and social identities are the crux of the refugee definition, sometimes the phase where identity is established fulfills all the requirements of the process. Identity alone is sufficient to ensure our belief in persecution and no further story about what has happened is needed. This is the case of those who established their identity as ethnic Albanians from Kosovo in the first half of 1999 or as Afghans fleeing the Taliban regime in 2001.

That identity alone sometimes grounds a refugee claim highlights the interaction I referred to earlier of self and group identities in the refugee definition. The jurisprudence directs a two-step analysis; the successful claimant is persecuted, and that persecution is carried out on the basis of one of the five underlying grounds. The formula is individualized, but some people, some identities, are persecuted so uniformly that an individual story of persecution becomes a redundancy. These are the easy cases – the exemplars of the refugee definition that was written in the aftermath of the Holocaust.

---

125 Robert I. Barsky has analyzed the pre-1989 refugee determination process in Canada (which differed significantly from current practice) as an exercise in "constructing a productive other." His analysis draws extensively on literary and discourse theory, and he pays particular attention to conditions of communication within a refugee hearing. While his methods are quite different from mine, as is the subject of his analysis, his conclusions parallel those I present in this section. He states: "In fact, one (albeit cynical) hypothesis is that the hearing could be seen as a test of the claimant's ability to construct an appropriate version of the 'Convention refugee'; in this sense the measure of one's success in *constructing a productive other* as a refugee could be seen as a measure of one's future ability to *construct a productive other* as integrated citizen": Robert I. Barsky, *Constructing a Productive Other: Discourse Theory and the Convention Refugee Hearing* (Philadelphia and Amsterdam: John Benjamins, 1994) at 6.

Examples from the late twentieth century include Rwandan Tutsis, ethnic Albanians in Kosovo, Iraqi Christians, at least for as long as the crisis endures.[126] But identity alone will not make a Tibetan in China a refugee, nor a Jew in Russia. The story of feared individualized persecution must be added. Group identity is one part of the equation, but personal identity as someone in whom the state takes an interest – or has chosen to ignore – is also crucial. When identity is not enough, the refugee must also *be identified by* the persecutor, be singled out and noted. The individualization movement in refugee identity is political in that it is defined by the state through identification and persecution or failure to protect.

When the group or self identity of the claimant can be constructed to fit the definition, the refugee identity is completed. Otherness and individualized persecution become the passkey into the new nation. The legal framework categorizes and names personal experience as "persecution" or "mere discrimination," as based on specific grounds or generalized enough to escape the refugee definition by prevalence alone.[127] The refugee identity certifies one's admission to the nation, but at the same time confines one's experience of that new nation. "Refugee" is not a free-floating identity category with an existence outside the law. It is generated by legal pronouncement and then awarded as a prize through a specific legal process. The hearing process *determines* who are refugees and who are not. Refugees can stay in Canada and Australia because of their identity *as refugees*. Refugee identity is linked to the purpose for which it is created. For the nation controlling the process and recognizing the definition as a constraint on sovereignty, the boundaries of the refugee identity are patrolled with an eye to controlling how large the constraint on sovereignty becomes. In the hearing room, the tribunal member must determine whether refugee identity will become the entry to the nation or the barrier. For claimants themselves, the difference Minow describes between choosing and being consigned to an identity is a tricky one. At the hearing, refugees chooses this identity and, if successful, become consigned to it as their identity within the new nation – an object of charity and beneficence. At one isolated point, this identity is

---

126   Of course, none of these people come within the refugee definition until they leave their homeland. Also, Australian Prime Minister John Howard stated in early 1998 at a time of intense ethnically motivated violence in the aftermath of the Asian economic crisis that Chinese Indonesians were welcome to benefit from Australia's refugee program. This statement met with strong protests and statements of "clarification" from the Department of Immigration and Multicultural and Indigenous Affairs (DIMIA). This example illustrates the fleeting nature of our certainty about who fits in the category, given its dependence on politics.

127   This is one analysis of the *Applicant A* case (*supra* note 17) in Australia, dealing with China's one-child policy. For some judges, this was simply an application of generally applicable law (see in particular McHugh and Gummow JJ.).

chosen as the best option. Nonetheless, the question of choices must also incorporate the range of choices available. This range, as much as choice itself, reveals the power configurations underlying the identities.

Refugee identity provides a particular kind of entrée to the new nation. Refugees are not recruited because of their skills or their ties with us. Regardless of the extent of a commitment to multiculturalism, we expect that refugee identity will be a passing phase on the way to becoming "us."[128] Refugee fits in the hierarchy of migration categories at differing points depending on one's perspective. As migration is supposed to serve the national interest, some versions of the hierarchy place refugees at the bottom of the heap: we are helping them, they have nothing to offer us. In others, though, refugee admissions are valued for their moral goodness; the value is not of the refugees themselves, but of the nation for admitting them. In either case, refugee is constructed as an identity within the nation, a label that individuals wear that conditions their legal entitlements.[129] While this identity label is supposedly temporary, it has a certain endurance. Speaking of the 1997 Young Australian of the Year who had settled in Australia sixteen years earlier, the minister for immigration stated that without a commitment inclusive to citizenship, "we would not have seen a five-minute standing ovation for this young Vietnamese refugee."[130] The pride with which Australians or Canadians identify their parents as having been refugees is one reminder that refugee itself is an identity, which has an existence beyond its legal category. The law sets up the category, but what happens beyond the law engages other social ordering systems as well.

128 At least when we admit refugees permanently, that is the expectation. The Kosovar crisis of 1999 marked the first departure from the tradition of admitting refugees for permanent resettlement in Australia. Australia agreed to admit 4,000 people for temporary protection, to be housed on unused military bases in remote areas – that is, to remain as isolated as possible from "us." This departure from tradition is due in part to reluctance to extend the annual admissions quota, and in part to a desire not to assist the Milosevic regime with its ethnic agenda. Canada agreed to accept 5,000 refugees and stressed in official statements (e.g., Press Release, then Minister Lucienne Robillard, 30 April 1999) that most would return to their homes. They were, however, eligible to lodge applications with the IRB, and so could potentially stay permanently in Canada.

129 Those determined to be refugee claimants are given more immediate access to state services than other migrants and are given access to settlement assistance. In Australia, recent changes in the law have reduced the entitlements of potential refugees to Medicare and work permits while awaiting determination or appeal results, in order to reduce the incentives for claiming refugee status. These changes are testimony to the discourses of control and abuse of the system. Those who arrive on boats are now entitled to temporary protection only, during which time they receive less access to welfare state provisions than others.

130 Honourable Philip Ruddock, Minister for Immigration and Multicultural Affairs, "Immigration Reform: The Unfinished Agenda" (Address to the National Press Club, Canberra, 18 March 1998), as reported on the minister's website at <www.minister.immi.gov.au>.

The implications of refugee as identity are complex. Discussing the operation of the Women at Risk program in Canada, Audrey Kobayashi argues that the refugee determination process assures one's "otherness" and "status outside the normative realm of independent immigrants."[131] While the successful claimant "is potentially granted 'rights' ... she is simultaneously marginalized as practises of gender- and racialization reduce her access to social justice in the larger sense."[132] As the nature of refugee identity and the refugee determination process locate the refugee as the ultimate other to the nation, the endurance and potential for marginalization of this label ought not surprise us. Barsky's insights are equally apposite, as he argues that the refugee hearing reduces an individual's identity so that "the Other who emerges from these transcriptions is diminished to the point of near non-existence,"[133] which in turn facilitates the construction of the new productive citizen. When refugees are admitted as permanent members of the community, they are literally invited to change their national identity. This shift in identity is facilitated through a process that judges the old nation as bad and emphasizes the goodness of the new nation.

In the current structure of both Australian and Canadian migration law, refugee identity is usually a stop on the way to new bonds of national attachment. Like family and economic migrants, this outsider can become a member. The conditions of that membership are their differences, their ultimate alterity, their essentialized identity. The refugee process constructs the ultimate other to the nation, and then allows them to enter the nation. These basic features of the refugee determination process are carried out similarly in Australia and Canada – similarly situated nations applying the same international legal standard. In turning now to the contrasts in those "others" constructed by these two nations, we find traces of Australian and Canadian national identities.

Images of the Nation

Australian and Canadian refugee admissions processes have much in common, and administrators in each country follow the actions of those in the other country closely. Despite the overwhelming similarities of situation, the similar rhetoric, the close working relationship, and the shared common law heritage, however, there remain significant differences in both the process and the outcomes of refugee determination that point to aspects of

---

131 Audrey Kobayashi, "Challenging the National Dream: Gender Persecution and Canadian Immigration Law" in Peter Fitzpatrick, ed., *Racism, Nationalism and the Rule of Law* (Aldershot, UK: Dartmouth Press, 1995) 61 at 70.

132 *Ibid.*

133 Barsky, *supra* note 125 at 3-4. He is referring to the pre-1989 version of the Canadian hearing, which is more similar to the bureaucratic phase of contemporary Australian practice than to the current Canadian practice.

national identity. In this area of the law, as with family migration and economic migration, the operations of the immigration regime leave an imprint of national mores. Refugee admissions represent the hardest case for this argument, as admission criteria in this category are not a direct statement of national needs and values. Even with refugee admissions, however, decisions about how the internationally agreed definition is applied and interpreted reflect national characteristics.

Refugee admission is treated more expansively in Canada than in Australia. The acceptance rate of the IRB is considerably higher (approximately 50 percent over the past few years) than that of the Australian departmental process (13 percent) and the RRT (approximately 10 percent over the past three years). It is tempting to conclude from this that the Canadian system is more lenient, or that the law is interpreted more generously, but given that the source countries that claimants come from are very different, this conclusion is not a firm one. What can be said conclusively is that more people per capita are permanently admitted each year, that the inland processing system is arguably better resourced, that there is no routine provision for the detention of some classes of refugee claimants, and that those awaiting determination receive more extensive access to the social welfare net. By contrast, the waiting time for an initial determination in Australia is considerably shorter than in Canada, and the Australian government assists more people per capita to arrive under its offshore humanitarian program. All of these factors point to refugee admission as having a more accepted place in Canadian culture. As I elaborated in Part 1, this does not make the Canadian system *better*. Since there is no just standard for who should be admitted to the liberal nation, it is impossible to conclude that admitting more refugees, or more refugees per capita, is better or morally superior. While individual morality will lead each of us to make a judgment about these issues, there is no standard for the liberal nation.

The conclusion that can be drawn from the comparison is about the character of the nation. Canadian culture is more accepting of refugees than is Australian. This is partially linked to an overall tolerance for higher rates of migration and partially related to the fact that refugee admission is the most challenging branch of the migration program to control, and strikes closest to the heart of national sovereignty. The two areas where I noted that the Australian refugee program is more expansive than the Canadian are instructive. A more efficient processing time allows the government to remove people who are determined not to be refugees in a shorter time, thereby reducing the amount of time that they are potentially assisted by the state and reducing the likelihood that they will develop significant ties to the Australian community, especially if they are in detention. The time difference may be illusory, as unsuccessful refugee claimants have access not only to the RRT at a review stage but also to the Federal and High Courts, but one aim of the system is clearly to have ineligible claimants leave as quickly as possible. The privative clause that became part of the law in late 2001 was aimed at furthering this goal, and will still have some scope do so following a 2003 High Court challenge.[134] The Australian preference for off-shore refugees also fits in with the control ideology, as offshore refugees have no legal claim to Australian protection and can be selected according to any criteria that Australia chooses. In a revealing comment, one Citizenship and Immigration Canada official stated that that department had tried to reduce the number of refugees admitted to be closer to the Australian scheme, but had simply not been as "successful" because of citizen pressure.[135] Canadian refugee policy taps directly into this public sentiment through the private sponsorship scheme.

The operation of refugee law in both countries leaves an image of the nation with the quality of a photographic negative – stripped of its colour and oddly reversed. Australia is identified as striving for a homogeneous identity despite its multicultural commitments, as concerned about the size of its population, as wanting a rigid and impenetrable border. As befits a nation with two founding cultures, Canada appears here as more committed to multicultures, given that the alternative is not possible, more concerned with fairness in process than with efficiency – even though the end result is not much different.

The control that the Australian nation imprints on its refugee law is an image of the control it wishes to exert over its national identity. Contemporary refugee law, even with its now grudging acceptance of the international definition of a refugee, does not escape the shadow of the White Australia policy and the carefully constructed migration schemes aimed at replicating the English nation. Canadian refugee law tells a somewhat different story, paralleling in some ways the more contested White Canada policies. In a curious precursor to contemporary bureaucratic observations, the constellation of policies that constituted White Canada were less successfully implemented. The interpretations of the *Refugee Convention* in the national courts also contribute somewhat to this picture, a point that is further addressed by engaging the relationship between rights and identity in Chapter 7.

Refugees in the Migration Laws of Liberal Nations

The differences in the refugee determination processes in Australia and Canada are revealing but are overshadowed by the similarities in the two systems that conform to the place of refugee admission in the migration laws of liberal nations. The process reflects and reinforces the identity of

---

134 *Plaintiff S157/2002 v. Commonwealth of Australia*, [2003] H.C.A. 2. This decision is
    analyzed in Chapter 7.
135 Interview, June 1997.

the refugee as the ultimate other to the nation, the extreme point of contrast. As well as occurring at the border of the nation, refugee determination occurs at the edge of the law, just beyond the reach of many of the core values of the common law. As refugee admissions are part of the immigration regime in both countries, they belong to the legal regime where there is no justice standard. For all these reasons, using identity as an analytic tool to examine the refugee admission process is appropriate. Other legal and ethical assessments are severely limited in their applicability to this realm of decision making precisely because it is an area of sovereign assertion that constructs an identity for the nation, an identity for the individual as refugee and finally, by reducing pre-existing identities to a few narrow points, an identity for the refugee as new member of the nation. A focus on the roles of identity in refugee law points to several conclusions about the place of refugees in liberal migration laws and about those laws more generally.

First, despite the placement of refugees within the immigration program, refugee admission and migrant admission raise different issues in the popular discourse of the nation as well as in its law. The Western settler nations with developed refugee admission programs have historically welcomed immigrants. To admit people who are not welcome in their own homelands today joins the tradition in both Australia and Canada of admitting others seeking to rebuild their lives in places with more freedom. What is different, however, is the immigrant–refugee distinction. This distinction is a product of the twentieth century and reflects the relationship of each group to the nation. The traditional mythology of immigration in both Australia and Canada portrays immigrants as the builders and founders of the nation. Their courage, independence, hard work, and sheer will are held up, in various ways, as important to establishing the prosperous nations in which their descendants live. The role of immigrants as service providers for the nation remains a key plank of migration law and migration rhetoric. Modern immigrants are supposed to bring economic resources or support for families. Refugees are not viewed in this way, however. In the collective imagining of refugees, it is the individual who benefits from admission to the nation. The nation is generous and good, sharing its prosperity with the huddled masses.

This is a late modern turn in migration discourse. The "mere economic refugees" for whom Australian and Canadian public discourse exhibits so much scorn are no different from most of the founding immigrants. But Australia and Canada are no longer in need of hardworking pioneers, and most of the founding waves of migrants would not be admissible under contemporary rules. The new world is no longer the unmapped frontier far from the safe hearths of Europe. These new nations of (former) migrants have established identities and by many measures have eclipsed the living

standards of the old world. National prosperity has grounded the establishment of the welfare state, and it is no longer only the toughest who can
survive here. In this climate, then, it is possible to divide newcomers into
immigrant and refugee categories, the former serving the nation, the latter
being served. This development becomes possible when the nation is no
longer identified with the frontier, demonstrating the ongoing creation of
the nation as contingent event.

A second set of conclusions about the liberal nation can be drawn from
the distinct slippage between the term "refugee" and the term "immigrant,"
a discursive confusion that demonstrates a degree of unease with separating
the categories and that offers a strong potential for political exploitation.
The unease arises because the distinction between refugees and immigrants
complicates the boundary between members and others. The outsiders
are differentiated by this distinction. Decisions about admitting immigrants
are made in part on the basis of what those people have in common with
members of the community; we select people who can speak our languages,
who can participate in our workforce, who already have close relatives among
us, and whose presence therefore meets the emotional needs of those we
already count as members. Decisions about refugees are envisioned on an
entirely different basis. Refugees are admitted because of what they lack:
legal and actual protections from dangers that we assume (usually rightly)
do not occur within our borders. But once refugees are admitted, they are
treated as immigrants, expected to become like us, to build the new identities we have created the space for by strategically reshaping and reducing
their previous ones. Thus refugees have a complex relationship with national identity building. They are expected to contribute in the way all immigrants do to the identity of the nation, by first reflecting and then adopting
national values and becoming members of the national community. Refugees, through their neediness, contribute to the identity of the nation as
good, generous, and prosperous, as does the refugee determination process,
which labels some other nation as "bad."

These dual facets of the refugee's relationship to national identity explain
part of the slippage between the refugee and immigrant roles. Another part
of the explanation is found in the complexity of the refugee definition and
the fact that it does not parallel common understanding of the word. The
opportunity for political manipulation is found in the lack of popular understanding of the differences between the two groups. One contemporary
example is the Australian practice of naming boat arrivals "queue jumpers,"
as if they could simply join in line and wait their turn, whereas in reality
they do not qualify for any immigrant queue.[136] Government officials can

136 This statement was part of the governing party's policy statement in the 2001 na-
      tional election: "The Coalition will not tolerate blatant queue-jumping. This practice

draw on public humanitarian goodwill towards refugees when immigration quotas are expanded, and can tap into public hostility towards more open immigration when introducing measures that make refugee admission harder. While the issues ought to be analytically separate, they overlap in popular discourse. When the Australian minister for immigration says that the young woman named Young Australian of the Year is a former Vietnamese refugee and an immigrant success story, he is of course telling a version of the truth. Although she was not an immigrant in a strict sense, the achievements that brought this honour to her belong to the mythology of migrants, not the abject need of refugees. The confusion in 1999 about whether refugees from Kosovo should be admitted to non-European nations permanently, temporarily, or not at all reflects part of this confusion. In Australia, public sentiment raged against plans to admit people temporarily and isolate them from the population.[137] Many members of the public wanted the newcomers treated as immigrants even though they clearly were not. The strength of sentiment was so strong in Australia that arguably the discursive confusion was successfully deployed against government interests, even though in the end the matter was resolved at the international level by a UNHCR decision to keep the majority of refugees close to their former home to emphasize their temporary status and facilitate a return home.

The final point to be made about the migration law of the liberal nation based on the discussion of refugee admittance emerges directly from the issues presented by this discursive conflation of the two identities. The international norms surrounding refugees fall short of an obligation to admit refugees, let alone to admit them as permanent members of the community. For some nations, admission of refugees is not a choice at all – refugees cross their borders uninvited and it becomes a real or political impossibility to invoke the coercive force of the state to remove them. It is no coincidence that this is not the case for most prosperous Western nations, for those who developed the refugee definition. Both Canada and Australia are distant from nations that are currently generating large numbers of refugees. The spectre of boatloads of Indochinese arriving on Australia's northern shores and Canada's long, largely unpoliced border with the United States notwithstanding, neither nation has ever coped with a Kosovar exodus. For these nations, admitting refugees is a political choice that partly reflects

---

unfairly benefits a minority at the expense of the majority with equal or superior claims to entry" (Liberal Party of Australia, *Immigration Building on Integrity and Compassion*, online: <www.liberal.org.au>, copy on file with author). See also Katharine Gelber, "A Fair Queue: Australian Public Discourse on Refugees and Immigration" (2003) 77 Journal of Australian Studies 23.

137 For some examples and discussion, see: D. Shanahan, "Anyone Who Had a Heart" *Australian* (10-11 April 1999) 27; James Murray, "Noblesse Oblige Should Begin at Home" *Australian* (17 June 1999) 13.

genuine liberal humanitarianism. That is, while the *Refugee Convention* may not effectively limit sovereignty, the humanitarian sentiment it embodies has a moral resonance in these nations. This cannot be a complete explanation; indeed, much of the structure of contemporary refugee law would not exist if it were.[138] The resonance of humanitarianism in this area of migrant admissions underscores the importance of looking behind that value to see its persistent importance to liberal understandings of migration law. I turn to this topic in Chapter 6.

---

138 Patricia Tuitt argues that "refugee law is not motivated by exclusively humanitarian concerns – indeed, if the concerns of the law are humanitarian it is only marginally and incidentally so": *supra* note 8 at 7.

6
Reflecting Ourselves:
The Mirror of Humanitarianism

In both Australia and Canada, the refugee program is only one of several ways migrants are admitted on a humanitarian basis. In this chapter, I consider humanitarian admissions outside the refugee process. Through this discussion, I extend the argument developed thus far in two directions. By considering the ways individuals and groups are admitted under the humanitarian rubric, I broaden the conclusions about the othering process discussed in Chapter 5. Second, by considering the overall mechanics of humanitarian admissions, I draw conclusions about the importance of humanitarianism for the identity of the nation. These aspects of the chapter refine and develop the Part 1 discussion of the humanitarian consensus in liberal migration discourses.

The core of the argument in Chapter 5 was that the othering process contributes to construction of the nation's identity through its emphasis on those who are outsiders to the nation, who do not belong and whose admission must be closely scrutinized. Through this process, the members of the in-group are identified in contrast. The others are everything that we are not, everything that we reject and quarantine. Considering the role of humanitarianism in migration law and in relation to national identification adds another dimension to the picture of national identity. Not only does migration law portray the nation and its members as having values and attributes distinct from those of outsiders, but through humanitarianism it also paints the insiders as good, generous, and magnanimous. Through this label both the nation and its members are portrayed as virtuous.

As established in Part 1, humanitarianism occupies a curiously central place in migration discourses. Upon expelling a group of unsuccessful refugee claimants, the office of the Canadian minister of citizenship and immigration issued a press release entitled "The Government of Canada Honours its Humanitarian Tradition."[1] The Australian minister for immigration has stated proudly that "how we respond to the humanitarian crises that continue to plague the world defines us as a nation ... We are a nation that can be proud of its record of responding to refugee and humanitarian problems."[2] Humanitarianism is a rallying cry for those who feel that more refugees should be admitted, and a point of pride held out by national representatives in international forums. In political discourses about immigration past and present, humanitarianism occupies a place that belies its relatively minor contribution to annual migration intake in both Australia and Canada. Examining the construction of humanitarianism in this discourse sheds light both on its crucial role in migration discussions and on how migration law serves the needs of the liberal nation and in the process contributes to the identity of the nation.

The analysis in this chapter begins by outlining how humanitarianism is written into the Canadian *Immigration and Refugee Protection Act* and the Australian *Migration Act*. Drawing on this description, I consider how the Canadian courts have developed the notion of humanitarianism and how the Australian minister exercises humanitarian discretion. The contrasts in Australian and Canadian deployments of humanitarianism provide grounding for the subsequent analyses of the differences between judicial and executive control of this aspect of the law, the particular identities of the beneficiaries of humanitarianism, and how humanitarianism highlights differences between Australian and Canadian perceptions of the national self.

Locating Humanitarianism in the Law

Although humanitarianism has a similar place in Australian and Canadian rhetoric about immigration, the place it takes in the laws of each country is markedly different. A comparative analysis of these provisions illustrates and allows for refinements of my analysis above of the liberal consensus about humanitarianism. It also enables me to demonstrate important differences between the two systems, and to draw insights about national self-identifications from those contrasts.

The Canadian *Immigration Act* and *Immigration and Refugee Protection Act*

The place of humanitarianism in the text of the Canadian law was shifted somewhat by the 2002 *Immigration and Refugee Protection Act* (the *IRPA*). The changes are most appropriately read as a response to two things: (1) a con-

---

1 Honourable Lucienne Robillard, Minister of Citizenship and Immigration, Press Release, "Situation of the Chileans in Montreal: The Government of Canada Honours its Humanitarian Tradition" (28 September 1998).
2 Honourable Philip Ruddock, Minister for Immigration, Address (Victorian Press Club, Melbourne, 26 March 1998).

cern expressed by many, including the 1997 legislative review, about the broad ambit of discretionary decision making under the old act; and (2) the Supreme Court of Canada's decision in *Baker v. Canada (Minister of Citizenship and Immigration)*.[3] There are, correspondingly, two types of changes in the new act. The former far-reaching provision for decision making based on humanitarian and compassionate concerns has been partially replaced by similar provisions specifically tied to each part of the *IRPA* where it is relevant. The overarching capacity to make exceptions on a humanitarian and compassionate basis has not been removed, however, and is now contained in s. 25.[4] The second change is that statements in the act about humanitarianism and compassion now often include reference to the best interests of any child affected by the decision, echoing *Baker*. It remains to be seen whether these changes will constrain humanitarian discretionary decision making. At this juncture, however, it is useful to understand both the old and the new schemes for two reasons: first, because the former scheme is the source of the extensive Canadian jurisprudence of humanitarianism that will continue to inform decision making under the *IRPA*; and second, because in my view the shift in format is largely a cosmetic rearranging of the legislation. Under both regimes, the combined effect of the legislation, the regulations, and the policy manuals ensures that the concept of humanitarianism can potentially play a role in almost all aspects of Canadian immigration law.

The place of humanitarianism in Canada's legislation begins with the statements of objectives. The former act's commitment was "to fulfil Canada's international legal obligations with respect to refugees and to uphold its humanitarian tradition with respect to the displaced and persecuted." In the new legislation, the objective "to grant, as a fundamental expression of Canada's humanitarian ideals, fair consideration to those who come to Canada claiming persecution"[5] has been located as one of the objectives related to refugees rather than immigration. In each formula, humanitarianism is linked with Canadian tradition and Canadian values – strongly associated with the "us" group. Construction of tradition and values is integral to building nation and national identity. Linking humanitarianism with refugees in the new act fits within the parameters of the liberal humanitarian consensus. It does not, however, fit with the form of the act, where references to humanitarianism appear throughout the immigration provisions, not just the refugee portions.

Both the old and new acts provide for the admission of classes of persons in "refugee-like" situations. Subsection 6(3) of the *Immigration Act* provided

---

3 [1999] 2 S.C.R. 817.
4 See discussion below at pp. 137-51.
5 Formerly s. 3(g), now s. 3(2)(c).

that the Governor-in-Council could designate classes of admissible immigrants, "the admission of members of which would be in accordance with Canada's humanitarian tradition with respect to the displaced and the persecuted."[6] This provision was used to allow for the admission of individuals who would not meet the legal definition of a refugee but who came from dire circumstances such that they would be considered refugees in popular parlance. In the past, humanitarian designated classes had more narrow identity-based labels, such as "self-exiled persons designated class" or "Indochinese designated class," which closely paralleled Australian practice. The *Immigration and Refugee Protection Act* has a similar provision for designating classes of individuals who will be accorded protection.[7] It also provides that persons facing a risk to their lives, or of torture, or of cruel and unusual punishment will be considered persons in need of protection.[8] Thus, one important aspect of humanitarian admission is a legislated protection mandate that extends beyond the *Refugee Convention*.

Several of the appeal provisions in both acts provide for the possibility of lodging what is effectively a humanitarian and compassionate appeal. This is a non-legal appeal and does not depend for its success on an error in the earlier decision. These appeals are possible for refugees and permanent residents who are subject to a removal order,[9] and also for Canadian citizens and permanent residents whose applications to sponsor the immigration of

---

6   For much of the 1990s, two classes were designated, a "country of asylum class" and a "source country class." The country of asylum class included individuals outside their country of origin who had been and continued to be personally and seriously affected by a massive human rights violation, armed conflict, or civil war in their country of origin, and in respect of whom there was no possibility, within a reasonable period, of a durable solution. The source country class included those still residing in their country of origin who (a) had been imprisoned for exercise of civil rights pertaining to dissent or trade union activity, or (b) had been affected by civil war or armed conflict in their country of origin, or (c) would fit within the definition of Convention refugee had they been outside their country of origin, and in respect of whom there was no possibility, within a reasonable period, of a durable solution.

7   Provided for by s. 97(2).

8   Section 97.

9   In the new act, ss. 63(2) and (3) and (4) and s. 67(3) are the relevant provisions. The parallel provisions in the former act were contained in s. 70. The provisions are broadly similar in both acts. The new act excludes from *all* appeals those who are inadmissible on security grounds or because of human rights violations or serious or organized criminality. The other difference in the new act is that the humanitarian provision has been altered to take account of the Supreme Court of Canada's ruling in *Baker*. The former provision stated: "(3) An appeal to the Appeal Division under subsection (2) may be based on either or both of the following grounds: on any ground of appeal that involves a question of law or fact, or mixed law and fact; and on the ground that, having regard to the existence of compassionate or humanitarian considerations, the person should not be removed from Canada." The humanitarian provision now says: "67(1)(c) other than in the case of an appeal by the Minister, taking into account the best interest of a child directly affected by the decision, sufficient humanitarian and compassionate considerations warrant special relief in light of all the circumstances of the case."

a family member have been refused on certain grounds.[10] Permanent residents facing removal orders were formerly able to appeal "on the ground that, having regard to all the circumstances of the case, the person should not be removed from Canada,"[11] a provision that was broad enough to bring in humanitarian and compassionate grounds.[12] Cases under this provision frequently discussed factors similar to those considered where the appeal is on the basis of humanitarian and compassionate considerations only, which is probably one reason why this separate formulation has been dropped in the new legislation.

These appeal provisions fit into the analysis of humanitarianism and identity in two ways: because they provide an avenue for the Federal Court to generate a jurisprudence of humanitarianism, and because they are accessible only to certain individuals. These avenues are open only to individuals who already belong to the Canadian community, as citizens, permanent residents, or protected persons, each a category that provides a right to remain and thus at least some form of membership. In the former act, those holding valid visas could also have access to some of these provisions; the removal of this privilege draws the linkage even more closely around the idea of community membership. In addition, these appeals are not available to people who have been convicted or suspected of serious criminal offences, human rights abusers, or those who pose security risks. The eligibility restrictions limit compassion directly, making it available to "upstanding members of the community." This clearly reflects that we do not want to misplace our generosity – it goes to deserving members. This is not the most needy group that comes in contact with our migration law, not the group that immediately springs to mind when we talk of compassion. What is going on here is evidently more than straightforward generosity.

The most important appearance of humanitarianism in the old *Immigration Act* was s. 114(2), which stated: "The Governor in Council may, by regulation, authorise the Minister to exempt any person from any regulation made under subsection (1) or otherwise facilitate the admission of any person where the Minister is satisfied that the person should be exempted from that regulation or that the person's admission should be facilitated owing to the existence of compassionate or humanitarian considerations."

---

10 Section 63(1), formerly 77(3). This provision is unavailable until the applicant is determined to be a member of the family class.

11 Section 70(1)(b).

12 The broader formula does not always lead to a more sympathetic result. In *Kirpal v. Canada (Minister of Citizenship and Immigration)* (1996), 35 Imm. L.R. (2d) 229 (F.C.T.D.), the court held that under the narrower humanitarian and compassionate formula it was inappropriate to consider ability to pay for medical care, and this need for care alone was the appropriate focus of consideration. In analyzing "all circumstances of the case" under s. 70(1)(b), ability to pay and cost to the state would also be relevant factors.

The regulation that supported this section was similarly broad,[13] and the delegation of this authority from the minister to departmental officials was approved by the courts.[14] This provision was broadly interpreted to create a duty of the minister to consider applications for exemption from various provisions of the act on compassionate or humanitarian grounds.[15] This section was the basis for frequent exemptions from the provision that visa applications must be made outside the country and for exemptions from various visa requirements.[16] The *Immigration Manual* also gave some examples of what might warrant a humanitarian and compassionate response to aid in interpreting s. 114(2),[17] but the Federal Court of Canada has plainly stated that the manual provides guidelines only.[18] The guideline status of the policy statements contributed to inconsistencies in the exercise of the s. 114(2) duty. Expressing disdain for the guidelines, the authors of the 1997 legislative review stated: "They are used differently by different managers. Some managers will routinely use their powers under this section of the Act to permit over age dependants or an elderly parent to accompany an independent immigrant; others will do so only in very unusual circumstances ... Entire programs involving thousands of individuals have effectively been created under this broad and undefined umbrella. Some applicants will know of these practices, and will quite reasonably take advantage of them; others will not and be unwittingly penalized."[19] The review further criticized the practice of allowing entire programs to develop under the s. 114 authority,

13 Regulation 2.1 stated: "The Minister is hereby authorized to exempt any person from any regulation made under subsection 114(1) of the Act or otherwise facilitate the admission to Canada of any person where the Minister is satisfied that the person should be exempted from that regulation or that the person's admission should be facilitated owing to the existence of compassionate or humanitarian considerations."

14 *Minister of Employment and Immigration v. Jiminez-Perez* (1984), 14 D.L.R. (4th) 609; [1984] 2 S.C.R. 565 [*Jiminez-Perez*].

15 *Ibid.*

16 Cecil L. Rotenberg, "Humanitarian and Compassionate" (1989) 8 Imm. L. Rev. (2d) 295, noting that these were two of the three most common uses of humanitarian and compassionate grounds. The third occurred in appeals under ss. 70 and 77 discussed above. The program managers of visa offices were authorized to waive selection criteria relating to independent immigrants as well as the requirement that an applicant must possess a valid passport or other travel document. To waive other requirements, a recommendation must be made to the minister.

17 The test in the former manual was that "unusual and undeserved or disproportionate hardship" is encountered. The manual lists eleven "general case types: spouses of Canadian citizens or permanent residents, parents and grandparents, separation of parents and children, common-law and same-sex partners, de facto family members, unexecuted removals due to generalized risk, personalized risk of inhumane treatment, refugees who apply for landing too late, abusive relationships, inability to obtain a travel document, former Canadian citizens": Vol. 1P5 – *Processing Inland Applications for Landing on Humanitarian and Compassionate Grounds* at 15-24.

18 *Yhap v. Canada (Minister of Employment and Immigration),* [1990] 1 F.C. 722 (T.D.) [*Yhap*].

19 *Not Just Numbers: A Canadian Framework for Future Immigration* (Ottawa: Citizenship and Immigration Canada, 1997) c. 10 at 1 [*Legislative Review*].

such as a provision for same-sex spouses to be recognized and a similar provision for spouses to apply for permanent residency from within Canada.

The concerns about this provision have been addressed in several ways in the *Immigration and Refugee Protection Act*. Same-sex partners are now formally recognized as part of the family class, and there are now specific provisions for partners within Canada to apply for permanent residency. These provisions will considerably reduce the number of applications for humanitarian exceptions to the law, at least in the short term. The new legislation contains a blanket provision similar to s. 114, and in addition it parcels out the ability to grant humanitarian and compassionate exceptions and links them directly to various sections of the act.[20] Section 25 states: "(1) The Minister shall, upon request of a foreign national who is inadmissible or who does not meet the requirements of this Act, and may, on the Minister's own initiative, examine the circumstances concerning the foreign national and may grant the foreign national permanent resident status or an exemption from any applicable criteria or obligation of this Act if the Minister is of the opinion that it is justified by humanitarian and compassionate considerations relating to them, taking into account the best interests of a child directly affected, or by public policy considerations." It remains to be seen whether this will alter the practice of granting humanitarian exceptions to the act. It would seem to at least make more transparent exactly what types of decisions are being made on the basis of humanitarian reading.

The combined effect of these features of the legislation, regulations, and policy manuals is that humanitarianism and compassion are both a duty and a ground for appeal. These factors have led to the growth of a jurisprudence of humanitarianism, which I discuss below. The extensive provisions allowing exemptions ensure that humanitarian and compassionate grounds can become a factor in almost any category of immigration decision. This is at odds with locating humanitarianism as an objective for solely refugee-type admissions. Considering the role played by these grounds alone provides a good illustration of how migration law is endowed with flexibility to meet the changing needs of the nation. As the standard of humanitarianism is difficult to pin down, and attempts to do so must be regarded as mere guidelines, its use in the law ensures that the boundary can expand and contract without any perceptible legal or rhetorical shifts. This allows for responses that address shifts in popular discourses. One example is the marked drop in so-called Minister's Permits issued in the late 1990s.[21] At the

---

20   See ss. 12, 65, 67, 68, and 69, and also regulations 66, 67, 68, 69, and 233.

21   These permits allow entry into Canada and, by policy, are used in cases of humanitarian and compassionate grounds or national interest. Formerly provided for in s. 37, they are now available under s. 24 or s. 25. The number granted annually must be made public, and fell in the 1990s from over 12,000 annually to less than 4,000. In 2001, 3,394 permits were issued, 5 more than in 2000: Minister of Citizenship and

same time, the proliferation of the phrase identifies the Canadian nation and its members as humanitarian and compassionate, constructing the tradition that the act's objectives name.

The Australian *Migration Act*

The Australian *Migration Act*, by contrast, is not a document about humanitarianism. Humanitarianism is not mentioned in the act's objectives or anywhere in the text of the act. Humanitarianism in the Australian scheme is located at either the regulatory or the policy level. For example, the department has at some points in time given processing priority to some types of applications with a humanitarian angle, such as orphaned relatives in compelling and compassionate circumstances and family members of those who hold a refugee or humanitarian visa.[22]

The immigration stream offering permanent entry to Australia for refugees and others located offshore, or those found to be refugees while in Australia, is named the Humanitarian Program. The label signifies that inland refugee claimants are not primarily regarded as rights claimants but as beneficiaries of Australian generosity. Approximately half of the admissions in this program are granted on the basis of membership in designated identity-based groups resembling the humanitarian designated classes used in Canada until 1997.[23] The Humanitarian Program provides the possibility of entering Australia to some individuals who do not meet the narrow refugee definition. Admission in many parts of the program is based on shared group identity characteristics, and the chances of receiving one of the visas available are enhanced by existing support from someone in Australia.[24] Under this program, in contrast to the Canadian situation, most humanitarian concessions are made to people outside the country.

The final significant avenue for humanitarianism to play a role in admission to Australia is found in the discretion of the minister to replace decisions unfavourable to applicants.[25] There is no legislative requirement that this substitution be made on a humanitarian basis. From 1994 to 1999,

---

Immigration Denis Coderre, News Release, "Coderre Tables Annual Report on Minister's Permits" (30 April 2002); Citizenship and Immigration Canada, News Release, 98-20, "1997 Report Shows the Number of Minister's Permits Issued Holding at the 1996 Level" (2 April 1998). In the year ending 30 March 1997, a total of 4,059 permits were granted, a drop of 75 percent since 1992, when 12,000 were granted.

22 Department of Immigration and Multicultural Affairs, *Annual Report 1996-97*.

23 In 2004, the categories were: Burmese in Burma; Burmese in Thailand; Cambodian; Citizens of the Former Yugoslavia; East Timorese in Portugal, Macau, or Mozambique; Minorities of the Former USSR; Sudanese; Sri Lankan; Ahmadi; Vietnamese.

24 *Migration Regulations, 1994*, s. 2, subclasses 201: In-country [i.e., country of origin and therefore not a refugee] special humanitarian; 202: global special humanitarian [the named groups in note 23]; 203: emergency rescue; and 204: woman at risk. Individuals can be nominated for a visa by someone in Australia.

25 See full discussion below at pp. 151-56.

guidelines dealing with failed refugee applicants suggested that this discretion would be used only for "persons of humanitarian concern," in situations that closely approximate refugee status. The guidelines have since been broadened, but their usage is most often accompanied by a reference to humanitarianism. Between 1995 and 2001, under two ministers, 1,211 decisions were reversed.[26] No statistics are available on the number of requests received, but in 1998 the minister's staff estimated that less than 1 percent of the requests received for personal discretionary consideration resulted in a new decision.[27] It is accepted among those working in refugee law in Australia that high-profile cases taken up by political friends of the minister are most likely to succeed.

The contrast in the place of humanitarianism in Australian and Canadian legislation is stark. At the broadest level, humanitarianism in Canada is written on the face of the act and bestowed on people within the community; in Australia it is kept from the legislation and predominantly reserved for those overseas. The contrast in the place of humanitarianism is somewhat surprising given the strong and similar place that it occupies in discourses of migration in each nation. The differential position of humanitarianism can provide some insights into national identities in each nation. Before proceeding to this analysis, however, it is important to consider how the structures of the two acts have influenced interpretations and uses of humanitarianism. In Canada, the prevalence of humanitarianism in the act has generated a "jurisprudence of humanitarianism." In Australia, the emergence in the 1980s of a rather different jurisprudence of humanitarianism is part of the explanation for the *Migration Act*'s current structure, and can be compared both with the Canadian rulings and with the minister's use of humanitarian discretion.

The Canadian Jurisprudence of Humanitarianism

Canadian courts have been called upon to consider the grounds for humanitarian and compassionate consideration when an applicant who has been refused the benefit of humanitarian and compassionate discretion under either the current or former legislation applies for judicial review of that decision, or when a permanent resident, a protected person, or a sponsor

---

26 Eight hundred sixteen (816) were decisions of the Refugee Review Tribunal (overturned under s. 417). The remaining reversals were of decisions of the Immigration Review Tribunal and later the Migration Review Tribunal, and of decisions originally reviewed by line bureaucrats.

27 Telephone interview, October 1998. Johanna Stratton was also unable to obtain statistics during her research in 2002. See Johanna Stratton, "Humanitarian Intervention in the Public Interest? A Critique of the Recent Exercise of s. 417 *Migration Act, 1958* (Cth.)" (LLB Honours Thesis, Australian National University, Faculty of Law, 2002 [unpublished; copy on file with the author].

appeals a negative decision. While the first group of cases are judicial review applications and the second are appeals, this difference has only minor effects on the resulting jurisprudence insofar as it contributes to giving some content to the question of humanitarianism. Many applications for judicial review are framed in such a way that judges cannot avoid, or do not want to avoid, commenting on the specific circumstances that make up the alleged humanitarian and compassionate grounds, even if the end result of a favourable ruling is only to turn the matter back to the bureaucrats. Similarly, most merit appeals are put forward both as arguments on the law or the facts, and as arguments for special relief on humanitarian and compassionate grounds. Accordingly, in many cases that canvass the question of humanitarian and compassionate grounds, the decision is made on the alternative argument and returned to the first-instance decision maker. Both types of cases, therefore, have generated a volume of commentary from the Immigration Appeal Division of the Immigration and Refugee Board (IRB) and from the Federal Court regarding the meaning of humanitarianism and compassion. The Supreme Court of Canada has handed down two significant decisions in this area: *Minister of Employment and Immigration v. Jiminez-Perez,*[28] where it affirmed the Federal Court's reasoning about humanitarian and compassionate grounds and, in 1999, *Baker v. Canada (Minister of Citizenship and Immigration),*[29] where the Court went some way towards addressing humanitarianism. I shall return to this case shortly after canvassing the lower court jurisprudence that preceded it.

There are a number of important caveats in considering this jurisprudence. The number of cases involved is vast, particularly those that involve requests for exemptions from a legislative provision.[30] In the period between mid-1989 and October 1990, there were almost 40,000 requests to the department for review on humanitarian and compassionate grounds under s. 114(2);[31] there is no reason to expect that this figure would have been significantly reduced in subsequent years and every reason to expect an increase. The cases that reach the Federal Court are those where the initial determination has been negative. Presumably, therefore, the jurisprudence of humanitarianism is tilted towards circumstances where the element of compassionate concern is not compelling enough to clear the hurdle at first instance and where the applicant has enough resources to continue the process. Finally, in order to narrow the cases, I have drawn on those appearing

---

28 *Jiminez-Perez, supra* note 14.
29 *Supra* note 3.
30 The Federal Court of Appeal held in *Jiminez-Perez, supra* note 14 (confirmed by the Supreme Court of Canada without reference to this point), that former s. 114(2) could exempt any application from a provision in the act or the regulations.
31 As reported in *Vidal v. Canada (Minister of Employment and Immigration)* (1990), 13 Imm. L.R. (2d) 123 at para. 30 [*Vidal*].

in the most comprehensive Canadian immigration law reporter and have cross-referenced this selection with the most well-known annotated version of the *Immigration Act*.[32] This significantly narrows the field of cases and undoubtedly generates more variance than would appear were it possible to consider the entire range of cases decided.

All this having been noted, examining a small sample of these cases does serve to give the flavour of this jurisprudence and is unlikely to be misleading, given that the final decision regarding when humanitarianism is important enough to override the strictly legal provisions of the legislation usually rests in bureaucratic hands and that the early and leading cases have explicitly held that humanitarian and compassionate grounds, while subject to departmental guidelines, must be determined on a case-by-case basis. Given that entire programs developed under former s. 114(2) and that access to the appeal provisions is limited, the circumstances that generate these cases have significant similarities and patterns can be discerned.

Many of the cases under s. 114(2) involved people seeking an exemption from the rule that applications for permanent residency were to be lodged outside the country, and a significant number in this group were spouses of Canadians or permanent residents. While there is now a different way for spouses or partners in Canada to apply for permanent residency, this possibility will remain for others.[33] Several themes emerge in the cases. First, it was clarified early on that while s. 114(2) uses permissive language suggesting that the decision is at the discretion of the minister, the minister or, more correctly, their delegate, was under a duty to consider all applications made for exemptions.[34] It was equally clear that the departmental guidelines were not determinative or exhaustive of potential outcomes.[35] These

32 To canvass the pre-*Baker* jurisprudence, I have drawn on cases reported in the *Immigration Law Reporter* (2d) between 1987 and 1998, and have selected them from the Quicklaw electronic database service. I searched for cases that made reference to the section of the act I was interested in, and to the term "humanitarian and compassionate grounds." This method generated a set of 110 cases relating to s. 114(2), 67 cases on s. 77, and 60 cases on s. 70 of the *Immigration Act*. Many of the s. 70 cases were not relevant, and the analysis relates primarily to the s. 114(2) and s. 77 cases. I also referred to Frank N. Marrocco and Henry M. Goslett, eds., *The 1998 Annotated Immigration Act of Canada*, rev. ed. (Toronto: Carswell, 1998). I have sampled the post-*Baker* jurisprudence from 2000, 2001, 2002, and early 2003 using Quicklaw databases only as the *Immigration Law Reporter* is no longer linked to the Quicklaw service. The absence of the reporter as a screening device results in vastly more decisions to be considered, close to 400 for the three years under consideration.

33 This type of application has become so routine that Citizenship and Immigration Canada provides a form to be completed entitled "Applying for Permanent Residence from within Canada: Humanitarian and Compassionate Cases" (IMM5291E).

34 *Nijjar v. Canada (Minister of Citizenship and Immigration)* (1997), 42 Imm. L.R. (2d) 54 (F.C.T.D.), holding that the immigration officer had a duty to submit the application for consideration on humanitarian and compassionate grounds even when the applicants had not specifically requested this.

35 *Yhap, supra* note 18.

principles appear likely to be applied similarly to the *Immigration and Refugee Protection Act* provisions. Beyond these points, however, the jurisprudence takes up several themes in inconsistent ways.

Although it is an established administrative law principle that the standard of procedural fairness to be applied to a particular decision varies with the context of that decision, in the case of s. 114(2) rulings the notion of context seems to extend to the particular circumstances of the case in the pre-*Baker* decisions. A line of cases established that a review of humanitarian and compassionate considerations does not require an oral hearing,[36] but conversely, in particular circumstances, failure to interview the applicant will constitute reviewable error.[37] In *Vaca* the Court went so far as to state that a "mere" thirty-minute interview was insufficient.[38] The Court seemed to be responding to a particularly high degree of bureaucratic ineptitude.[39] This theme recurs in the cases and it is hardly surprising that executive incompetence raises the courts' ire.[40] What is more surprising, however, is that humanitarianism and compassion become the legal response to this annoyance. If this option did not exist in the legislation, the courts would be forced to choose between expanding the traditional grounds of reviewable error[41] and allowing some ineptitude to escape sanction. The "humanitarian" solution may, therefore, be a particularly apt one. However, it creates a basis for humanitarian concern that is at odds with a commonsense understanding of humanitarianism and compassion. Compassion becomes compensation for having to deal with a frustrating bureaucracy rather than with personal hardship. It communicates something about Canadian values but nothing about the person who is granted membership in that community.

36 *Nanatakyi v. Canada (Minister of Citizenship and Immigration)* (1994), 30 Imm. L.R. (2d) 97 (F.C.T.D.); *Selakkandu v. Canada (Minister of Employment and Immigration)* (1993), 22 Imm. L.R. (2d) 232 (F.C.T.D.); *Carson v. Canada (Minister of Citizenship and Immigration)* (1995), 95 F.T.R. 137 (F.C.T.D.); *Charran v. Canada (Minister of Citizenship and Immigration)* (1995), 28 Imm. L.R. (2d) 282 (F.C.T.D.).
37 *Chhokar v. Canada (Minister of Employment and Immigration)* (1991), 13 Imm. L.R. (2d) 282 (F.C.T.D.); *Vaca v. Canada (Minister of Employment and Immigration)* (1991), 15 Imm. L.R. (2d) 123 (F.C.T.D.) [*Vaca*].
38 *Vaca, ibid.*
39 The scheduled hearing had not been held because the applicants' file was misplaced, and the delay forced the applicants into the refugee-processing stream, to their disadvantage.
40 See also *Muoz v. Canada (Minister of Citizenship and Immigration)* (1995), 30 Imm. L.R. (2d) 166 (F.C.T.D.) [*Muoz*]; *Rizzo v. Canada (Minister of Citizenship and Immigration)* (1997), 41 Imm. L.R. (2d) 86 (F.C.T.D.); *Marques v. Canada (Minister of Citizenship and Immigration)* (1997), 35 Imm. L.R. (2d) 81 (F.C.T.D.), where costs were awarded to the applicant as an exceptional response to bureaucratic error; *Sandhu v. Canada (Minister of Citizenship and Immigration)* (1997), 40 Imm. L.R. (2d) 142 (F.C.T.D.).
41 See s. 8.1 of the *Federal Court Act*, R.S.C. 1985, c. F-7.

The cases also take a variety of approaches to economic factors. Intuitively, we reserve our compassion for those who are the most needy. Equally, money is our most common way of quantifying and comparing need. We might expect, therefore, that the benefit of a humanitarian and compassionate legal provision would go to those with the least money or, to put it another way, to those with the most need. Canadian courts treat economic factors in a variety of ways, none of which correspond closely with a commonsense understanding of compassion. The policy manual states that "establishment factors" alone are not sufficient to ground an application for exemption on humanitarian grounds,[42] and this has been repeated by the Federal Court.[43] Despite this, "establishment factors" often loom large in humanitarian and compassionate reviews[44] and it is difficult to predict when they will be a deciding influence. Certainly, any competent application will include reference to how well established the applicant is in the Canadian community, and practitioners claim that these factors are highly important. At the extreme, the court may regard establishment factors as decisive, as in *Muoz* where Justice Muldoon stated: "The exhibited documents attached demonstrate what valuable members of Canadian society are the applicants, parents and children alike. From praiseworthy accomplishments in employment to praiseworthy accomplishments in education and praiseworthy participation in their general residential community, it is evident that Canada is the better for their presence here ... From the evidence which the court sees herein, it would be highly astonishing if their h. & c. assessment [sic] were not positively favourable."[45] It is of course compassionate not to dislocate successful, happy families. But to use established success as a measure – even as one indicator among many – of who we ought to be most charitable towards is again counterintuitive. The Muoz family was far from being among the most needy in the community.[46] In *Vaca*, the Court attempts to separate the economic element from the factors under consideration in the humanitarian assessment, in recognition that

---

42 *Supra* note 17. Many "establishment factors" have an economic dimension, such as holding a job, having a Canadian educational or training qualification, or owning a house. Others include having friends and family in Canada and community ties such as links to voluntary organizations.

43 *Vidal, supra* note 31; *Pereira v. Canada (Minister of Citizenship and Immigration)* (1994), 31 Imm. L.R. (2d) 294 (F.C.T.D.).

44 *Muoz, supra* note 40; *Cabalfin et al. v. Canada (Minister of Employment and Immigration)* (1990), 12 Imm. L.R. (2d) 287 (F.C.T.D.); *Vaca, supra* note 37.

45 *Muoz, supra* note 40 at para. 5.

46 These cases do often go the other way, but the reasoning has the same counterintuitive ring to it. In *Pereira*, the court held that self-sufficiency *alone* does not warrant a positive humanitarian and compassionate consideration and that the applicant would be denied an exemption because she had stronger family ties in her home country than in Canada. Neither factor has much to do with what we think of as humanitarian outside the migration law context.

economic success alone ought not guarantee that one can circumvent the usual application of the rules. Justice Cullen states: "The myriad letters and affidavits of support from family, friends and neighbours, the English language certificate, the doctor and the priest's support, the purchase of a home, the participation in a business, all go to compassionate and humanitarian grounds – but they were not considered other than as economic establishment."[47] While this list reaches beyond economic factors, it does not reach beyond success indicators and demonstrating that Mr. Vaca was not among the most needy who would seek to remain in Canada.

The role of establishment and economic factors is simply unclear. One judge rules that it is appropriate to consider ability to pay for medical expenses when weighing up factors in a humanitarian assessment;[48] another explicitly rules this factor out of bounds.[49] One judge allows a spouse to apply for permanent residency from within Canada to avoid having the rest of the family become dependent on the state.[50] Another upholds a denial of the benefit of s. 114(2) to an individual in part because they had been receiving social assistance for some time.[51] The courts are obviously interested in the question of dependence on the state and it is never presented in a favourable light, despite what could be considered a logical argument that those most in need of compassion may need state support as a matter of course.

The pre-*Baker* jurisprudence under the appeal provisions is scarcely more coherent. Interpretations of humanitarianism arise most often when an application for sponsored immigration of a family member has been rejected. In all of these cases, therefore, there is an argument to be made about the humanitarian value of reuniting the family. In this area as well, the Appeal Division and the Federal Court appear inconsistent. Allowing an appeal on humanitarian and compassionate grounds and noting in particular the sponsor's genuine commitment to her mother and sister, the Immigration Appeal Division asserted that "in assessing compassionate and humanitarian grounds the Board must give effect to the Act's objective to facilitate the reunion in Canada of Canadian citizens and permanent residents with their close relatives from abroad."[52] In refusing a similar

---

47 *Vaca, supra* note 37.
48 *Sema v. Canada (Minister of Citizenship and Immigration)* (1995), 30 Imm. L.R. (2d) 249 (F.C.T.D.).
49 *Kirpal v. Canada (Minister of Citizenship and Immigration)* (1996), 35 Imm. L.R. (2d) 229 (F.C.T.D.). Both these cases were s. 77 appeals, but this issue of what is appropriately considered under the term "humanitarian and compassionate grounds" is identical to that in the s. 114(2) cases.
50 *Smith v. Canada (Minister of Employment and Immigration)* (1992), 18 Imm. L.R. (2d) 71 (F.C.T.D.).
51 *Orantes v. Canada (Minister of Employment and Immigration)* (1990), 34 F.T.R. 184 (T.D.).
52 *Rudrakumar v. Canada (Minister of Citizenship and Immigration)* (1996), 38 Imm. L.R. (2d) 82 (IRB-AppDiv) [*Rudrakumar*]. Other cases where the closeness of the family is among

application,[53] the same Board stated: "It clearly cannot be that every appeal with respect to a close relative will warrant granting of special relief, notwithstanding the broad policy objective of s.3(c) [reuniting Canadians citizens and permanent residents with their close relatives from abroad][54] ... The desire to be reunited with family is the basis of all sponsorship appeals and is not a special factor warranting special relief."[55] While arguably the difference is that some families are closer than others, the language used to describe the families differs little, and the family image against which assessments are made is that of a stereotypical Canadian family. Even if such a standard as degree of closeness were discernible, it is not being applied consistently in the jurisprudence. There are inconsistencies in what the Immigration Appeal Division says about the families it encounters, and it is these inconsistencies that leave a jurisprudential trace to be followed by courts, tribunals, and bureaucratic decision makers in the future.

Another theme that is prevalent in the appeal cases is the fragility of the line between an appealable error and a humanitarian consideration. This is especially apparent in cases where the application has been refused because one of the family members in the application is medically inadmissible.[56] Following the important *Uppal* decision,[57] the courts are prepared to scrutinize medical opinions in detail and to consider alternative evidence.[58] *Uppal*

---

the principal humanitarian and compassionate grounds include *Mena v. Canada (Minister of Employment and Immigration)* (1990), 13 Imm. L.R. (2d) 147 (IRB-AppDiv); *Chan v. Canada (Minister of Citizenship and Immigration)* (1994), 28 Imm. L.R. (2d) 317 (IRB-AppDiv) [*Chan*]; *Sall v. Canada (Minister of Employment and Immigration)* (1993), 22 Imm. L.R. (2d) 66 (IRB-AppDiv) [*Sall*]. In *Parmar v. Canada (Minister of Employment and Immigration)* (1993), 21 Imm. L.R. (2d) 102 (IRB-AppDiv) [*Parmar*] and *Chan v. Canada (Minister of Employment and Immigration)* (1993), 21 Imm. L.R. (2d) 259 (IRB-AppDiv), the IRB examined the facts and found that the family was not particularly close and used this factor in their reasoning to reject the appeal on humanitarian and compassionate grounds.

53 *Parmar, ibid.* In both cases the sponsorship had initially been rejected because a mentally retarded family member was included in the application.

54 *Ibid.* at 16 of QL version.

55 *Ibid.* at 26 of QL version.

56 Under the *Immigration and Refugee Protection Act,* close family members who are partners or children of their sponsor are no longer inadmissible because of potential "excessive demand" on Canadian health or social services, but may still be inadmissible on the grounds of health conditions that pose a danger to "public health" or "public safety" (s. 38). Most of the cases being considered relate to the former "excessive demand" bar.

57 *Uppal v. Canada (Minister of Employment and Immigration)* (1987), 2 Imm. L.R. (2d) 143 (F.C.A.) [*Uppal*].

58 *Tan v. Canada (Minister of Citizenship and Immigration)* (1997), 40 Imm. L.R. (2d) 113 (IRB-AppDiv); *Partab v. Canada (Minister of Employment and Immigration)* (1989), 8 Imm. L.R. (2d) 282 (IRB-AppDiv); *Nagra v. Canada (Minister of Citizenship and Immigration)* (1997), 38 Imm. L.R. (2d) 197 (IRB-AppDiv); *Rudrakumar, supra* note 52; *Sidhu v. Canada (Minister of Employment and Immigration)* (1994), 28 Imm. L.R. (2d) 236 (IRB-AppDiv); *Lai v. Canada (Minister of Employment and Immigration)* (1993), 22 Imm. L.R. (2d) 185

provided a way of arguing that the medical refusal is invalid in law, when arguably the court is being influenced by what might accurately be called compassionate considerations. The difference is significant, as winning in law usually results in the matter being returned to the original decision maker, whereas the IRB Appeal Division or the Federal Court will exercise what is alternatively known as its "discretionary" or its "equitable" jurisdiction to grant special relief when it grounds its decision in humanitarian or compassionate considerations.[59] A humanitarian and compassionate win is superior to a legal win not because of the stated law but because of what the Appeal Division is willing to do by way of remedy in the name of humanitarianism. In some cases, the original decision is simply overturned without a clear statement as to whether this is being done because of an appealable error or humanitarian consideration. While this is clearly shoddy decision making, it highlights the affinity between an "unreasonable" medical opinion about a close family member who would never be left to burden the state, and a decision drawing explicitly on the extra-legal humanitarian and compassionate jurisdiction. These patterns show again that the concept of humanitarianism is being used to patch over difficulties in the law, rather than in developing a jurisprudence that attaches some stable and inherent meaning to the term. It is arguable that there have been fewer humanitarian and compassionate grounds cases than there would otherwise have been if the medical refusal jurisprudence were not itself so malleable.

One part of the story of the humanitarian jurisprudence, therefore, is that the theoretical flexibility of the concept is well reflected in the judicial interpretations. It does tend to support Seidman's observation, considered in Chapter 4, that humanitarianism is a good basis for political compromise but not a workable legal standard. The Federal Court has stated that the words "'humanitarian and compassionate' have some kind of objective meaning intended by Parliament."[60] Indeed, I have referred to some objective core of meaning in talking of the intuitive or commonsense meanings. An early formulation by the Immigration Appeals Commission, which has been regularly referred to since, including in post-*Baker* cases, captures most

---

(IRB-AppDiv); *Chan, supra* note 52; *Sall, supra* note 52; *Sidhu v. Canada (Minister of Employment and Immigration)* (1991), 15 Imm. L.R. (2d) 122 (IRB-AppDiv). A considerable number of these cases involve family members who have been refused because of mental retardation. The additional evidence used to counter the medical opinion in these cases is frequently a video of the person in question carrying out day-to-day tasks. The treatment of mental health in Canadian immigration law receives detailed treatment in Judy Mosoff, "'Excessive Demand' on the Canadian Conscience: Disability, Family and Immigration" (1998-99) 26 Man. L.J. 149.

59 *Jeganathan v. Canada (Minister of Citizenship and Immigration)* (1997), 42 Imm. L.R. (2d) 186 (IRB-AppDiv); *Rudrakumar, supra* note 52; *Sidhu v. Canada (Minister of Employment and Immigration)* (1994), 28 Imm. L.R. (2d) 236 (IRB-AppDiv).

60 *Vidal, supra* note 31 at para. 9.

of that essence and also illustrates a key to understanding the fluidity of the term when it states that compassionate or humanitarian grounds will depend upon "those facts, established by evidence, which would excite in a reasonable man in a civilized community a desire to relieve the misfortunes of another."[61] But the standard is hard to assess. In one case, failure to allow a pregnant woman to apply for permanent residency inland constitutes failure to "consider the application as a reasonable person would have done."[62] In another, a man whose house, farm, and village were buried by a volcano while he was visiting Canada does not meet the threshold for humanitarian exception to the rule.[63] One explanation is that the situations are incomparable. Leaving the decision to the individual bureaucrat ensures that the courts do not have to establish a hierarchy of human tragedy. Nonetheless, the idea that some individuals deserve our humanitarian consideration while others do not relies on the assumption of just such a hierarchy. In yet another case, a man whose wife had withdrawn her sponsorship of his application, claiming he was involved in criminal activities and was physically violent towards her, was allowed permanent residency on humanitarian and compassionate grounds because the Board did not believe her allegations.[64] While this case is an exception, it is worth noting the extent to which the term "humanitarian and compassionate grounds" can stretch. There was nothing dire about his circumstances. The decision concentrates on his professional education and earning capacity and her lack of credibility.

The Supreme Court of Canada's *Baker*[65] decision has not ended the diversity of views in the lower courts. Such an outcome was unlikely, of course, given the setting of discretionary bureaucratic and ministerial decision making.[66] The ruling does, however, set out clear directions, at least some of

---

61 *Chirwa* (1970), 4 I.A.C. 338.
62 *Drame v. Canada (Minister of Employment and Immigration)* (1994), 29 Imm. L.R. (2d) 304 (F.C.T.D.).
63 *Mendoza v. Canada (Minister of Citizenship and Immigration)* (1997), 41 Imm. L.R. (2d) 71 (F.C.T.D.).
64 *Hundal v. Canada (Minister of Employment and Immigration)* (1994), 26 Imm. L.R. (2d) 47 (IRB-AppDiv). The Federal Court of Appeal upheld this decision in *Canada (Minister of Employment and Immigration) v. Hundal* (1994), 167 N.R. 75, a ruling that has become the leading case on the separate issue of when a visa is valid. The wife did not give evidence before the IRB. The IRB notes that the applicant's sister did not believe his wife's allegation and also notes that Mr. Hundal held an engineering diploma and had gotten a good job in Canada while waiting for his appeal to be heard. The IRB found the applicant to be trustworthy and rejected evidence that an immigration officer had found potential evidence of links to a Sikh militant movement in his possession when he arrived in Canada. The case is one of the more bizarre humanitarian and compassionate successes I have read.
65 *Supra* note 3.
66 But note that Justice L'Heureux-Dubé for the majority wrote: "It is, however, inaccurate to speak of a rigid dichotomy of 'discretionary' or 'non-discretionary' decisions": *ibid.* at para. 54.

which are reflected in the subsequent jurisprudence. Ms. Baker had been illegally resident in Canada since 1981. She had four Canadian-born children and was the sole carer for two of them. She had been diagnosed as paranoid schizophrenic. As such, her case combined establishment and medical factors and presented an individual in genuine need of state support. The officer reviewing her case stated:

> The PC [person concerned] is paranoid schizophrenic and on welfare. She has no qualifications other than as a domestic. She has FOUR CHILDREN IN JAMAICA AND ANOTHER FOUR BORN HERE. She will, of course, be a tremendous strain on our social welfare systems for (probably) the rest of her life. There are no H&C factors other than her FOUR CANADIAN BORN CHILDREN. Do we let her stay because of that? I am of the opinion that Canada can no longer afford this kind of generosity. However, because of the circumstances involved, there is a potential for adverse publicity. I recommend refusal but you may wish to clear this with someone at the Region.[67]

The Court held that the decision was both biased and unreasonable. Bias was found in the officer's emphasis on Baker as a single mother with a mental illness, with apparent disregard for other evidence available. Acknowledging that standards of bias vary with the context of the decision, Madam Justice L'Heureux-Dubé wrote:

> The context here is one where immigration officers must regularly make decisions that have great importance to the individuals affected by them, but are also often critical to the interests of Canada as a country. They are individualized, rather than decisions of a general nature. They also require special sensitivity. Canada is a nation made up largely of people whose families migrated here in recent centuries. Our history is one that shows the importance of immigration, and our society shows the benefits of having a diversity of people whose origins are in a multitude of places around the world. Because they necessarily relate to people of diverse backgrounds, from different cultures, races, and continents, immigration decisions demand sensitivity and understanding by those making them. They require a recognition of diversity, an understanding of others, and an openness to difference.[68]

Accordingly, the assessment of bias must take into account the interests of the nation as a whole, and in particular its interests as a nation with a found-

---

67 *Ibid.* at para. 5. Capitals in original.
68 *Ibid.* at para. 47.

ing mythology rooted in immigration. This is a vital imprint of national self-interpretation.

The decision was unreasonable because it departed from the values underlying the grant of discretion: humanitarianism and compassion. Madam Justice L'Heureux-Dubé wrote:

> These words and their meaning must be central in determining whether an individual H&C decision was a reasonable exercise of the power conferred by Parliament. The legislation and regulations direct the Minister to determine whether the person's admission should be facilitated owing to the existence of such considerations. They show Parliament's intention that those exercising the discretion conferred by the statute act in a humanitarian and compassionate manner ... [W]hen considering it, the request must be evaluated in a manner that is respectful of humanitarian and compassionate consideration.[69]

While the content of humanitarianism is not specified, Justice L'Heureux-Dubé's intent is that individuals like Ms. Baker are at least potential beneficiaries. The ruling also exemplifies the annoyance with the bureaucracy that is a theme in the lower court decisions. In particular, Justice L'Heureux-Dubé held that decision makers must be "alert, alive and sensitive" to the best interests of any children affected by the decision.[70] She makes reference to the international *Convention on the Rights of the Child*, which Canada has ratified but not incorporated into its domestic law, but asserts that her reasons are based on principles of administrative law solely, not international obligation. Her assertion was not sufficiently convincing for Justice Iacobucci, who wrote in dissent that unincorporated treaties ought not be referred to, particularly as the majority had chosen to resolve the case without recourse to the *Canadian Charter of Rights and Freedoms*.[71]

The upshot of the Supreme Court of Canada's one substantial decision on the question of humanitarian and compassionate decision making in the immigration realm has been, first and foremost, to link the best interests of children affected by migration decisions to the humanitarian context explicitly. One expression of this is the formulation of some humanitarian and compassionate exceptions clauses in the *Immigration and Refugee Protection Act* with specific reference to children.[72] The IRB and the Federal Court have also grappled with how to fit considerations relevant to children's

---

69 *Ibid.* at para. 66.
70 *Ibid.* at para. 75.
71 Recourse to unimplemented international treaties is an acceptable tool for *Charter* interpretation.
72 Examples include ss. 25 and 67, discussed above. The High Court of Australia also made reference to the similarly unincorporated *Convention on the Rights of the Child* in

interests into the humanitarian jurisprudence. A good number of the cases following *Baker* have grappled with the question, which seems to have been sorted out by the Federal Court of Appeal in *Legault v. Canada (Minister of Citizenship and Immigration).*[73] The Court holds that the best interests of the children, which will presumably most often be to remain in Canada, do not create presumption in favour of granting humanitarian exceptions: "This expression [best interests of the child] is ofttimes understood to mean that the interests of the children are superior to other interests, it can cause the agent to believe that this factor is, before all others, more important, which in light of *Suresh* and in the absence of clear legislative or regulatory limitations stating otherwise, cannot be the case. It would be better to use the expression 'children's interests.'"[74] It is, therefore, permissible and correct to consider "public interest" factors at the same time as children's interests; in this particular instance, those factors are the criminal convictions of the parent. Thus it remains evident that humanitarian and compassionate grounds are not exclusively factors that would inspire generosity but include any factors that are of interest to the public that might choose such generosity.[75]

The *Legault* reasoning was applied, by the same judge in the same year, to a different result in *Hawthorne v. Canada (Minister of Citizenship and Immigration).*[76] Here the child's mother was being deported and the child's father was a permanent resident. She did not know her father well and her mother was her source of financial support. The mother had no immigration status in Canada, but the Court also considered that she had been steadily employed and had not relied on social assistance. The mother also alleged that the father had sexually assaulted his stepdaughter. The original decision

---

Minister for Immigration and Ethnic Affairs v. Teoh (1995), 128 A.L.R. 353, with the argument that at least the executive branch, which had ratified the document, could be considered to be following its principles in deportation decisions. Ironically, the legislative response in Australia was to draft legislation to limit the effect of unincorporated treaties.

73 [2002] F.C.J. No. 457. Leave to appeal was declined by the Supreme Court of Canada. This decision reviews the contradictory approaches of the Federal Court to interpreting *Baker*.

74 *Ibid.* at para. 13.

75 In a related case, the Supreme Court of Canada in *Chieu v. Canada (Minister of Citizenship and Immigration)*, [2002] 1 S.C.R. 84 – followed in *Al Sagban v. Canada (Minister of Citizenship and Immigration)*, [2002] 1 S.C.R. 133 – held that in merit reviews considering "all the circumstances of the case" the former provision defining the "equitable" jurisdiction of the Appeal Division of the IRB under the former legislation could, and indeed should, consider the circumstances in the country to which the individual would be returned. This reach of "all the circumstances" seems to have been carried over into "humanitarian and compassionate" circumstances as well.

76 *Hawthorne v. Canada (Minister of Citizenship and Immigration)*, [2002] F.C.J. 1687, per Decary J.A. for the majority, Evans J. separate concurring opinion [*Hawthorne*].

refers to these factors, but in the view of the Court did not give them sufficient consideration. Interestingly, the Court also stated that while "'hardship' is not a term of art ... children will rarely, if ever, be deserving of any hardship."[77] Despite the Court's assurances to the contrary, it is difficult not to consider that this outcome amounts to a reweighing of the factors involved.

Baker has provided important guidance regarding standard of review – that reviewing courts will give considerable deference to discretionary decision makers and will not, therefore, engage in a reweighing of the factors to be considered in any decision. This has ensured that humanitarianism and compassion do not need to be closely defined. *Baker* has also clarified that a hearing is not required and that reasons must be given, at least upon request.[78] It is evident, nonetheless, that conflicting impulses will continue to dominate this jurisprudence.

The question of criminality is one example of this. The notion of whether to grant an exception to an individual with a criminal record links humanitarianism with desert directly. At the most serious end of the spectrum of criminal behaviour, the IRB has held that being excluded from refugee status under the crimes against humanity provision is not an unassailable bar and all the circumstances of the offence and the offender must be examined.[79] On the other hand, a hijacking offence has been regarded as so serious that it may outweigh any other factor.[80] An individual with twenty-one convictions over a lengthy period may be considered to be rehabilitated.[81] A person facing an allegedly politicized conviction for drug trafficking in Tunisia may be returned there, particularly if the person has lied about it.[82] It is permissible to remove the mother of two young children when her four years in Canada have been marked by complete reliance on social assistance and a pattern of upmarket thievery, especially where the children's father has already been allowed to remain on humanitarian grounds.[83] In *Haq*, the IRB found not only that minor criminal convictions from thirty years earlier could be overlooked but also that the applicant should have been assessed as rehabilitated by the original decision maker.[84] It is, of course, possible to tell the story of these cases in a way that asserts a principled consistency between them. It is equally possible to do the opposite. Matters

77 *Ibid.* at para. 9.
78 *Rylott v. Canada (Minister of Citizenship and Immigration)*, [2003] F.C.J. 187.
79 *Javdani v. Canada (Minister of Citizenship and Immigration)*, [2001] I.A.D. 1819 [*Javdani*]. Application refused.
80 *Saini v. Canada (Minister of Citizenship and Immigration)*, [2003] F.C.J. 225 [*Saini*].
81 *Malicia v. Canada (Minister of Citizenship and Immigration)*, [2003] F.C.J. 235.
82 *Majerbi v. Canada (Minister of Citizenship and Immigration)*, [2002] F.C.J. 1145 [*Majerbi*].
83 *Vajda v. Canada (Minister of Citizenship and Immigration)*, [2002] I.A.D.D. 326.
84 *Haq v. Canada (Minister of Citizenship and Immigration)*, [2002] I.A.D.D. 304.

of humanitarianism and compassion seem inevitably marked by this characteristic, which parallels the malleability of humanitarianism at a theoretical level.

Other issues that recur in this jurisprudence include a strong condemnation of those who lie during the immigration or refugee process,[85] an ongoing consideration of when people who are close to the low-income cut-off for sponsorship will be allowed to overcome this legal provision,[86] and when the risks faced upon return would reach a level of hardship that is, in the terms of the guidelines, "undeserved."[87] The cases are compelling, and upon reading them it is difficult to resist the impulse to consider one's own weighing of the factors involved. Even in the cases where children are involved, *Baker* has not led to predictable outcomes, particularly following *Legault*. All of this typifies a discretionary setting. It is not, however, necessary to link the discretion to humanitarianism, but doing so adds something to simple legal discretion. Making these decisions in the name of humanitarianism and compassion serves to inject these themes strongly into the law, putting them in the place of plausible alternatives such as "all the circumstances of the case" or "the public interest." While these terms are not absent from the jurisprudence, they are interpreted within a humanitarian setting. Justice L'Heureux-Dubé's work towards describing some substantive content for the notion of humanitarianism is not the part of *Baker* that has been taken up, and the term remains fluid.

Even without accepting a complete radical indeterminacy of law, the humanitarian jurisprudence shows trends broad enough to contain a series of contradictory interpretations. A considerable part of the jurisprudence concerns factors that do not accord with non-legal meanings of humanitarianism. This is likely to increase under the *Immigration and Refugee Protection Act* because of the removal of the generally defined "equitable" jurisdiction in some appeals in favour of an expansive reading of humanitarian considerations. While neither legal nor non-legal understandings will ever be completely stable, the legal meanings clearly function as a guise at least some of the time. This accords with the place of the humanitarian consensus in liberal theory and with the place of migration law in the liberal nation. "Humanitarianism" is a loose enough term on which to build a consensus

---

85 *Beneche v. Canada (Minister of Citizenship and Immigration)*, [2002] I.A.D.D. 216 [*Beneche*]; *Javdani, supra* note 79; *Traore v. Canada (Minister of Citizenship and Immigration)*, [2002] F.C.J. 1197 [*Traore*]; *Qui v. Canada (Minister of Citizenship and Immigration)*, [2003] F.C.J. 24; *Rylott v. Canada (Minister of Citizenship and Immigration)*, [2003] F.C.J. 187.

86 *Jugpall v. Canada (Minister of Citizenship and Immigration)* (1999), 2 Imm. L.R. (3d) 222; *Dang v. Canada (Minister of Citizenship and Immigration)*, [2000] 1 F.C. 3.2.1; *Tahir v. Canada (Minister of Citizenship and Immigration)*, [2001] I.A.D.D. 1895; *Agbayani v. Canada (Minister of Citizenship and Immigration)*, [2001] I.A.D.D. 1776; *Beneche, supra* note 85.

87 *Saini, supra* note 80; *Majerbi, supra* note 82; *Hawthorne, supra* note 76; *Traore, supra* note 85.

among the diverse strands of liberalism. The range of its interpretation, even just within the Canadian setting, demonstrates how fragile that consensus is and that it therefore cannot generate a standard for the moral behaviour of liberal nations. This same flexibility allows humanitarianism to function as a key feature of migration law's project of accommodating shifting national identities and priorities. Despite still fitting in the framework of liberal migration laws, the Australian approach to humanitarianism in migration law diverges greatly from the Canadian. The next section provides a sketch of that approach to facilitate comparative analysis.

Australian Acts of Grace

Under the *Migration Act,* most humanitarian admissions to Australia are made in response to applications from overseas, and only traces of what humanitarianism means in that setting are found in the visa criteria. Discretionary decisions about people within Australia seeking exceptional permission to remain are a close parallel to the Canadian jurisprudence of humanitarianism, and thus I have chosen to use them for comparison. This decision-making setting also engages my theoretical framework directly, as the "outsiders" are already "within" the nation and are seeking to avoid an exercise of state power aimed at removing them. Finally, these decisions generate reasons of a sort.

Ministerial authority to substitute a more favourable decision extends to decisions of the Migration Review Tribunal,[88] the Refugee Review Tribunal (RRT),[89] the Administrative Appeals Tribunal,[90] and, formerly, to internal review decisions that are not subject to tribunal scrutiny.[91] Requests to overturn decisions of the RRT are the most significant of these, as they make up the largest group of requests and the largest group of resulting ministerial actions.[92] Between May 1994 and May 1999, these decisions were made under the "guidelines for stay in Australia on humanitarian grounds." New guidelines issued in May 1999 are entitled "Ministerial Guidelines for the Identification of Unique or Exceptional Cases Where It May Be in the Public Interest to Substitute a More Favourable Decision Under s345, 351, 391, 417, 454 of the *Migration Act*," and were still in use in mid-2004. However, aside

---

88 Section 351. The jurisdiction of the MRT belonged to the Immigration Review Tribunal until 1 June 1999, when the latter was disbanded.
89 Section 417.
90 Sections 391 and 454. The option of either specialist tribunal referring a case to the AAT rather than deciding it is rarely used.
91 Former s. 345.
92 Official statistics on the numbers of requests received are not recorded by either the department or the minister's office. Ministerial staff confirm that requests to overturn RRT decisions make up a significant majority of requests received. An examination of the tabled papers demonstrates that RRT decisions make up the majority of the minister's personal decisions here.

from more formal presentation and explicit warnings that this is a non-compellable discretion, little else has changed. Unlike the Canadian discretionary review on humanitarian and compassionate grounds, the minister must use these powers personally and has no duty to even consider these requests.[93] In both Australia and Canada, the decision is discretionary, but the breadth of that discretion differs enormously.

The guidelines are issued from the minister's office and are not subject to scrutiny outside the department before being made public. The 1994 guidelines were accompanied by a press release stating that they were aimed at people who were unable to sustain a refugee claim but whose "claims evoke a strong humanitarian response." The nature of that humanitarian response was circumscribed by noting that "Ministerial discretion is not designed to cover people seeking residence on compassionate, non-refugee related grounds such as family, medical or economic reasons."[94] The current guidelines open by stating that "the public interest may be served by the Australian government responding with care and compassion to the plight of certain individuals in particular circumstances." They provide a list of factors that may be relevant considerations, including threats to the person's security, human rights, or human dignity; individualized persecution; former refugee status; and risk of facing torture or breaches of the *Convention on the Rights of the Child* or the *International Covenant on Civil and Political Rights*. This formula encapsulates both the idea that this protection is aimed at those in refugee-like circumstances who fall outside the strict definition of a refugee, and the principle that behaving in a humanitarian way is in the public interest.

This principle is at the heart of my inquiry. While public immigration discourse so frequently echoes this coupling of humanitarianism and public interest that it seems correct, its content is nebulous or worse. The public cannot be served by being humanitarian in the same direct way that it can be by selecting migrants on the basis of economic need or family reunification. The public interest that is served by being humanitarian, however, is the need *to be seen to be* humanitarian. We as a nation, at the level of the individual, at the level of the political actor, and at the level of the nation

---

93 These parameters were established by the Federal Court in *Ozmanian v. Minister for Immigration, Local Government and Ethnic Affairs* (1996), 137 A.L.R. 103, and affirmed by the High Court in *Re Minister for Immigration and Multicultural and Indigenous Affairs; Ex parte Applicants S134/2002*, [2003] H.C.A. 1. The Federal Court also stated that it was permissible for a delegate to review requests and consider which ones should be put to the minister for consideration.

94 Minister for Immigration and Ethnic Affairs, Media Release, B28/94 (24 May 1994). People in such situations would ask for ministerial dispensation under another section not covered by these guidelines but nonetheless open to humanitarian concerns. The tabled papers reveal that humanitarian considerations are sometimes listed in these instances.

as actor on the international stage, derive some value from being humanitarian. The public interest that is served here is an identity-building, a nation-building, interest. The commitment to humanitarianism represented in these guidelines provides evidence for that enterprise. Through this commitment to do more than required by law, and to consider circumstances on an individual basis, we construct an identity for ourselves – the "in" group – as "good."

This role of humanitarianism is reinforced by examining the tabled reasons for ministerial reversals under s. 417.[95] What is most remarkable about these reasons is the scant information they contain. In most instances, it is impossible to discern even which country the individual concerned has come from.[96] The ministerial statements are vague and formulaic, but we do learn about the formula. Each statement is three or four paragraphs. The first paragraph or two describe the process the applicant has followed to this point. Next, there is a paragraph with either some generally worded information about the case or a brief description of the refugee law framework. The final paragraph talks about Australia's humanitarianism, generosity, or compassion – and sometimes all three. For example: "In the circumstances, I have decided that as a discretionary and humanitarian act to an individual with a genuine on-going need, it is in the interest of Australia as a humane and generous society to grant the applicant a ... visa." Only four statements of 816 tabled under s. 417 did not refer to humanitarianism. This specifies that the interest for Australia in humanitarian admissions is its interest as a humane and generous society. That interest is in both being – and being perceived as – humane and generous. If the perception were not important, this part of the formula would be unnecessary. This is also an important part of the formula given the incredibly small success rate of these applications. Rejecting almost all of these last-ditch humanitarian appeals could be regarded as less than compassionate, and perhaps this rhetoric provides some bulwark against that assessment.

The second paragraph of the formula, which might be called the detailed one, is also notable. The key to this aspect of the formula is the importance of the public interest and the particular circumstances and personal characteristics of the individual involved. The emphasis on the uniqueness of the individual reinforces that this is an exceptional admission and that, as there are unlikely to be similar circumstances, arguments for similar treatment

---

95 I examined all 1,211 "statements under the *Migration Act*" tabled between 1995 and December 2001, as compiled at my request by the staff of the Parliamentary Table Office. I have retained a copy of each statement in my files.

96 In the case of the 816 statements tabled under s. 417, 8 contained the name of the country and 5 contained the name of a person. A further 29 were accompanied by a list of names (from which country of origin could be speculated), but the names were not linked to the stated reasons.

will be futile. There is no description of what the public interest in admitting this unique individual might be. Sometimes the paragraph mentions nothing more than these two factors. In most cases, when additional information is given it echoes one of the phrases in the guidelines, such as "personal hardship," "safety at risk," "genuine subjective fear," "trauma," or even – in a perfect tautology – that to return the person would be "inhumane." One set of applications refers to assimilation to the Australian community and having been here for more than three years.[97] It is also notable that additional details are more common in reasons relating to sections other than s. 417 – that is, to claimants who did not go through the refugee process – and that earlier statements contained more detail than later statements. The level of vagueness ensures that the merits of the ministerial decision cannot be publicly impugned, and that the assertion by practitioners that only high-profile applicants whose cases are taken up by colleagues of the minister will be successful cannot be tested.[98] The requirement to table reasons amounts to little when this type of formulaic presentation is used and there is no way to link ministerial statements to tribunal rulings on particular facts. There is also no way of comparing favourable decisions with instances where an application for grace is made but rejected. This reinforces the argument that humanitarianism is a useful concept in migration law partly due to its vagueness. Nothing more is revealed than the fact that it serves the interest of the generous nation and is an exception related to unique circumstances. The guidelines and the humanitarian categories give us some further information, but in the end this is even less than the Canadian jurisprudence of humanitarianism reveals.

The humanitarian aspects of the Australian law have not always been so carefully concealed. The current absence of humanitarianism as a clearly named concept in the *Migration Act* can be interpreted as a response to the courts' interpretations of the pre-1989[99] provision that permanent residency could be granted to any non-citizen legally in Australia who could demonstrate "strong compassionate or humanitarian grounds for the grant of a

---

97 This formula is reminiscent of the Canadian "establishment factors." However, little can be drawn from the comparison as the Australian formulation does not contain enough information to elaborate.

98 Interviews with refugee law practitioners in Melbourne, December 1997, and in Sydney, January 1998 and May 2002.

99 In 1989, the *Migration Act* was significantly amended (*Migration Law Amendment Act 1989*, proclaimed December 1989) with the aim of reducing discretionary decision making under the act. For a discussion of the amendments, see Kathryn Cronin, "Concerning Equity and Control: A Look at the New Immigration Law" (1990) June, 28 Law Society Journal 50. Other articles in the June 1990 *Law Society Journal*'s "Forum: Immigration Law" discuss the effects of the amendments on particular parts of the immigration program. One of particular interest is Adrian Joel, "The Edifice of Compassion" (1990) June, 28 Law Society Journal 67.

permit."[100] This provision gave the courts an opportunity to interpret the concept of humanitarianism, which proved to have a broad range of applications and contained the potential to develop in the disparate directions of the Canadian jurisprudence.

The Australian courts were no more able or willing than the Canadian to define humanitarianism. In *Ates,* the Federal Court linked humanitarianism to the good of the nation with this expansive language:

> In the administration of good government there is not only room, but a legal duty, to consider, even, on occasion with compassion, the circumstances of particular cases. The prima facie strictness of the law is designed to achieve population security and national security. That strictness is to be justified also on the basis that, in the area of entry to this country, the law may be seen to be strictly enforced. But in this case there is no security or even economic consideration ... The law must be administered by the Minister in the best interests of Australia. So to do extends Australia's interests broadly regarded and embraces, on occasion and according to circumstances, the taking of decisions by reference to a liberal and even compassionate outlook appropriate to a free and confident nation and conscious of its reputation as such.[101]

The High Court, in *Kioa v. West,*[102] accepted without comment the bureaucratic decision that a Tongan family with an Australian-born daughter[103] who had overstayed their visas to earn money to assist relatives whose homes had been destroyed by a cyclone did not present strong humanitarian and compassionate considerations. The merits of the decision were beyond review and, notably, natural justice was found to have been breached. But the High Court was much more restrained than the Canadian courts in its *obiter dicta*, however. Commenting on the humanitarian admission provision, Justice Mason (as he then was) stated that strong compassionate or humanitarian grounds "may be very much a matter of opinion."[104] Justice Wilson stated that humanitarian grounds may have a relevance, "albeit attenuated" to a discretionary decision to deport, and that this may strengthen a claim that natural justice in this situation requires a hearing.[105]

100   Section 6A(1)(e).
101   *Ates v. Minister of State for Immigration and Ethnic Affairs* (1983), 67 F.L.R. 449 at 455-56; note that s. 6A(1)(e) was not at issue.
102   *Kioa v. West* (1985), 159 C.L.R. 550 [*Kioa*], discussed in detail in Chapter 7.
103   At that time, birth in Australia assured Australian citizenship. The *Australian Citizenship Act 1948* (Cth.) has since been amended to provide that Australian-born children become Australian citizens at birth only if one of their parents is a citizen or permanent resident. Otherwise, they inherit their parents' visa status: s. 10(2).
104   *Supra* note 102 at 582.
105   *Ibid.* at 600.

Both *Damouni*[106] and *McPhee*[107] provide examples of the Federal Court attempting to weigh up factors for and against granting a visa on "strong humanitarian and compassionate grounds." Justice French in *Damouni* began by dissecting dictionary definitions of humanitarianism and compassion and isolated "hardship" as the common element to all the circumstances addressed.[108] Factors going to granting the visa on these grounds included fear of returning to their home country to face death or imprisonment, inability to go elsewhere, three young children at school in Australia, and family support in Australia. On what Justice French termed "the debit side" were entering Australia on false premises, falsely claiming not to know their visa conditions, and the majority of their family members residing elsewhere.[109] Justice French remitted the case to the decision maker below with specific suggestions about humanitarian considerations. Mr. McPhee was similarly awarded reconsideration of his circumstances when the Court ruled that his juvenile record should not have weighed in the delegate's deliberations, and that the delegate failed to allocate sufficient weight to McPhee's sense of frustration.[110] While the approach of the Australian courts to humanitarianism was not permitted much time to develop, the balancing of factors that doubles as a notion of desert is present, as it is in the Canadian jurisprudence. As well, humanitarianism was at least sometimes linked to the good of the nation in expansive terms, and certainly the potential for further expansion seemed to have been obvious to lawmakers.

During the nine years that this provision for judicial humanitarianism was in place, admissions increased each year, paralleling the courts' expansive treatment of the provision.[111] Removing humanitarianism and other types of discretionary decision making from the act ensures that control over the content of the term "humanitarian" remains with the executive. As is evident in the Canadian jurisprudence, once humanitarianism is put to the courts in any fashion, the language of duty and fairness inevitably becomes part of the equation and precedent has a role to play. This is part of the reason that the Canadian interpretations of humanitarianism are so counterintuitive. Humanitarianism, outside this narrow migration law context, is not about fairness and desert; it is about bestowing something out of goodness. The Australian executive control approach, characterized by merciful individuated decisions, may preserve a meaning for humanitarian-

---

106   *Damouni and Anor v. Minister for Immigration, Local Government and Ethnic Affairs* (1989), 87 A.L.R. 97 (F.C.) [*Damouni*].

107   *McPhee and Ors v. Minister for Immigration and Ethnic Affairs* (1988), 16 A.L.D. 77 (Full Fed. Ct.) [*McPhee*].

108   *Supra* note 106 at 102-3.

109   *Ibid.* at 110-11.

110   *Supra* note 107 at 80.

111   Mary Crock, *Immigration and Refugee Law in Australia* (Sydney: Federation Press, 1998) at 131.

ism that is closer to its extra-legal meaning, even as far more people per capita and per application are turned away and the circumstances of those refusals are rendered invisible.

Humanitarianism and Identity

The contrasts between how humanitarianism is deployed in the Australian and Canadian laws allow for analyses of the relationship between humanitarianism and identity in Australia and Canada and for reflection on liberalism's humanitarian consensus. Three aspects of the legal positioning of humanitarianism are important to completing the portrait of its role in liberal theory and in liberal migration laws. First, significant differences can be explained by contrasting the effects of locating humanitarian decision making with the courts or with the executive. Second, attention to identity in the analysis requires considering who the beneficiaries of these decisions are. Finally, drawing on these two phases of the analysis, the mirror of humanitarianism in which both the nation and its members are reflected can be understood.

Legislative or Executive Control

The use of the term "humanitarian" throughout both the *Immigration Act* and the *Immigration and Refugee Protection Act* ensures that Canadian courts have a significant role in determining interpretations and appropriate uses of the term. By contrast, in Australia, humanitarianism is reserved to the executive through overseas visas and ministerial discretion. One consequence of this difference is that we have far more evidence of Canadian interpretations of the term, and therefore it is much easier to see how the term is used in disparate situations, often counterintuitively, by the Canadian courts. Fewer conclusions can be drawn in the Australian case about the meaning of humanitarianism. Because humanitarian decision making in Australia is carried out on a case-by-case basis, there is at least a possibility that it may be informed solely by concerns that are very close to extra-legal meanings.

The principal conclusions to be drawn from the locus of humanitarian decision making go beyond what can be said about its meaning to the crucial questions of control and sovereignty. When the executive makes these decisions, the government of the day retains control over the decision making. Australia's quick abandonment of s. 6A(1)(e) provides one example of this. Executive control over migration decisions keeps these decisions at the heart of the sovereign nation. Two important strands of analysis come together at this point. The first is that immigration has long been associated with the core of national sovereignty.[112] Legomsky argues that British immigration

---

112 This is a cornerstone of Stephen Legomsky's explanation for the inordinate deference of British and American courts to immigration decisions. See Stephen H. Legomsky, *Immigration and the Judiciary: Law and Politics in Britain and America* (New York: Oxford

law is at least overshadowed by the royal prerogative, under which decisions relating to foreign affairs or to acts of state were completely beyond judicial review.[113] Even in Britain this doctrine has lost much of its historical importance, and the federal constitutions of Australia and Canada dint its impact, yet the line of cases that Legomsky draws on to demonstrate the influence of the prerogative in immigration law is part of the common law of both these former colonies.[114] The strong historical link of control over immigration and nationhood itself is seen in these century-old prerogative decisions, as well as in the early-twentieth-century removal of citizenship and migration concerns from the international legal sphere to the domestic[115] and in the use of control over immigration at a national level as an argument for the establishment of both the Australian and Canadian confederations. Control over immigration, over its own borders, is defining of the nation. It marks out the nation *qua* nation, rather than mere colony or quasi-dependent state.[116] In the twenty-first-century context, "cracking down" on extra-legal migration is one response of nations threatened by the forces of globalization.[117] The second strand of analysis engaged by executive control in this area is that if migration law is to be harnessed to the needs of the liberal nation, there are strong incentives to control the contents and interpretations of the law.

Australian and Canadian approaches to humanitarianism reveal important differences about the strength of the national need for control over migration, which in turn tell us something about national myths and identity building. Writing humanitarianism all over the legislation allows the Canadian courts the latitude to "leave the door ajar." Canadian discourses about immigration are much less concerned with leaving that door swinging than Australian discourses are. Canada lets in many more immigrants each year on a per capita basis, and sits north of what we proudly learned in primary school was the "longest undefended border in the world." Even if Canada wanted to develop the same kind of "control culture"[118] as island

---

University Press, and Oxford: Clarendon Press, 1997), especially Chapter 4, "Patterns and Trends: A Descriptive View."

113   *Ibid.* at 87-105 and following.

114   *Musgrove v. Chun Teeong Toy,* [1981] A.C. 272 (P.C.); *Poll v. Lord Advocate,* [1899] 1 F. 823 (Ct. Sess.); *Attorney-General for Canada v. Cain,* [1906] A.C. 542 (P.C.).

115   Discussed in Sean Brawley, *The White Peril: Foreign Relations and Asian Immigration to Australasia and North America 1919-1987* (Sydney: UNSW Press, 1995).

116   Article 1 of the *Montevideo Convention on Rights and Duties of States,* 1933, 165 L.N.T.S. 19, states: "The State as a person of international law should possess the following qualifications: (a) a permanent population; (b) a defined territory; (c) government; and (d) capacity to enter into relations with other States."

117   I make this argument fully in Catherine Dauvergne, "Sovereignty, Migration and the Rule of Law in Global Times" (2004) 67 Mod. L. Rev. 588.

118   This term was coined and applied to Australian migration law by Kathryn Cronin in "A Culture of Control: An Overview of Immigration Policy-Making" in James Jupp

Australia, it could not. The encroaching hordes imagery, which still lurks at the edges of Australian migration discourses, is not there either.[119] There has never been a sense in Canada that the massive population of the United States might suddenly want to come north. Thus, Canadian politicians are much more confident in leaving humanitarianism to the courts, in relinquishing a bit of control. Control over the border, and the quest for an impermeable border, are close to the core of Australian nationhood. The universal visa system and the national panic over "boat-people" are evidence of this.[120] Canada is by no means free of the culture of control, but there are more counters to it. One important cultural difference is played out in the way the population debate intertwines with concerns about immigration. In Australia, there is an ongoing popular and academic debate about the maximum population of the nation. While there is disagreement about the number, the idea of a maximum is agreed upon.[121] Despite geographic similarities (large tracts of empty land that are not easily made productive), this question never arises in Canadian debate. When migration and population meet in popular discourse, the concern is that the population rate of increase may be affected one way or another by migrant intake. This is another manifestation of the control discourse, of the importance of control to the national imagination of itself. Locating discretionary humanitarian decisions with the executive, at the sovereign core of the nation, facilitates these nation-building, nation-controlling objectives.

Closely related to the difference in judicial or executive determinations is the construction of humanitarian decision making as discretionary decision making. Here the most fruitful aspect of the analysis is considering the

---

and Marie Kabala, eds., *The Politics of Australian Immigration* (Canberra: Australian Government Publishing Service, 1993) c. 5.

119 This mythology is reflected in the minister for immigration's comment that "whole Middle Eastern villages" are planning to pack up and come to Australia by boat, which attracted widespread attention in the Australian media in late 1999. R. McGregor, "10,000 Illegals on Way, Says Ruddock" *Australian* (16 November 1999) 1; M. Saunders, "Ruddock 'Hysteria' Makes Waves: Beazley" *Australian* (7 December 1999) 4.

120 Australia is the only major tourist destination and only major "Western" nation requiring every non-citizen entering the country to hold a visa. Regarding boatpeople, between the first arrivals in the late 1980s and mid-1999, approximately 3,000 people arrived in Australia by boat. These arrivals prompted reform of the *Migration Act* to allow for non-reviewable detention of these people. Yet, if all boat arrivals had been allowed to stay, their numbers would have made up less than 5 percent of the annual migration intake for any one of those years. Beginning in 1999, the Australian press used the compound word "boatpeople" to the exclusion of gramatically correct alternatives.

121 Philip Ruddock, "Temporary Influx of the Highly Skilled Makes Sense" *Australian* (17 November 1999) 17; A. Hodge, "Plea to Populate to 50m or Perish" *Australian* (25 November 1999) 3; D. Pradd, "Refugee Alert Sounds Like a Wake-up Call" *Australian* (25 November 1999) 13; D Campbell, "Just How Big a Nation Should We Aim to Be?" *Australian* (15 October 1996) 13.

interaction between humanitarianism and discretion rather than drawing out differences between the Australian and Canadian situations.[122] In both systems, decisions about humanitarian and compassionate consideration for those within the borders are made almost entirely on a case-by-case discretionary basis. In many ways, these decisions are paradigmatic discretionary decisions. The indeterminacy of humanitarianism fits well in the discretion paradigm, which Lacey describes as "allowing the ideological gaps between the rhetoric and substance of the law to be managed."[123] In humanitarian admissions, the ideological gap between rhetoric and substance is particularly large. The nebulous content of humanitarianism allows for even more slippage than standard discretionary decision making, and the legal device of discretion limits, even in the Canadian setting, judicial inquiry. While the classic description of the relationship between law and discretion states that law sets the boundaries within which discretion is to work,[124] writing humanitarianism into the law allows the discretionary element of the decision to overlap its legal borders. This is important to ensuring the complete flexibility of the migration law framework. In order for migration law to function at the behest of the constantly changing national need, and at the same time retain its appearance of stability and support the rule of law ideology, porous concepts like humanitarianism – to repair porous borders – are essential tools.

This type of discretionary decision making fits within Schneider's "rule-building discretion" category because the rapidity of change makes the rules controversial, the discretion and the extent of the change are uncertain, and the rules must be replaced frequently.[125] Schneider asserts that this type of discretion is most useful in times of great social change, and could take issue with my use of his categorization scheme on that basis.[126] But it is because of this that my assignment is most appropriate. Migration law is a perpetual setting of great social change. This is precisely why it is an important site of the construction of national identity, as a work in progress. I

---

122   Although this could certainly be done. The Australian humanitarian decisions fit within definitions of strong discretion; the Canadian ones are much closer to definitions of weak discretion. The Australian discretion is exercised at the highest level of the executive, the Canadian at a range of levels and sometimes even at the lowest. The range of discretionary decisions is much smaller in Australia than in Canada. These factors contribute to the earlier analysis of a stronger control culture in Australia.

123   Nicola Lacey, "The Jurisprudence of Discretion: Escaping the Legal Paradigm" in Keith Hawkins, ed., *The Uses of Discretion* (Oxford: Clarendon Press, and New York: Oxford University Press, 1992) 361 at 364.

124   Discussed and summarized in J. Bell, "Discretionary Decision-Making: A Jurisprudential View" in Hawkins, *supra* note 123, 89 at 93.

125   C.E. Schneider, "Discretion and Rules: A Lawyer's View" in Hawkins, *supra* note 123, 47 at 64.

126   His other categories are khadi-discretion, rule-failure discretion, and rule compromise discretion: *ibid.* at 61-65.

discussed in Part 1 the important dual function of migration law in establishing the appearance of stability and yet accommodating ongoing shifts in understanding of the national self. The framework of the legislation ensures that every shifting political whim and national need can be poured into the sieve and made law. The rules in migration are controversial, do require frequent change, and are highly uncertain, especially in humanitarian decision making. What the combination of the term "humanitarianism" and discretion allow is for this incessant change to be hidden, and for the law, the border of the community, our constituted identity, to appear stable. The Canadian law, with its high levels of humanitarianism and discretion, is amended much less frequently than the Australian. This is the counterbalance to direct executive control. But stability is required, nonetheless, and hence upholding the control ideology is even more vital in Australia.

The Chosen Ones
Because a humanitarian admission is an act of grace, the identity of the beneficiary is highly important, just as it is in the humanitarian subcategory of refugee. If precious membership in our national community is to be bestowed on one who does not bring us a direct benefit and to whom justice requires that we owe nothing, that *individual* must be deserving. The importance of the identity of the individual in humanitarian admissions is seen in the Canadian jurisprudence and is hinted at in the Australian ministerial decisions.[127] As these types of admission are not pegged to a particular national benefit, identity is closely scrutinized. This scrutiny, as the cases, guidelines, and arguments show, goes two ways: towards ensuring that the person is sufficiently destitute to be deserving of our mercy, and towards ensuring that the person is acceptable as a member of the community. This accounts for some of the diversity in the law, such as the contradictory emphasis in the Canadian cases on both need and establishment factors. The other in this scenario must be both apart and acceptable.

This dual scrutiny of identity is also related to the emphasis on individuality. As both the Australian and Canadian courts have said, humanitarianism is matter of emotion, of what stirs a compassionate response in an individual. Further, humanitarianism is analytically an exception to the rule, a way to circumvent the law, and so cannot be open to everyone but only to individuals. It is both individually defined and individually applied. This provides double-strength resistance against any floodgates argument, which is indispensable to the control ideology. This is similar to the role of

---

127 My argument here provides further support for Legomsky's observation that judicial responses to immigration cases are highly sensitive to the status of the individuals involved. Legomsky, *supra* note 112 at 265-66.

individualization in the refugee definition but is heightened here, as there is no group identity aspect to the analysis.

The humanitarian admission categories contribute to this analysis. In Australia, and in Canada until very recently, certain categories have been designated for priority humanitarian admission. While this may seem to depart from the linkage between humanitarianism and individuation, the category labels are highly identity-specific, even more so than the refugee definition. Examples of categories that Australia has opened at some time in the past decade include women at risk, citizens of the former Yugoslavia, minorities of the former USSR, Sudanese, Sri Lankans, and Ahmadis in Pakistan.[128] In addition to these requirements and others, each category contains a detailed list of specific identity requirements that an applicant must construct themselves to conform to. For example, to come within the women at risk category, a woman must be subject to persecution, identified as "of concern" by the United Nations High Commissioner for Refugees (UNHCR), without the protection of a male relative, in danger of violence, victimization, or abuse because of her gendered identity, and not fit with another part of the refugee or humanitarian program. Humanitarian program visas are also available to those with a connection with someone already in Australia.[129] Like the refugee, the humanitarian migrant must be not like us in order to need our protection, but must also able to shed that identity and merge with the nation when required. The paradoxical requirement to be both other and not-other is overt here. These humanitarian entry categories are so narrowly defined that they do not detract from the argument that humanitarian concern is tied to individuals to facilitate control over it. Control is also facilitated by ensuring, in both Australia and Canada, that the categories can be created and dismantled by the executive, as can the number of visas accorded to each.

These identity-specific categories, the more generic categories that make up the remainder of the Australian program (in-country humanitarian visa, global special humanitarian visa, emergency rescue visa), and all of the current Canadian designated class program are all alternatives to a broader definition of refugee. To that extent, they could be subject to the same analysis of identity as the refugee definition in Chapter 5. What is crucial in relation to these supplementary humanitarian categories is that both

---

128 See *supra* notes 23 and 24. Similarly constructed identity categories were in use in Canada prior to 1997.

129 Formerly, visas in this program were prioritized on the basis of degrees of connection with Australia: highest priority to those with relatives in Australia, next to those with other close ties in Australia (friends, more distant relatives, past visits, especially for education or business), and third to those with "resettlement potential." These factors, and the current quasi-sponsorship rules, make the humanitarian categories mimic the priorities of family and economic migration.

Australia and Canada (and other nations as well) choose this option rather than a more expansive definition of refugee. Using ad hoc humanitarian categories allows for direct manipulation of the identities to be admitted. The narrow framing of each category, like the narrow refugee definition itself, enables identity constructions at the border to be closely scrutinized.

Considering who is chosen as deserving also communicates national values. In the Canadian humanitarian jurisprudence, values of family independence and self-sufficiency are enshrined alongside a strong work ethic and a vision of economic and academic success as contributions to the national community. Family rather than state responsibility for weak members is valued. Australian decision making is veiled, but in the brief time when humanitarianism and compassion were before the courts, the value of nuclear family and of certain contributions to society were referred to. The tabled discretionary decisions do communicate somewhat the importance of being able to become established in Australian society.

Reflecting Ourselves: The Mirror of Humanitarianism

From all of these elements, we can frame the mirror of humanitarianism. In the case of humanitarian admissions, the national need most readily catered to is the need to be fair and right and even just, and the perhaps identical need to be perceived in this light. This need of the liberal nation is intertwined with the liberal consensus, and both contribute to migration discourses of humanitarianism. The philosophical dissonance over the meaning of humanitarianism is paralleled by the various ways in which the law represents humanitarianism. The instability inherent in the term also makes it an apt device for easing the coupling of national need and migration law. It simultaneously accounts for how intuitive and extra-legal interpretations of humanitarianism can so often diverge from the legal uses of the term.

Looking at the use and position of humanitarianism in Australian and Canadian migration law, we see a subtly expressed difference in the power of a public and political discourse about control over immigration, control over borders, and therefore control over community membership and identity. This control function was named by then-Justice Brennan when he defined the purpose of the migration legislation as "control of the membership of the Australian people."[130] In the comparison between the two nations, we also see that the Canadian law is far more concerned with humanitarianism. While this multiplies the easily demonstrated contradictions and inconsistencies in legal manipulation of the term, it cannot detract from the fact that the Canadian law has a more generous face. This, backed up by the numbers, adds up to a more generous or humanitarian law no matter the extent of textual indeterminacy. Humanitarianism is closer

---

130 *Kioa, supra* note 102 at 626.

to the heart of the Canadian rhetoric about migration than it is in Australia, closer to the tradition Canadian lawmakers seek to construct, closer to the mythology that Canadians as individuals are willing to honour and reify.

The comparison of Canadian and Australian humanitarianism also deepens our understanding of the liberal humanitarian consensus. The consensus is exposed as illusory, strengthening the conclusion that liberal theory provides little guidance to moral behaviour in migration law-making. This absence of guidance is linked both to the hegemony of nation-states – that each can and evidently does build its own humanitarian mirror – and to liberal legalism's hermeneutics – that once a term is adopted and made legal, the techniques of the law turn the term into a category and remove it from its extra-legal moorings.

Humanitarianism is about identity. The individual identity of the other who benefits from our grace is important, but only because of the light it reflects back on us. When we admit the deserving, we are good. We bestow grace and hold up that mirror to admire ourselves. The instances of this in Australian and Canadian migration discourses are myriad. Humanitarianism in migration law is often a self-serving ruse.

There are two critical qualifiers, however. Despite all of this, humanitarianism is the touchstone of consensus in liberal migration laws. It has theoretical and rhetorical weight across a wide range of liberal theory, and it resonates in popular discourses. For these reasons, it is the strongest mobilizing principle we have for rallying to alter the law. To seek change in migration law so that more people for more reasons may be admitted to share our prosperity, we must appeal to vanity through the mirror.

For the final qualifier I must address the obvious: that both Australia and Canada have over history taken in large numbers of some of the neediest people in the world.[131] The people in these waves of humanitarian migration have arrived from great distances, with national assistance, have remade their lives and found good and positive ways to make these nations their own, intertwining their identities with the other. These migrations have had little to do, however, with the texts of our migration statutes, and most of these people would be inadmissible today. They have largely been facilitated through spontaneous eruptions of popular and political goodwill. Australian Prime Minister Hawke's invitation to Chinese nationals after the Tiananmen Square massacre or Prime Minister Howard's more recent

---

131   This must be understood in the context of the distance of these countries from situations of human crisis. Howard Adelman made the point in 1994 that Canada addresses fewer refugee claims per capita than the average among Western nations: Howard Adelman, "Justice, Immigration and Refugees" in Howard Adelman et al., eds., *Immigration and Refugee Policy: Australia and Canada Compared* (Melbourne: Melbourne University Press, 1994) 63 at 90. This observation is not challenged by more recent statistics. Australia addresses fewer claims.

– if recanted – invitation to ethnic Chinese in Indonesia[132] are good examples, as is the outpouring of private-citizen sponsorship of Indochinese refugees in the early 1980s, for which the Canadian people, *as a nation,* won the UNHCR Nansen medal. This kind of humanitarianism is not counterintuitive, but it is counter-legal. Once humanitarianism is moved into the texts of our law and policy, it loses what is most attractive about it.

The image of the nation that humanitarianism creates stands in stark contrast to the image of the nation when migration law intersects with rights discourse. When the other asserts a claim to justice rather than petitioning for mercy, the nation responds in kind. This intersection of rights, identities, and the liberal nation is the subject of Chapter 7.

132 This invitation was made at a time of heightened violence against them in 1998, as part of the social turmoil following the Asian economic crisis.

7
Identities, Rights, and Nations

This chapter scrutinizes the interrelationships between migration law and national identity through the perspective of rights discourses. In doing so, it takes up another aspect of the law and identity analysis set out in Part 1 and pushes the reasoning thus far in a new direction. Chapter 5 considered the othering of the refugee determination process and the reciprocal emergence of national identity in contrast to this ultimate other to the nation. Chapter 6 looked at how humanitarianism is located within liberal migration law to reflect a beneficent image of the nation and its members. Those two chapters examine the identity construction process from contrasting perspectives: first from the outside, considering how the absent other reflects contours of the nation, and then from the inside, by looking at how the nation seeks to present itself. In taking up the analysis of national identity through the perspective of rights discourses, these two analytic positions come together.

Many legal analyses focus solely on rights discourses in the highest courts. The advantage of moving to this level of analysis after canvassing the first two is that the interrelationship between what happens in the highest courts and what happens in other adjudicative and administrative settings is made visible. In addition, it is crucial to recall at this instance that migration law is one site where national identities can be observed. It is not the only site where this is possible, nor is national identity the only factor influencing migration law decisions. Some decisions will have nothing at all do to with national self-identification. However, looking at the cases as a whole, overarching patterns are visible that cannot be explained by any other factor, and that fit in with a consistent explanation linking judicial, administrative, and appellate practices.

Rights are the paradigm of legal discourse, and identity-based critiques of rights discourses have emphasized how they embed both categorizations, such as refugee, and normative perspectives, such as the beneficent nation. Rights claims are raised at many instances in and around migration law. To some extent, rights discourse does replicate the insider–outsider dichotomy, but attention to identities in migration law reveals that rights play a variety of more nuanced roles in migration law as well. My analysis in this chapter uses identity as a hermeneutic tool as well as using national identity as a subject of analysis. Attention to identity allows an exploration of variations in rights discourses in the migration law setting, and analysis of how these discourses contribute to the construction and contingent nature of national identities. Rights discourses are anchored in a discourse of justice and entitlement that sharply contrasts with the discourse of humanitarianism. Accordingly, the analysis in this chapter deepens the understanding of humanitarianism by looking at how claims from the humanitarian admissions stream are "translated" into a rights-dominated setting.

My analysis of rights in migration law adds insights to the identity-based critique of rights discussed in Part 1. In this chapter, I take up and examine rights as "images of power,"[1] look at rights as a phenomenon of collective identity,[2] and consider how the position of rights in migration law offers a particular illustration of Minow's thesis that there is a central instability in rights discourse that hinges on the inability of this discourse to offer an adequate reckoning of sameness and difference.[3] In contrasting Australian and Canadian migration law rights discourses, an important qualifier to the critique of rights discourses emerges. Since the rights deployed in migration law are themselves hierarchically arranged, it is important to consider how rights interact differently with identities at differing positions in the hierarchy. In some contexts, "strong" rights open a space for more robust identities of rights claimants. The potential for multifaceted relationships between rights and identities is one of the themes I take up here. An understanding of these relationships is also of strategic importance, as it provides insights into when rights might carry the potential for social transformations and when they will be inevitably tied to existing constellations of power relationships in society. This analysis, therefore, contributes also to that ongoing aspect of the critique of rights discourses.

The final step in the analysis of the interrelationship between migration law and national identity is to situate rights discourse in migration law at the border of the liberal nation – that is, to link my analysis of rights discourses in migration law to my broader analytic framework for migration law. While the analysis to this point allows for nuancing and extension of the identity-based critique of rights, locating the analysis in that broader

---

1 Patricia Williams, *The Alchemy of Race and Rights* (Cambridge, MA: Harvard University Press, 1991) at 233-34.
2 Alan Hunt, *Explorations in Law and Society: Toward a Constitutive Theory of Law* (London and New York: Routledge, 1993) at 247.
3 Martha Minow, *Making All the Difference: Inclusion, Exclusion and American Law* (Ithaca, NY: Cornell University Press, 1990) at 108.

framework demonstrates the importance and strength of that critique. In the realm of migration law, once a claim is articulated as a rights claim, the liberal nation's "right" to exclude all outsiders is triggered as an almost automatic response. For this reason, the most significant differences in migration rights discourses in Australia and Canada do not relate to Canada's constitutionally entrenched human rights and the absence of such in the Australian constitution, but to differing perceptions of national identity.

In Chapters 5 and 6, I focused on the day-to-day workings of refugee determination and humanitarian decision making. In this chapter, I consider instead the most significant judicial pronouncements concerning humanitarian admissions to Australia and Canada. These highest-court judgments provide a contrast to the day-to-day workings of the law discussed earlier. I proceed through the chapter by first locating the array of rights discourses in migration law. I then take up the Chapter 5 discussion of refugee claims as rights claims, and the conclusions to be drawn here about the hierarchy of rights. The next section considers the substance of process rights, and the subsequent one considers cases decided under Canada's *Charter of Rights and Freedoms*. In the final section, I draw out the linkages between rights discourses and the liberal nation that are foundational to my broader argument.

Rights in Migration Law

The rights discourses of migration law cluster around two dichotomies I explore in this chapter: the right–privilege distinction and the substantive rights–procedural rights distinction. The short version of the story is that admission to the nation for non-members is a privilege and never a right, and therefore the "rights" of those seeking entry are at most procedural. The simplicity of the story is an important part of understanding the limited potential for making rights claims the basis of legal change in migration law. It is also crucial to understanding the pre-eminent role of the nation's identity to migration law provisions and outcomes. As outsiders claim no rights, this law reflects national self-identifications and priorities exclusively, rather than other claims.

That non-members have no right of entry is the brightest beacon guiding the development of migration law. In the words of Canada's Justice Sopinka, "The most fundamental principle of immigration law is that non-citizens do not have an unqualified right to enter or remain in the country."[4] The Canadian *Immigration and Refugee Protection Act* draws the right–privilege distinction under the subheading "Entering and Remaining." Subsection 19(1) states: "Every Canadian citizen within the meaning of the *Citizenship*

---

4 *Chiarelli v. Canada (Minister of Employment and Immigration)* (1992), 90 D.L.R. (4th) 289 (SCC) at 303 [*Chiarelli*].

Act and every person registered as an Indian under the *Indian Act* has a right to enter and remain in Canada." This strong statement contrasts with subs. 19(2), under which "an officer shall allow a permanent resident to enter Canada if satisfied following an examination on their entry that they have that status." While this effectively translates into a right to enter for permanent residents, it is a qualified and contingent one. The most interesting aspect of these provisions, which were formerly called the "principles of Canadian immigration policy" is that the *Indian Act*[5] has a role in defining the membership of the nation.

The distinction of right versus privilege is the core principle of Canadian immigration policy. While permanent residents, refugees, and Indians[6] also have rights to remain (and enter in the case of permanent residents and Indians), these rights are qualified claims. For the first two groups, the limits are drawn by criminal behaviour. Over the past decade, the limits on these rights have been expanded by progressively broadening the criminal behaviour exclusions.[7] The rights of status Indians are also subject to the provisions of a separate governing regime. While it is difficult to deprive a person of Indian status, not every member of a First Nation holds or chooses to seek this status. The rights of Indians within the *Immigration and Refugee Protection Act* underscore the uneasy relationship of First Nations with migration law. First Nations are awkwardly positioned as neither members nor others, and thus distanced from the monolithic nation created in the law. This was underscored when the Federal Court of Appeal held in *Watt v. Canada (Minister for Citizenship and Immigration)*[8] that the right to enter Canada may extend to First Nations members who are not registered under the *Indian Act,* but on judicial review in the matter at hand, could not fully determine the issue. The place of Indians in the immigration law text echoes the absence of First Nations in the migration mythologies of the Canadian nation.

The Australian *Migration Act* has the same effect, but achieves it in a more direct way by stating in section 4 that its objective is to regulate "the coming into and presence in, Australia of non-citizens."[9] This introduces a theme

---

5 R.S.C. 1985, c. I-5.
6 The identity label "Indian" is used in the *Immigration and Refugee Protection Act* and is the legally relevant category under Canada's *Indian Act.* This term is no longer culturally appropriate in Canada, where the First Nations people are increasingly use the name of their nation, or are "categorized" generically as First Nations peoples.
7 These exclusions were contained in ss. 19 and 27 of the *Immigration Act* and are now set out in ss. 34, 35, 36, and 37 of the *Immigration and Refugee Protection Act,* 2002. Criminal inadmissibility now extends to those there are reasonable grounds to believe have committed an act anywhere that would constitute an offence if committed in Canada or who are members, broadly read, of any group involved in organized criminal activities or terrorism.
8 (1998), 169 D.L.R. (4th) 336.
9 Notably, each of the four subsections refers to the non-citizen–citizen dichotomy directly.

that resonates in many of the comparisons to be drawn between Australia and Canada in this chapter. Canadian migration law is more overtly concerned with substantive rights. While in Australian law permanent residents and refugees can be excluded for approximately the same reasons as in Canada,[10] their rights to remain are not enshrined as "principles" of Australian migration policy. The significance lies in what the nation chooses to say about itself in its law. To broaden the list of those with some basic rights claims makes the membership of the nation more diverse and more inclusive. That its promise may not be met in the Canadian setting can then become a legal argument with different rhetorical weight than the parallel Australian argument that a given subsection of the act is being wrongly interpreted. This is a clear instance of the nation writing its aspirational self into its migration law. The specific reference to Indians in the Canadian act focuses attention on the contested place of First Nations. A similar relationship exists, of course, in Australia, but the *Migration Act* proclaims the message "we are all Australians," submerging troublesome distinctions in that universalizing statement. It also has implications for the hierarchy of rights and the covert power of rights discourses that are explored later in this chapter.

Another lesson to be drawn from how the right–privilege dichotomy is written into migration law comes from its alignment with citizenship. Citizenship is the cornerstone of rights discourse because its universalizing and homogenizing impulse extends only to the border of the nation. That is, citizenship as a generic category is not homogenizing in itself; rather, it is the citizenship of some particular geographically and historically located nation that is universalized. Rights gain their power from their ability to be enforced by national legal systems. Citizens have the most secure and complete access to those systems. Citizens and rights are both attached to the nation. From the identity of the nation, citizens gauge some aspects of their self-identification. From that same identity of the nation, rights garner some of their substantive content.

The allotment of procedural rights in migration law forms concentric circles with citizenship in the centre. A refugee in an overseas camp hoping to resettle in either Australia or Canada has no rights at all when that government's representative is making selection decisions. A person arriving in Australia with no documents and not asserting a refugee claim at the border does not even have the right to be told of their right to have legal assistance or of their right to make a refugee claim.[11] Someone applying for permanent residency status in Canada at an overseas post does not have a

---

10 *Migration Act,* ss. 200-3.
11 *Fang v. Minister for Immigration and Ethnic Affairs* (1996), 135 A.L.R. 583 (Full F.C.A.) [*Fang*].

right to be heard in person by the decision maker.[12] Someone arriving in Australian territory that has been legislatively "excised" from the "migration zone" does not have the right to make a refugee claim.[13] Someone detained in Australia because of arriving without a visa has only a limited right to have their detention reviewed by a court.[14] An unsuccessful refugee claimant in Canada does not have a right to have that decision judicially reviewed.[15] A rejected refugee claimant in Australia has the right to a hearing on merit review,[16] but their access to judicial review is sharply curtailed by legislation.[17] A permanent resident of Canada who has applied to sponsor a new immigrant can appeal the rejection of that sponsorship, although the individual who was rejected cannot.[18] A permanent resident facing deportation from Australia has access to the full range of review and appeal possibilities.[19]

The concentric circles are not the same in each nation, but the principle is. The closer one is to belonging to the nation, the more rights one has in the migration realm. Citizenship is the centre of the circle, where one has the full bundle of rights, so much so that migration law is almost completely inapplicable to citizens save for some provisions providing sanctions for citizens who aid others in circumventing the law or where citizens can assist others in joining the nation through sponsorship.[20] As the circles become smaller, the connection between the nation and the individual is more tightly drawn, until the centre, where the nation and the individual are co-identified. This image of the array of rights in migration laws mirrors the linkages between rights and power. It also demonstrates the relationship between rights and community. There is a hierarchy of belonging

12 *Muliadi v. Minister of Employment and Immigration* (1986), 18 Admin. L.R. 243 (Fed. C.A.). This principle is not disturbed by the new legislation.

13 *Migration Amendment (Excision from Migration Zone) Act, 2001* (No. 127, 2001).

14 *Lim v. Minister for Immigration* (1992), 176 C.L.R. 1.

15 Although they do have the right to seek leave of the Federal Court to conduct judicial review. They may also seek humanitarian and compassionate review, but compassion is not a right.

16 *Migration Act,* s. 411.

17 At present by the privative clause in the *Migration Act,* s. 474, and previously by the removal of natural justice and unreasonableness as grounds of judicial review from the Federal Court.

18 *Immigration and Refugee Protection Act,* s. 63.

19 With some limited exceptions (on national security grounds), this person could seek merit review followed by limited judicial review in the Federal Court and then the High Court of Australia.

20 In both Canada and Australia, the argument that not all citizens are fully equal is sustained by considering distinctions between how citizenship was attained, and by the capacity to look behind grants of citizenship. This distinction does not disturb the present argument but presents an interesting dilemma for citizenship law, which shares many of migration law's themes. For a full discussion in the Australian context, see Kim Rubenstein, *Australian Citizenship Law in Context* (Sydney: Law Book Company, 2002).

inscribed in migration law, and its gradients are reflected in the allocation of legal markers – of rights.

The concentric circles allow for comparison between Australia and Canada as well. By using this image to visualize these rights, we can see that one can get further away from the centre in Australia than in Canada. That is, once a person has physically arrived on national soil, they can have no rights at all in Australia, except rights they need not be informed of and a right to be released from unlawful detention. In similar circumstances in Canada, a person must by law be told of their right to counsel. This may not amount to much if we imagine the situation in which one might seek to enforce this right. How much does an uninformed and uncomprehending individual at a port of entry really benefit from it? There are two counters to this. First, not all individuals at point of entry are uninformed or uncomprehending; and second, an accretion of minor rights distinctions does eventually add up to a noticeable difference between the migration laws of Australia and Canada.

Australian and Canadian migration laws are also an appropriate backdrop to considering the legal power and potential for social transformation of constitutionally protected human rights. Since 1982, Canadians have engaged in a robust conversation about whether the *Canadian Charter of Rights and Freedoms*[21] reduces or entrenches social and legal inequalities. The *Charter* does not replicate the *Immigration and Refugee Protection Act*'s statements about rights to enter and remain in Canada, but it does provide that "every citizen of Canada has the right to enter, remain in and leave Canada" and that both citizens and permanent residents have the right to "(a) move and take up residence in any province; and (b) to pursue the gaining of a livelihood in any province."[22] Aside from this provision and from the right to vote and to minority language education, the *Charter* does not refer to citizenship, setting out instead rights for individuals, persons, and First Nations. The Supreme Court of Canada's first and ground-breaking equality rights decision, while not a migration matter, struck down a distinction between citizens and permanent residents.[23] The decision had considerable implications for the meaning of membership of the Canadian community, but few for crossing the membership hurdle. In *Re Singh*,[24] the Supreme Court of Canada established that anyone physically present in Canada has the benefit of the *Charter*, setting the stage for a meaningful test of the utility of the *Charter* for those apply-

---

21 *Constitution Act, 1982,* Schedule B, Pt. 1.
22 *Ibid.,* s. 6.
23 *Andrews v. Law Society of British Columbia,* [1989] 1 S.C.R. 143. Permanent residents challenged a requirement of citizenship to enter legal practice.
24 *Re Singh and the Minister of Employment and Immigration* (1985), 17 D.L.R. (4th) 422 [*Re Singh*].

ing inland to become members of the community. In the section "Testing the *Charter of Rights and Freedoms*" below, I consider *Charter* arguments that have been raised in the area of migration law.

While the Australian Constitution does not enshrine rights of the individual, it has nonetheless had a role in shaping outcomes in migration law. Section 75 of the Australian Constitution, which creates an original jurisdiction for the High Court of Australia, has proven a bulwark against executive ousting of the courts in the migration area. The provision that individuals may go to the High Court to seek administrative law remedies in the form of writs of mandamus or prohibition, or an injunction, against an officer of the Commonwealth, has ensured that while access to the courts may be limited, it will not disappear completely. In the migration realm, where procedural rights have driven more outcomes than substantive rights, this jurisdictional provision has proven vital.

International law adds little or nothing to the array of rights available to those who seek access to a country where they are not already citizens or residents. There is no international right to enter a foreign country, or to leave one's own. Even the narrow potential right of genuine refugees not to be returned to face harm is so limited that it is at best a very weak rights claim. Similarly, what narrow rights claims may be won in an international arena still rest on national governments and domestic courts for their enforcement. A powerful example of this is provided by Australia's reaction to the United Nations Human Rights Committee finding that their detention regime for asylum seekers was in breach of international law.[25] The Australian government largely ignored the ruling.

My next step in analyzing the relationship of rights, identities, and nations is to explore why the claims of refugees fail as rights claims and how this contributes to refugee identity and to the identity-based critique of rights.

Refugee Claims as Rights Claims

While *prima facie* at international law refugees have no right to enter any country except that of their nationality, I argued in Chapter 5 that the *Refugee Convention*'s provision[26] that refugees must not be returned to countries where they risk persecution does not completely translate into a right to remain. I agree with Hathaway's assertion that "the notion of refugee law as

---

25 *Australia v. Applicant A*, Communication No. 560/1993, UN Doc. CCPR/C/59/D/560/ 1993 (30 April 1997), finding breaches of the *International Covenant on Civil and Political Rights*.

26 *Convention Relating to the Status of Refugees*, 1951, 189 U.N.T.S. 150 (entered into force 22 April 1954) with *Protocol Relating to the Status of Refugees*, 1967, 606 U.N.T.S. 267 (entered into force 4 October 1967) [*Refugee Convention*].

a rights based regime is largely illusory."[27] The reasons for this are related to the refugee's position as the ultimate other to the nation, and to the refugee's role as a humanitarian claimant seeking the mercy of the nation. A claim for compassion does not effectively function as a right because rights are grounded in equality but compassion is grounded in generosity and inequality. Efforts to shift the claims of refugees to some other basis have not been successful, in part because of the liberal humanitarian consensus surrounding the admission of outsiders. These factors draw the relationship between refugee identities, rights, and the nation into a curious alignment that provides a fuller picture of the reasons for the weakness of refugee rights discourses.

The Refugee Definition in the Highest Courts

Opinions of the highest courts in Australia and Canada interpreting the refugee definition can be analyzed by considering the extent to which the interpretation is conducted within, alongside, or at a distance from rights discourse. Broadly speaking, decisions that have been most favourable to refugee claimants have analyzed that claim in the context of fundamental human rights – that is, they have identified refugees as "right holders" of some sort, even while keeping some distance from the proposition that the *Refugee Convention* provides a right to remain in the country of refuge.

Canada (Attorney-General) v. Ward[28] is the most comprehensive of the relevant decisions of the Supreme Court of Canada and the High Court of Australia as it deals systematically with many aspects of the refugee definition. It is also a rare unanimous pronouncement of the Supreme Court of Canada.[29] Writing for the Court, Justice La Forest began by exploring "the rationale underlying the international refugee protection regime"[30] and made thorough use of the traditional sources of treaty interpretation including *travaux préparatoires,* academic commentary, and prevailing authorities.[31] He drew on the Preamble to the *Refugee Convention* to conclude that "underlying the *Convention* is the international community's commitment to the

---

27 James C. Hathaway, "Reconceiving Refugee Law as Human Rights Protection" (1991) 4 Journal of Refugee Studies 113. Hathaway argues that positive reforms in refugee law could be achieved by reformulating the law around the concept of a fundamental right to return to one's own state.

28 *Canada (Attorney-General) v. Ward* (1993), 103 D.L.R. (4th) 1 (SCC) [*Ward*].

29 The case was argued before a five-member panel (of a possible nine), and Stevenson J. did not participate in the judgment.

30 *Ward, supra* note 28 at 12.

31 Interestingly, Justice La Forest moves to these sources without elaborating his reasons for doing so, in marked contrast to the High Court of Australia's approach in *Applicant A and Another v. Minister for Immigration and Ethnic Affairs and Another* (1997), 142 A.L.R. 331 [*Applicant A*]. One explanation for this may be that the refugee definition is written directly into the Canadian law.

assurance of basic human rights without discrimination ... This theme outlines the boundaries of the objectives sought to be achieved and consented to by the delegates. It sets out, in a general fashion, the intention of the drafters and thereby the inherent limit to the cases embraced by the *Convention*."[32]

Justice La Forest kept the principle of human rights without discrimination at the forefront of his approach to all aspects of the refugee definition. It provided the justification for his use of *Charter* interpretation techniques[33] and his definition of a "particular social group."[34] The *Ward* decision sorted and categorized a number of Federal Court of Appeal decisions that had preceded it. In keeping with the human rights focus, the decision took a reasonably sympathetic approach to aspects of the definition presented to the court, such as state complicity in persecution, the test for determining fear of persecution, and exclusions from the refugee definition. Justice La Forest, however, could not overlook Ward's dual citizenship, and the case was returned to the IRB to consider whether Ward, an Irish citizen, could be adequately protected in Britain, where he also held citizenship. He was ultimately denied refugee status.

The effect of the Justice La Forest's human rights focus is easier to appreciate in cases where there are varying opinions. In *Chan v. Canada (Minister of Employment and Immigration)*,[35] the majority dismissed the appeal on the basis of the evidence given before the Convention Refugee Determination Division (now Refugee Protection Division). In an unjustifiable twist on the refugee definition, Justice Major wrote that the applicant had failed to establish "that his fear of forced sterilization was objectively well-founded,"[36] neatly sidestepping the issue of whether forced sterilization amounts to persecution and using the relaxed evidentiary requirements of a refugee hearing to argue that more anecdotal evidence should have been introduced. Justice Major made no mention of rights in any guise in his judgment.

32 *Ward, supra* note 28 at 29.
33 *Ibid.* at 32-33.
34 *Ibid.* at 33-34. He states: "The meaning assigned to 'particular social group' in the Act should take into account the general underlying themes of the defence of human rights and anti-discrimination that form the basis for international refugee protection" (at 33).
35 (1995), 128 D.L.R. (4th) 213. The IRB had found that Chan was not a refugee and the Federal Court of Appeal agreed. (While formally the Federal Court of Appeal was engaged in judicial review, the decision amounts to an agreement.)
36 *Ibid.* at 268. Major J. also "assumes without deciding" that *Cheung v. Canada (Minister for Employment and Immigration)* (1993), 102 D.L.R. (4th) 214 (F.C.A., deciding that a woman who had fled China in fear of forced sterilization was a refugee on the basis of persecution for being a member of a particular social group) was correctly decided (at 258) and refers to the standard of proof in a refugee hearing as a "balance of probabilities" (at 268). These statements could have introduced considerable confusion into Canadian refugee jurisprudence were this decision not so clearly based on the majority's suspicion of the evidence given through an interpreter to the IRB.

In his strongly worded dissent, Justice La Forest cast his analysis in the human rights discourse he introduced in *Ward*. He linked refugee claims to human rights violations directly, and rejected the argument that support for his position could lead to a flood of refugees to Canada's borders: "To alter the focus of refugee law away from its paramount concern with basic human rights frustrates the possibility that foreign persecution may be eventually halted by international pressure. To accept at a judicial level that fundamental human rights violations do not serve to grant Convention refugee status minimizes one of the principle incentives the international community has to denounce foreign persecution and attempt to effect change abroad: to avoid a flood of refugee claimants."[37] He repeated the reference to "basic human rights" throughout the judgment and used it to rework the definition of "particular social group" that he outlined in *Ward*.[38] One of the most significant aspects of Justice La Forest's approach is that he did not qualify in any way the human rights violations referred to. While the rights violated must be "basic," the violations need not be "serious," "repeated," or otherwise narrowed.

A similar analysis applies to the Supreme Court of Canada's decision in *Pushpanathan v. Canada (Minister for Citizenship and Immigration)*[39] considering exclusions to refugee protection under the *Convention* definition. Although the question of the appropriate standard of review for an IRB decision was not argued in the Trial Division of the Federal Court, or in the Federal Court of Appeal, Justice Bastarache, for the majority, began his analysis of the case from this point. Following the Supreme Court of Canada's "functional and pragmatic" approach to standard of review, this analysis starts with a focus on the legislative intent of the statute creating the tribunal under review. In a chain of reasoning that involves some slippage from strict logic, Justice Bastarache looked to *Ward* to determine that the purpose of the *Refugee Convention* is to protect human rights without discrimination. He then argued that the Convention Refugee Determination Division is not expert in human rights decision making, and used this as a strong plank in his conclusion that a correctness standard of review should apply.[40] After thus setting the opinion on a human rights footing, Justice Bastarache linked the exclusions from the refugee definition to human

---

37 *Chan, ibid.* at 237.

38 In "Chinese Fleeing Sterilisation: Australia's Response against a Canadian Backdrop" (1998) 10 Int'l J. Refugee L. 77 ["Chinese Fleeing Sterilisation"], I argued that La Forest's definition is awkwardly worded and that this dissent provides further evidence of how unworkable it is.

39 *Pushpanathan v. Canada (Minister for Citizenship and Immigration)*, [1998] 1 S.C.R. 982; [1998] S.C.J. No. 46 (QL; paragraph references are to this electronic version) [*Pushpanathan*].

40 *Ibid.* at para. 42-47. This is the least deferential standard of review available under the Canadian pragmatic and functional approach.

rights.[41] He summarized the logic of the exclusions as "that those who are responsible for persecution which creates refugees should not enjoy the benefits of a *Convention* designed to protect those refugees."[42] Following this, his conclusion that drug trafficking does not "come ... close to the core or even form a part of the corpus of fundamental human rights"[43] comes as no surprise.

Justice Cory, in dissent, opened his opinion by stating, "Mr. Pushpanathan was a member of a group convicted of trafficking in heroin with a street value of $10 million."[44] Justice Bastarache had minimized this aspect of the case by noting that the facts in the case were not in dispute. While the majority opinion canvassed principles of treaty interpretation and UN human rights instruments, Justice Cory examined international drug trafficking and the links between drugs and crime. Significantly, he agreed with Justice Bastarache that the *Refugee Convention* is a human rights instrument,[45] but he also stated that human rights violations are not the only conduct central to the UN's purpose and principles.[46] Justice Cory sidelined the role of human rights in interpreting the *Refugee Convention* without dismissing it altogether. He was careful to reject the Federal Court of Appeal's proposition that refugee status is a mere privilege, and asserted instead that "the right to claim refugee status constitutes an important right, and any exclusions from that right must be interpreted in accordance with accepted principles."[47] Unlike Justice Bastarache, Justice Cory did not, however, use human rights discourse as the core interpretive principle for the *Refugee Convention*. In the Canadian jurisprudence, those judges who aim to achieve a generous or broad interpretation of refugee status have done so by invoking the discourse of fundamental human rights.

A similar analysis of the High Court of Australia cases is revealing. The leading Australian decision on the interpretation of the refugee definition, *Chan v. Minister for Immigration and Ethnic Affairs,*[48] establishes that a refugee must face a "real chance" of persecution and that the assessment of refugee status is to be made at the time of the determination in the receiving state rather than at the time of the claimant's decision to leave home. Beyond

---

41 Pushpanathan, a permanent resident, had been sentenced to eight years jail after pleading guilty to trafficking heroin. When he was paroled, the Canadian government issued a deportation order. Pushpanathan applied for refugee status and the IRB determined that he was not a refugee because of the exclusion in Article 1F(c) of the *Refugee Convention* for those who are "guilty of Acts contrary to the purposes and principles of the United Nations."

42 *Pushpanathan, supra* note 39 at para. 63.

43 *Ibid.* at para. 72.

44 *Ibid.* at para. 78.

45 *Ibid.* at para. 127.

46 *Ibid.* at para. 126.

47 *Ibid.* at para. 136.

48 *Chan v. Minister for Immigration and Ethnic Affairs* (1989), 169 C.L.R. 379.

these two points, little is agreed upon in the five opinions. The references to human rights in the judgment are not used as interpretive devices, but rather as references to actions that may *not* constitute persecution. For example, Justice Dawson stated that it is unnecessary to determine whether "other serious violations of human rights for the same reasons would also constitute persecution."[49] Justice McHugh stated that exile or imprisonment "is such a gross invasion of his human rights as to constitute persecution for reasons of political opinion,"[50] and that "not every threat of harm to a person or interference with his or her rights for reasons of race, religion, nationality, membership of a particular social group or political opinion constitutes 'being persecuted.'"[51] Both justices left open the possibility that some human rights violations would not constitute persecution. While undoubtedly the Canadian Supreme Court would agree with this proposition, it signifies a different approach to the refugee definition and a distinctly different interpretive principle informing the jurisprudence.

Two of the justices in *Chan v. Minister for Immigration and Ethnic Affairs* cast the intent of the *Refugee Convention* as humanitarian. Justice Toohey asserted that the "real chance" test "gives effect to the language of the *Convention* and to its humanitarian intendment,"[52] and Justice Gaudron argued that the "humanitarian purpose of the *Convention*," along with the difficulty of finding facts in refugee determinations, should "curb enthusiasm for judicial specification of the content of the expression 'well-founded fear.'"[53] The significance of these statements lies in the distinction between humanitarian discourse and rights discourse. The difference between categorizing the *Refugee Convention* as being about human rights and being about humanitarianism seems innocuous on its face, but it positions subsequent interpretations differently within liberal legal discourse. The legal and rhetorical power of rights is missing from discussions of humanitarianism.

The analytic importance of rights discourse is highlighted in *Applicant A,* where the Australian High Court interprets the phrase "membership of a particular social group" in the case of two nationals of the People's Republic of China fleeing the reach of the one-child policy.[54] For Chief Justice Brennan in dissent, fundamental human rights are the key to interpreting the refugee definition. They inform the interpretation of persecution and, in turn, of particular social group:

49   *Ibid.* at 400.
50   *Ibid.* at 434.
51   *Ibid.* at 429.
52   *Ibid.* at 407.
53   *Ibid.* at 413.
54   *Applicant A, supra* note 31.

If a putative refugee's enjoyment of his or her fundamental rights and freedoms is denied by a well-founded fear of persecution for a reason that distinguishes the victims as a group from society at large, it would be contrary to the "principle that human beings shall enjoy fundamental rights and freedoms without discrimination" [*Refugee Convention* Preamble]. It would therefore be contrary to the object and purpose of the Convention to exclude that putative refugee from the protection which the Convention requires Contracting Parties to accord.[55]

The other dissentient, Justice Kirby, takes the opposite approach, stating: "The appeal is not about 'fundamental human rights' as such, although clearly upon one view, they are affected. The appellants seek no more than the enforcement of Australia's domestic law."[56] The distinction here is crucial. It plainly indicates the superior power of domestic rights claims and the potential weakness that fundamental human rights, because of their universality, carry with them. Those claiming a right directly under the *Migration Act* raise a superior, specific, claim against Australia.

For the majority justices, fundamental human rights are discussed only in reference to arguments based on Canadian cases.[57] Their comments reflect the High Court's unanimous, but flawed, view that the Canadian jurisprudence results from the *Charter of Rights and Freedoms*.[58] The framework of this decision closely resembles the *Pushpanathan* decision, with an emphasis on human rights corresponding with broader interpretations of all aspects of the refugee definition. Justice Kirby's view, which moves the rights discourse within the nation by setting it in domestic law, is even more expansive.

The relationship of humanitarian discourse and rights discourse is present in the High Court's ruling in *Chen Shi Hai v. Minister for Immigration and Multicultural Affairs*,[59] which is related to the earlier *Applicant A* decision because it concerns China's one-child policy. Here, all five members of the panel found that children discriminated against as "black children" because of their birth in contravention of the policy can constitute a particular social group. The joint majority judgment writes of the "standards of civil society which seek to meet the calls of our common humanity" in describing the discrimination suffered by so-called black children.[60] This language evokes a humanitarian impulse. Justice Kirby's judgment, while opening

---

55 *Ibid.* at 336.
56 *Ibid.* at 385.
57 Dawson, McHugh, and Gummow J.J.
58 I discuss this in "Chinese Fleeing Sterilisation," *supra* note 38.
59 (2000), 170 A.L.R. 553.
60 *Ibid.* at 560 per Gleeson C.J., Gaudron, Gummow, and Hayne J.J.

with reference to the broad humanitarian purpose of the *Refugee Convention,* strongly emphasizes the "legal rights" of the child in question under Australian law, and links these rights to identity: "Under Australian law, the child was entitled to have his own rights determined as that law provides. He is not for all purposes subsumed to the identity and legal rights of his parents."[61] While all members of the Court agreed that "black children" were a particular social group, Justice Kirby's separate opinion places additional emphasis on the distinct rights claim of the child, a point that is minimized in the joint judgment. Nothing turns on this point in this case, but it sets a standard for future judgments. In language replete with the logic of humanitarian bestowing, the majority opinion emphasized the blamelessness of children born in contravention of the one-child policy.

In *Minister for Immigration and Multicultural Affairs v. Ibrahim,*[62] Justice Gummow, writing the lead judgment for the majority described the purpose of the *Convention* as limiting humanitarianism and restricting rights. His starting proposition was that the right of asylum is a right of states, not of individuals.[63] He noted the international right to seek, but not to obtain, asylum, and the absence of any right to enter a state to do so. Drawing on Hathaway's work about the restrictive purposes of the *Convention,* Justice Gummow found that "it is generally accepted that the *Convention* definition, based on individual persecution, limits the humanitarian scope of the *Convention,*"[64] and concluded, therefore, that "it would be ... wrong to depart from the demands of language and context by invoking the humanitarian objectives of the *Convention* without appreciating the limits which the *Convention* itself places on the achievement of them."[65] Against this interpretive backdrop, Justice Gummow found that the decision of the Refugee Review Tribunal (RRT) regarding limits to persecution during civil war characterized by clan warfare did not constitute error of law. In agreeing with Justice Gummow, Chief Justice Gleeson again noted that not all "invasions" of human rights will constitute persecution.[66] Justices Gaudon, McHugh, and Kirby each penned strongly worded dissents. Justice Kirby took direct issue with Justice Gummow's discussion of the *Convention's* purpose and urged instead an emphasis on the Preamble's commitment to fundamental rights and freedoms.[67] For the majority judges, the vital rights at stake were those of the nation, not of the individual.

61 *Ibid.* at 573. Kirby J.'s discussion of rights begins at 572.
62 [2000] H.C.A. 55. Ibrahim was a Somali national.
63 *Ibid.* at para. 137.
64 *Ibid.* at para. 141.
65 *Ibid.*
66 *Ibid.* at para. 6.
67 *Ibid.* at para. 198.

The *Ibrahim* decision was followed in 2002 by two further High Court decisions interpreting the refugee definition, each with regard to a narrowly framed point. In *Minister for Immigration and Multicultural Affairs v. Khawar,*[68] the Court held that a woman from Pakistan might be able to make out her claim on the basis of persecution for reasons of membership in a particular social group, and returned the matter to the RRT for further consideration of the evidence. In this instance, where the decision was favourable to the applicant, Justices McHugh and Gummow linked a denial of fundamental rights and persecution.[69] Justice Kirby continued to analyze the *Refugee Convention* in rights terms.[70] The case determined little because of the scant evidence considered by the tribunal, and does not settle how the parameters of the particular social group in question ought to be drawn.[71] In such a setting, a discussion of individual rights is used without hesitation.

Minister for Immigration and Multicultural Affairs v. Singh[72] is similar in its narrow focus on tribunal error. This was the first case where the High Court considered the exclusion clauses of the refugee definition. The Court held that the RRT had erred by concluding that because a murder was motivated at least in part by revenge, it could not be a "political crime."[73] The reasons are generally focused closely on this question and do not consider the *Refugee Convention* broadly. Justice Kirby's reasons are an exception. He asserted that the *Refugee Convention* was a compromise between the reasonable desire of national communities to exclude criminals of any type and the legal right to protection. He also noted that comparisons with extradition provisions must be carefully measured, as extradition does not constrain sovereignty in the same way as refugee law.[74] In this judgment, he contrasted the rights of individuals and nations, finding that the nation's rights are limited.

---

68 [2002] H.C.A. 14.
69 *Ibid.* at paras. 79, 85.
70 *Ibid.* at paras. 111-15, for example. Justice Callinan was the sole dissentient in the case, agreeing with the RRT's characterization of any harm as private in nature. He also expressed skepticism at whether "women" could ever be a "particular social group" because of the size of the group, which seems to contradict the majority holding in *Applicant A.*
71 *Dranichnikov v. Minister for Immigration and Multicultural Affairs,* [2003] H.C.A. 26 also contributes to the High Court's elaboration of the meaning of "particular social group," stating that in this instance the RRT had defined the group too broadly, making the required nexus with persecution impossible.
72 *Minister for Immigration and Multicultural Affairs v. Singh,* [2002] H.C.A. 7 [*Singh*].
73 Article 1F(b) excludes from *Convention* protection those who have "committed a serious non-political crime outside the country of refuge prior to his admission to that country as a refugee." The case holds that it is permissible, in spite of the wording of the paragraph, to address the question of exclusion before considering whether the claimant falls within the positive aspects of the refugee definition.
74 *Singh, supra* note 72 at paras. 94-105.

This was precisely the opposite of the limiting described by the *Ibrahim* majority.

The 2003 ruling in *Appellant S395/2002 v. Minister for Immigration and Multicultural Affairs*[75] that I considered in Chapter 5 can also be analyzed through a rights and identity discourse. The dissentients emphasized that the *Refugee Convention* does not aim to guarantee all human rights.[76] In contrast, the two sets of majority reasons make reference to international human rights standards and to human dignity.[77] What is more important in the reasoning, however, is that the majority judges found that the tribunal relied on an incorrect understanding of sexual identity: "Sexual identity is not to be understood in this context as confined to engaging in particular sex acts or, indeed, to any particular forms of physical conduct. It may, and often will, extend to many aspects of human relationships and activity. That two individuals engage in sexual acts in private ... may say nothing about how those individuals would choose to live other aspects of their lives that are related to, or informed by, their sexuality."[78] The more expansive reading of identity leads to a positive outcome for claims. Rights and identity are twinned in this decision, just as in the procedural rights cases discussed below.

Decisions of the highest courts interpreting the *Refugee Convention* are few. Even though recent Australian efforts to limit judicial review in the Federal Court have pushed more and more cases into the constitutional jurisdiction of the High Court, most of these have been decided on procedural questions that do not touch on the refugee definition itself. Refugee law is a relatively new area of jurisprudential concern and the barriers to reaching the highest court are myriad. Nonetheless, each decision sets the standard for lower courts and refugee tribunals. The role of human rights discourses in these decisions is closely aligned with the courts' approaches to refugee identities, a key point that builds on the Chapter 5 analysis of how these identities are constructed.

Rights and Refugee Identities

The story told by these cases complicates the critique of rights discourses. When the refugee definition is interpreted within a rights discourse, that of fundamental human rights, the result is a broader reading of the law and consequently greater likelihood of a successful claim. That is, rights discourse is favourable for refugee claimants to this extent at least. Nonetheless, the role of human rights discourses reinforces the narrow version of

---

75 [2003] H.C.A. 71.
76 *Ibid.* at para. 107.
77 *Ibid.* at para. 45 and para. 66.
78 *Ibid.* at para. 81, per Gummow and Hayne JJ.

refugee identity that I elaborated and falls short of ensuring that refugee claims are treated as rights claims in domestic courts.

The discourse of fundamental human rights provides guidance in interpreting the *Refugee Convention* that draws on a vision of refugee identity and is strongly linked to international law discourses. In this discourse, the refugee is identified as a holder of certain rights and as a victim of fundamental human rights abuses. The rights that are held are those fundamental to our humanity, rights that are held by all individuals. They are not rights to enter or remain in any nation, nor are they rights to be protected by a "foreign" nation. The discourse of fundamental human rights is linked to the international law context where it evolved, and is marked with characteristics of that setting. Two of those characteristics are the simmering instability of fundamental human rights in the face of cultural relativity, and the difficulties of enforcing human rights norms. A specific enumeration of fundamental human rights is difficult to achieve. There are strong links between the phrase and a sense of dignity and humanity, as is echoed by Canadian Justice Linden in describing people refusing forced sterilization as "united or identified by a purpose which is so fundamental to their human dignity that they should not be required to alter it."[79] What is "fundamental" about fundamental human rights is often the emotional reaction provoked by their breach. This commonality – which parallels the definition of humanitarianism in Chapter 6 – is not sufficient for the blunt reasoning of the law. It leaves a troublesome sense that we will know a fundamental human right when we see it. In combination with this difficulty of precise enumeration comes the recognition that fundamental human rights are related to our humanity, not tied to a national legal system. There is a strength and unity in this discourse that grounds legally powerful and strongly emotive decisions, but it is not the same degree of strength that derives from, for example, constitutionally protected rights in domestic legal systems.

When the refugee definition is linked to the discourse of fundamental human rights, the refugee is identified as a right holder. The refugee thus occupies one of Patricia Williams's "islands of entitlement." But the island is a small one. The entitlement accorded to the refugee is nothing more than we would accord to anyone. As such, the rights entitlement is minimal indeed, and the floodgates case for keeping it that way is strong. A successful refugee claim is based on fitting into the narrow configurations of the refugee definition – that is, identifying oneself as distinct from all others who have fundamental human rights in some ways. When the discourse of fundamental human rights is the interpretive tool, it reinforces

---

79 *Cheung v. Canada (Minister of Employment and Immigration)* (1993), 102 D.L.R. (4th) 214 (F.C.A.).

the identity of the refugee as a certain type of victim, because the breach of fundamental human rights is only part of the definition. This accords with what the examination of the refugee determination process in Chapter 5 demonstrated – a narrowing of identity to a mere pinprick and a strong appeal to the liberal humanitarian consensus.

The discourse of fundamental human rights identifies the refugee as a holder of certain rights, and also identifies the refugee as a victim of certain types of rights breaches. It is because refugee identity is rooted in the breach of rights rather than in holding the rights themselves that the humanitarian impulse to view the refugee as deserving of compassion rather than justice is triggered. Identity as refugee is restrictive because in order to fit within it, the individual must continue to be a figure worthy of compassion.

Even when a refugee claim is analyzed using the discourse of fundamental human rights, which these cases show occurs only some of the time, it falls short of being a rights claim. The rights that are accorded to members of the nation are rights to enter and to remain. The *Refugee Convention*'s provision that refugees not be refouled could constitute a right to remain only because it is impossible to expel individuals into some empty non-national space. Analyzing the refugee definition using a discourse of fundamental human rights is not enough to counter the weight of quotas, political pressure, and national sovereignty that ensure that refugees are allowed to remain because of the goodness of the nation rather than because of their fundamental right to stay. Moreover, the discourse of human rights is used to analyze what the other nation has done or failed to do for the refugee claimant. It assists us in understanding what persecution is, when a fear is well founded, how to define a particular social group. Fundamental human rights are things breached by the others, not claims made against us. The analysis of fundamental human rights in these cases is focused outside the nation, not turned inward to look at *our own* behaviour or *our own* obligations. When the refugee raises a fundamental human rights argument, it is linked to something that happened to them in the past and will happen to them in the future, rather than being some entitlement that they are claiming in the present.

An important aspect of any critique of rights discourse is the understanding that rights are hierarchically arranged legal categories – that is, that some rights are better than others. The rights that command the most persuasive power are those most closely associated with the liberal legal tradition, and hence most relevant to the mythic struggle between the individual and the state. For this reason, the rights of the criminal accused are often more powerful than the more recently devised "rights" of victims of crime; and the civil and political rights expressed in the *International Covenant on Civil and Political Rights* are regarded as more important than the social and group rights of the *International Covenant on Economic, Social and Cultural Rights*.[80] The potential right of a refugee not to be returned to a persecutory state is far from the core of liberal legalism as most liberal frameworks consider only what happens inside the state, and it is consequently low in any version of the hierarchy of rights. While the individual may be involved in a struggle with the state, as a non-member their claims do not resonate within the nation. This is one more factor contributing to the failure of refugee claims to function effectively as rights claims.

Despite all of this, the discourse of fundamental human rights remains the most persuasive alternative presently available for interpreting the refugee definition. As the highest courts' decisions demonstrate, it is the discourse of fundamental human rights that is invoked when judges seek to rule in favour of refugee claims, and broad appeals to fundamental human rights are effective in patching over infelicities in legal reasoning.[81] As well, any rights-based discourse contains at least some transformative potential, some chance that the right in question may ascend the hierarchy of rights.[82] An identity as a right holder is a stronger base from which to mount an argument that resonates within liberal legalism than any other. The following section on process rights illustrates this point further.

The Substance of Process Rights

The traditional process rights are crucial in migration law's administrative decision-making setting. Given the linkage of admission decisions to the historically non-reviewable royal prerogative and the absence of a substantive right to enter a nation, the development of procedural safeguards in migration law processes reveals a great deal about identities of the nation and the potential right holder. Procedural rights are crucial to the liberal dichotomy between the individual and the state. The way these rights are constructed and deployed depicts both sides of that dichotomy. The range of potential differences is seen in contrasting judicial opinions regarding process rights in the migration area. Justice Kirby classifies the refugee claimant as similar to all other people in Australia by stating that judicial review does not entitle an applicant to be accepted as a refugee; "it simply secures

---

80 *International Covenant on Civil and Political Rights*, 1966, 999 U.N.T.S. 171 (entered into force 23 March 1976) and *International Covenant on Economic, Social and Cultural Rights*, 1966, 973 U.N.T.S. 3 (entered into force 3 January 1976).

81 See especially Justice La Forest in *Ward*, Justice Bastarache in *Pushpanathan*, and Justice Brennan in *Applicant A*, all discussed in the preceding section.

82 Evidence of this is found in the *Pushpanathan* decision, where Justice Cory, in dissent, states that there is an important "right" to make a refugee claim (*supra* note 39 at para. 136) even though his approach to interpreting the definition is not grounded in rights discourse and his conclusions are unfavourable to the applicant. Depending on future developments, this may constitute some early evidence of a shift in Canadian legal discourse about refugees.

to him or her the basic entitlement, enjoyed by every person sheltering under the laws of this country, citizen or not."[83] In contrast, Justice Callinan reinforces a strict distinction between "us" and "them" regardless of whether "they" are already in Australia and subject to the Australian legal system, with the view that the limited provisions for judicial review under the *Migration Act* "gave entrants to Australia ... certain rights in respect of what would otherwise be matters for the executive exclusively."[84] The distance between these two Australian perspectives denotes the length of the spectrum. In discussing the substance of process rights, I argue in turn that process rights depict those who hold them in substantial ways; that procedural rights are at the core of liberal legality and therefore closely linked to the nation itself; and that the Canadian *Charter* jurisprudence enhances the important slippage between substance and process rights.

The 1985 Watershed Decisions: *Singh* and *Kioa*

In both Australia and Canada, an important procedural rights decision marks the watershed for migration law in the highest courts and introduces the contemporary era of migration jurisprudence. The Supreme Court of Canada handed down its decision in *Re Singh and the Minister of Employment and Immigration*[85] in April 1985, eight months before the High Court of Australia decision in *Kioa v. West*.[86] Both cases concerned the meaning of natural justice for potential refugee or humanitarian entrants who were already in the country, particularly whether claimants were entitled to be heard in person.

Singh was argued during the early days of the Canadian *Charter*, but the Supreme Court split three to three on whether to decide the case under the *Charter* or under the moribund *Canadian Bill of Rights*.[87] Justice Wilson's *Charter*-based decision is the part of the judgment that is frequently cited and that looms large in Canadian mythic jurisprudence. The decision is mythic because it has come to stand for the importance of the *Charter* in immigration law despite its specific contents.

Justice Wilson reasoned that the use of the term "everyone" in s. 7 of the *Charter* meant that the provision applied to all who were physically present in Canada, regardless of citizenship and of whether they had been allowed

---

83 *Minister for Immigration and Ethnic Affairs v. Wu Shan Liang* (1996), 185 C.L.R. 259 at 292.

84 *Abebe v. The Commonwealth; Re Minister for Immigration and Multicultural Affairs,* [1999] H.C.A. 14 at para. 277 [*Abebe*].

85 *Re Singh, supra* note 24.

86 *Kioa v. West* (1985), 159 C.L.R. 550 [*Kioa*].

87 S.C. 1960, c. 44. Justice Beetz penned the opinion based on the *Bill of Rights,* with Justices Estey and McIntyre concurring. The opinion must have surprised those involved in the case, as no *Bill of Rights* arguments had been put to the Court. The right–privilege distinction had previously been fatal to use of the *Bill of Rights,* and in the realm of migration law it would surely have been seen by 1985 as almost entirely pointless.

through border controls or not.[88] The second step in Justice Wilson's analysis was to determine that the substantive right of a refugee not to be refouled triggered the interests in life, liberty, and security of the person protected under s. 7.[89] This reasoning introduces the important slippage between substantive and procedural rights in *Charter* jurisprudence that I discuss below. It also provides some hint of a possibility of treating a refugee claim as a substantive right, within a confined framework.[90] Upon concluding that both liberty and security of the person were threatened by definition when a refugee was refouled, Justice Wilson concluded that procedures for refugee determination had to conform to s. 7's "principles of fundamental justice." Although she concluded that s. 7 would not always trigger a need for an oral hearing, "where a serious issue of credibility is involved, fundamental justice requires that credibility be determined on the basis of an oral hearing." In ruling that s. 1 of the *Charter*[91] did not save the s. 7 infringement, Justice Wilson stated:

> It is important to bear in mind that the rights and freedoms set out in the *Charter* are fundamental to the political structure of Canada and are guaranteed by the *Charter* as part of the supreme law of our nation. I think that in determining whether a particular limitation is a reasonable limit prescribed by law which can be "demonstrably justified in free and democratic society" it is important to remember that the courts are conducting this inquiry in light of a commitment to uphold the rights and freedoms set out in the other sections of the *Charter*.[92]

Both Justices Wilson and Beetz were concerned in *Singh* with an opportunity to know the case against oneself, with the reasons for decision, and with determining procedural protections based on the consequences for the individual involved. Each concluded that while fundamental justice – either *Charter* or *Bill of Rights* style – may not always require an oral hearing,

---

88 *Re Singh, supra* note 24 at 456; see also 462-63, where a distinction is drawn from the American approach to the same question.

89 Section 7 reads: "Everyone has the right to life, liberty and security of the person and the right not to be deprived thereof except in accordance with the principles of fundamental justice."

90 For example, Justice Wilson stated: "On these appeals this court is being asked by the appellants to accept that the substantive rights of *Convention* refugees have been determined by the *Immigration Act, 1976* itself and the court need concern itself only with the question whether the procedural scheme set up by the Act for the determination of that status is consistent with the requirements of fundamental justice articulated in s. 7 of the *Charter*": *Re Singh, supra* note 24 at 463-64.

91 Section 1 reads: "The *Canadian Charter of Rights and Freedoms* guarantees the rights and freedoms set out in it subject only to such reasonable limits prescribed by law as can be demonstrably justified in a free and democratic society."

92 *Re Singh, supra* note 24 at 468.

it does always require an oral hearing for those claiming refugee status when inside Canada. Bringing the decision under the *Charter* provided a way for Justice Wilson to link the issue directly to the values of Canada as a nation.

Mr. Kioa did not claim refugee status but rather sought to remain in Australia under the former s. 6A(1)(e) of the *Migration Act,* strong compassionate and humanitarian grounds for the grant of a permanent entry permit. All four of the majority judges held that the decision whether to grant an entry permit on this basis required that the decision maker adhere to principles of natural justice.[93] They also agreed that in the particular circumstances of this case, natural justice included an opportunity to be heard.[94] There was a range of disagreement, however, over which particular facts triggered the need to be heard. Justices Mason and Wilson held that the implication that Mr. Kioa had been involved in illegal activities or had generally been deceptive triggered a natural justice requirement that he be able to respond to this potential basis for a discretionary decision.[95] Justice Wilson also stated that as strong humanitarian and compassionate grounds were at issue, "this may strengthen the claim to an expectation to be heard in relation to such a decision."[96]

Justice Brennan found that while a hearing had been required on these facts, the requirement could be overridden by the control objectives of the *Migration Act:*

> When the purpose for which the provision is conferred – control of the membership of the Australian people and their visitors – would be frustrated by giving a hearing, the principles of natural justice do not require that a hearing be given. But there is no reason to think that giving a hearing to Mr. Kioa would impair the Minister's control over the disposition of the Kioa family.[97]

Justice Brennan thereby subordinated process rights to the needs of the nation, in reasoning that is consistent with strong executive control over admission to the nation and the royal prerogative pedigree.

---

93 Chief Justice Gibbs dissented. Justices Mason, Wilson, Brennan, and Deane comprised the majority.
94 *Kioa, supra* note 86, per Mason J. at 587, Wilson J. at 602, Brennan J. at 626 and Deane J. at 633.
95 Justice Mason stated the proposition this way: "In the ordinary course of granting or refusing entry permits there is not occasion for the principles of natural justice to be called into play ... But if in fact the decision-maker intends to reject the application by reference to some consideration personal to the applicant on the basis of information obtained from another source which has not been dealt with by the applicant in his application there may be a case for saying that procedural fairness requires that he be given an opportunity of responding to the matter": *ibid.* at 587.
96 *Ibid.* at 600.
97 *Ibid.* at 626.

Justice Deane, on the other hand, wrote an opinion agreeing that Kioa ought to have been heard before a decision was made and speculating that few situations would justify denying such an opportunity. He stated:

> Putting aside cases of necessity however and in the absence of any clear legislative intent excluding or modifying the requirement of procedural fairness, it is difficult to envisage a case in which the particular circumstances would either exclude those requirements completely in relation to the making of a deportation order or so modify them that the person affected was not entitled to an adequate opportunity of being heard before he was subjected to the adverse effects of such an order.[98]

Like Justice Brennan, Justice Deane situated his reasoning in relation to the needs of the nation. He opened his analysis by asserting that "an alien who is unlawfully within this country is not an outlaw," and emphasized that "an alien is not without status or standing in the land" and "can invoke the protection of the law."[99] Justice Deane recognized the importance of procedural rights to identities and how the removal of procedural rights reduces the substance of identity: "The making of a deportation order against a prohibited immigrant drastically and adversely changes his rights and, to some extent, dehumanizes his status."[100] While Justices Deane and Brennan reached the same conclusion in *Kioa*, their agreement is almost coincidental. Justice Brennan privileged the identity of the nation and Justice Deane the identity of the person. What their opinions share is an overt acknowledgment of the interests at stake.

Singh and *Kioa* were both regarded as important victories for those in the most needy group of people hoping to join the Canadian and Australian communities. Both judgments contain passages in which the judges reflect on how the decision before them is linked to the needs and self-perceptions of the nation, and both judgments demonstrate the paucity of the term "procedural" rights for outcomes that are linked to substantive rights. For *Singh*, this is true because of the influence the potentially substantive right not to be refouled had on Justice Wilson's reasoning. In *Kioa*, it is the case because he has remained in Australia. This link is underscored by how the respective governments responded to the decisions. In Canada, *Singh* was an important trigger for the establishment of the present refugee determination procedure before the IRB. In Australia, *Kioa* was followed shortly by curtailment of the operation of citizenship by birth. In argument and in the press, the fact that Kioa had an Australian-born daughter who was a citizen was emphasized. While nothing overt turned on it in the

98   *Ibid.* at 633.
99   *Ibid.* at 631.
100 *Ibid.* at 632.

judgment, each of the opinions addressed this fact. The Australian *Citizen-ship Act* was amended soon after to provide that only children born to citizens and permanent residents would become Australian citizens at birth.[101] As well, since *Kioa,* the discretion to allow someone to remain on humanitarian grounds has been made non-compellable and non-reviewable. Review of decisions under the *Migration Act* has been progressively curtailed, culminating in the 2001 privative clause.[102] The story since *Kioa* is of increasing assertion of executive power over the migration area. By contrast, the post-*Singh* story in Canada is of moving refugee determination further from the core of executive control, including a formal expansion of the IRB's jurisdiction in 2002 to include other protection obligations, such as those under the *Convention Against Torture and Other Cruel, Inhuman or Degrading Treatment or Punishment.*

Narrowing Process Rights and Identities

Decisions since this time have continued to reflect the initial directions established by these governmental responses, with the Australian High Court being called upon to assess a successive range of executive assertions of control in this area and the Canadian Supreme Court operating under the maturing *Charter's* monopoly over rights discourse in that country. As well, decisions of both courts have continued to be notable on the basis of their positioning of the nation and the other in process rights scenarios.

In *Lim v. Minister for Immigration,*[103] the High Court held that the provisions requiring mandatory detention of people arriving in Australia by unregistered boat were constitutional with the exception of the provision that "a court is not to order the release from custody of a designated person,"[104] which the majority held had to be read down to permit a court to order the

---

101 *Australian Citizenship Act 1948* (Cth.), s. 10(2).
102 Introduced by the *Migration Amendment (Judicial Review) Act 2001* (Cth.).
103 *Lim v. Minister for Immigration* (1992), 176 C.L.R. 1 [*Lim*].
104 *Migration Act 1958* (Cth.), s. 177 (called s. 54R at the time the case was argued). The mandatory detention provisions at that time applied only to "designated persons" defined as:
     a non-citizen who:
       has been on a boat in the territorial sea of Australia after 19 November 1989 and before 1 December 1992; and has not presented a visa; and is in Australia; and has not been granted an entry permit; and is a person to whom the Department has given a designation by:
       determining and recording which boat he or she was on; and giving him or her an identifier that is not the same as an identifier given to another non-citizen who was on that boat;
       and includes a non-citizen born in Australia whose mother is a designated person.
     Section 177 has since been reworded slightly. Section 189 provides for mandatory detention of unlawful non-citizens who are not boat people. Detention can be terminated by the grant of a bridging visa.

release of persons unlawfully detained.[105] The impugned legislation had been explicitly enacted "in the national interest"[106] and was an attempt to remove all process rights from a narrowly defined group of "aliens." Having concluded that the power to detain aliens applying for refugee status was incidental to the power to exclude or deport aliens, and further that this "application detention" was not punitive in nature, the Court therefore held that it was not a prohibited exercise by the executive of judicial power.[107] It was precisely at the removal of process rights that the court balked. In this legislation, the various process rights attendant to having detention reviewed by a court are the barest minimum of what constitutes procedural rights.[108] Protection against arbitrary detention by executive decree is a core value of the common law system, intertwined with the evolution of all process rights beginning with habeas corpus.[109] The decision underscores how integral process rights are to liberal legalism and its rule of law ideology.

While the decision preserves these rights, its tenor is considerably different from that of *Kioa,* as it revolves around the constitutional "aliens" power. The identity of the appellants in the case is primarily as "alien." Attempts made in argument to raise issues related to the *Refugee Convention* or the *International Covenant on Civil and Political Rights* – which would have framed the applicants as something other than alien – are not taken up in the opinions.

---

105 Chief Justice Mason and Justices Toohey and McHugh in dissent held that the section was to be read in this manner as it was written, and hence that it was valid.

106 *Migration Act,* s. 176.

107 See Brennan, Deane, and Dawson JJ. in *Lim, supra* note 103 at 30-32, Mason C.J. at 10, Gaudron J. at 53, and McHugh J. at 71.

108 As Justices Brennan, Deane, and Dawson stated, "citizens of this country enjoy, at least in times of peace, a constitutional immunity from being imprisoned by Commonwealth authority except pursuant to an order by a court in the exercise of the judicial power of the Commonwealth": *ibid.* at 28-29.

109 Habeas corpus was itself at issue in the litigation that surrounded the rescue by the *MV Tampa* of 438 people attempting to reach Australia from Indonesia in August 2001. As the Norwegian-owned *Tampa* approached the Australian territory of Christmas Island, the government refused it permission to land and then closed its territorial sea. By a message passed via the ship's captain, those on board confirmed the speculation that they intended to seek asylum in Australia. Lawyers in Australia asserted that those on board were their clients and sought a writ in the nature of habeas corpus on their behalf. The Federal Court initially granted such a writ, but it was denied on appeal by the Full Federal Court on the basis that those on board were not "detained" but were free to leave at any time, although not free to leave the ship for as long as it remained in Australian waters. The High Court declined special leave to hear the argument, as the people had been moved to other countries by the time of the special leave hearing and thus, if they were detained, it was not under Australian law. See *Victorian Council for Civil Liberties Inc v. Minister for Immigration and Multicultural Affairs,* [2001] F.C.A. 1297; *Ruddock v. Vardalis* (2001), 110 F.C.R. 491; *Vardalis v. MIMA and Ors M39/2001* (27 November 2001, High Court Transcript). For further analysis, see Pene Mathew, "Australian Refugee Protection in the Wake of the *Tampa*" (2002) 96 Am. J. Int'l L. 661; Kim Rubenstein, "Citizenship, Sovereignty and Migration" (2002) 12 Public Law Review 102.

Alien identity is intertwined with the legislation, which empowers the executive to "designate" individuals for detention by naming the boats on which they arrive and then assigning "identifiers" to particular individuals. Under the impugned legislation, the state asserts complete control over the identity of the other. The state names each of the boats that these people arrive on and then numbers each of the people. The combination of naming and numbering is the executive act that brings individuals within the scope of the legislation. Someone who arrives on a boat illegally, but whose identity is not redefined in this way by the state, is beyond the reach of the legislation.

The assumptions embedded in this us–them distinction were put at issue by Justice Gaudron, who cautioned against equating "non-citizen" with "alien," noting that "membership of the community constituting the Australian body politic, for which the criterion is now, but was not always, citizenship, is a matter of such fundamental importance that, in my view, it is necessary that the questions be acknowledged even if they are not answered."[110] Justice McHugh also brought the Australian community to the forefront in his analysis by characterizing the purpose of the legislation as "to prevent the alien from entering into the community until the determination [regarding an entry permit or refugee status] is made."[111] This emphasizes how detention contains these outsiders, despite the fact that the applicants are already within Australian territory. The case contrasts those identified as aliens, whose names and numbers are assigned by the state, with the Australian community. *Lim* leaves the nation with control over the identifiers of individuals and accepts reduction of their procedural rights on the basis of their alien status.

A series of cases since *Lim* have tested additional reductions in procedural rights accorded to refugee claimants and upheld them in each case, with the opinions relying in part on contrasts between national and outsider identities. In *Fang v. Minister for Immigration and Ethnic Affairs,*[112] the Full Court of the Federal Court considered the case of a group of ethnic Chinese who had been born in Vietnam and expelled to China, where they had allegedly been resettled.[113] The majority found that while the group had been denied procedural fairness and the protection of provisions of international treaties, this had been done expressly by Parliamentary intent and therefore could not be interfered with by the Court.[114] The procedures that

---

110   *Lim, supra* note 103 at 53.
111   *Ibid.* at 71. See also *ibid.* at 73.
112   *Fang, supra* note 11. Although this is not a High Court case, I have included it because its holdings are remarkable.
113   The group included some in a younger generation who had been born in China. Their claims included claims of very poor treatment and social ostracism in China.
114   Summing up his judgment, Justice Nicholson stated:
      This is a case in which Parliament has negated the possibility of common law concepts of procedural fairness applying in favour of the non-citizen appli-

were upheld included not informing those arriving of their right to make a visa application, not informing them of their right to legal advice, and requiring precise language to constitute a refugee claim. Rejecting the traditional statutory interpretation rule that strict compliance with particular forms is not fatal because of the evident Parliamentary intention to the contrary, the Court in *Fang* found that "the prescription of the form is one of substance and is not merely procedural."[115] This demonstrates perversely the substantive dimension of process rights. The majority's acknowledgment that these applicants were likely to have cultural and linguistic difficulties, as well as being traumatized, isolated, and detained,[116] did not inspire them to find ambiguity in the legislation.

Fang approved an important set of the executive's moves to limit procedural rights at the front end of the refugee application process. The cases that followed upheld a narrowing of procedural rights in the post-decision phase. In *Minister for Immigration and Ethnic Affairs v. Wu Shan Liang*,[117] the High Court held that a shift in the language of the *Migration Act* from empowering the minister to make a determination as to refugee status to allowing that the minister "may determine" that a person is a refugee "if the Minister is satisfied that the person is a refugee"[118] altered the focus of judicial review.[119] The decision had the effect of increasing the degree of curial deference to refugee determination decision makers. In the plurality judgment, the issue was presented as one of pure procedure. In his separate judgment, where he concurred regarding "satisfaction,"[120] Justice Kirby situated the decision at the border of the nation:

---

cants. Parliament has achieved this by the enactment of ss 45-57 and ss 193 (2) and 198 (4) of the *Migration Act*. The inference from the findings of the trial judge is that the representatives of the relevant arm of the executive were well informed of this and avoided acting so as to place the applicants in the position where they had the means to apply for a protection visa when the course remained open to them, prior to its preclusion by legislation. While that executive conduct does not accord with internationally expressed goals relating to conduct in relation to refugees, the conditions for application of international law, as prescribed by Australian domestic law, are not present to enable international law to control that conduct. Furthermore, such conduct was supported by the enactments of the Australian Parliament which, to that extent, evince an intention in relation to non-citizens to negate the application of those internationally commended basic procedural requirements. (*Fang, supra* note 11 at 634-34)

115 *Ibid.* at 617.
116 *Ibid.* at 633 and following.
117 *Minister for Immigration and Ethnic Affairs v. Wu Shan Liang* (1996), 185 C.L.R. 259 [*Wu Shan Liang*].
118 *Migration Act,* s. 22AA (at that time).
119 *Wu Shan Liang, supra* note 117 at 275. The Court does also hold that it is no longer the case that a decision as to "satisfaction" is unreviewable.
120 *Ibid.* at 295.

> The decisions committed to them [refugee decision makers] are extremely important for the persons involved. But they are also important to Australia as a recipient nation. This is because the composition of the community is in question. Its conformity with an important international convention is at stake. Its reputation as a country of refuge which decides claims of refugee status according to the law is involved.[121]

While this broader perspective did not lead to a different conclusion in the case, it serves as an important reminder of the contrast being played out between individual-outsider and the nation and the role of these decisions in constituting the boundary of the nation. The deference to the RRT is confirmed in *Minister for Immigration and Ethnic Affairs v. Guo*,[122] in which the High Court warns the Federal Court against "reading such [RRT] reasons with an over-zealous eye."[123]

In two crucial decisions of the late 1990s, the High Court upheld the 1994 amendments to the *Migration Act* that reduced the grounds of review available to the Federal Court in considering refugee decisions.[124] In both *Abebe v. The Commonwealth; Re Minister for Immigration and Multicultural Affairs*[125] and *Minister for Immigration and Multicultural Affairs v. Eshetu*,[126] the High Court confronted cases where the RRT had dealt with credibility issues in problematic ways.[127] Despite this, the highest degree of deference was shown to RRT decision makers. The *Abebe* case approved the reduction of grounds of review scheme and *Eshetu* affirmed that the Court would not permit the one plausible end run around this scheme that had remained.[128]

---

121   *Ibid.* at 292.
122   (1997), 144 A.L.R. 567 (H.C.).
123   *Ibid.* at 593 (per Kirby J. in a separate concurring judgment).
124   Part 8 of the *Migration Act,* introduced by *Migration Legislation (Amendment Act) 1992* (Cth.). This legislation restricted review of the RRT by removing unreasonableness or breach of the principles of natural justice as grounds for review in the Federal Court. This section was superseded by the 2001 privative clause.
125   *Abebe, supra* note 84.
126   *Minister for Immigration and Multicultural Affairs v. Eshetu,* [1999] H.C.A. 21 [*Eshetu*].
127   With regard to Ms. Abebe, the RRT stated: "The applicant now has a long history, much of it admitted by her, of having told untruths. Her claims as to fear and confusion wear thin after six or seven occasions of 'clearing the state' as it were" (cited in *Abebe, supra* note 84 at para. 76"). In Mr. Eshetu's case, the Full Federal Court found the RRT's conclusions about his evidence to be so unreasonable that no reasonable decision maker could have reached them. See Chapter 6 regarding the difficulties of making credibility determinations in the RRT. Both sets of RRT reasons emphasize reliance on Department of Foreign Affairs and Trade (DFAT) information and a process of comparing evidence that would not likely be acceptable under IRB procedures. In each set of reasons, it is clear that the RRT has developed an attitude of exasperation towards the claimant.
128   On the basis of s. 420 of the *Migration Act,* an argument was put to the Court that "substantial justice" incorporated necessarily the principles of "natural justice." This argument was defeated in *Eshetu, supra* note 126.

As two of the dissentients in *Abebe* stated, "to define the jurisdiction of a federal court to determine controversies with respect to those rights and liabilities by excluding grounds for relief which otherwise would be available has the effect of restricting or denying the right or liability itself."[129] The judges concluded that this "stultifies the exercise of the judicial power of the Commonwealth"[130] and is therefore a constitutional wrong. The more serious wrong is, of course, to the right holders. To hold a right with nowhere to exercise it makes it merely rhetorical.[131]

The *Eshetu* and *Abebe* rulings led to a flood of applications for judicial review in the original jurisdiction of the High Court, as rejected refugee claimants who could no longer take their arguments to the Federal Court sought constitutional relief. This drastically altered the work load of the High Court and resulted in a sharp increase in High Court commentary on the procedural rights of refugee claimants because the standard for granting of these constitutionally enshrined remedies is that of jurisdictional error, and a breach of natural justice by the RRT will constitute such error.[132] The importance of natural justice has also meant a role for the *Kioa* reasoning in many of these cases, as it has been a leading natural justice decision in Australia.

It is predictable that given the jurisdictional error standard and the judicial review setting, most of the applications for constitutional relief will be rejected. Among the practices of the Department and the RRT that have been considered by the High Court *not* to constitute a jurisdictional error are: failing to read all of the documents in the file under review;[133] failing to provide all of the actual documents relied on at first instance to the merit reviewer;[134] failing to contact overseas witnesses when requested by an

---

129 *Abebe, supra* note 84 at para. 143, per Gummow and Hayne JJ. Gaudron J. also dissented.

130 *Ibid.*

131 It is for this reason that I take issue with the conclusion of Justices Gaudron and Kirby that "the effect of s. 476(2) is not to relieve the Tribunal from observance of the rules of natural justice or to authorize the making of unreasonable decisions. Rather, it is to forbid the Federal Court from reviewing a decision on those grounds": *ibid.* at para. 64.

132 Several justices complained bitterly and repetitively about the increased workload. See, for example, *Re The Minister for Immigration and Multicultural Affairs; Ex parte Durairajasingham*, [2000] H.C.A. 1; *Re Refugee Review Tribunal; Ex parte Aala*, [2000] H.C.A. 57 [*Aala*], per Kirby J. This has also led to a reinvigoration of the difficult doctrine of jurisdictional error, which was effectively abandoned in the United Kingdom following *Anisminic Ltd. v. Foreign Compensation Commission*, [1969] 2 A.C. 147 (H.L.). To unfairly oversimplify, jurisdictional errors are generally the more serious errors in exercising executive power. Of course, as this is now the only type of relief possible, the doctrine is becoming ever more elastic.

133 *Re Minister for Immigration and Multicultural and Indigenous Affairs; Ex parte Applicants S134/2002*, [2003] H.C.A. 1.

134 *Muin v. Refugee Review Tribunal; Lie v. Refugee Review Tribunal*, [2002] H.C.A. 30 [*Muin*]. This point arose as a question of statutory compliance in the case and did not need to

applicant to do so;[135] not providing access to adverse information relied upon by the decision maker when that information was not recent and was generally available;[136] taking into account some factors that were nonexistent;[137] making findings of fact only in relation to facts considered by the RRT to be material;[138] and not interviewing applicants for refugee status before making a first-instance decision.[139] The High Court has also rejected claims of bias on the part of the minister[140] and of a member of the RRT.[141]

The cases where the High Court has found breaches of natural justice amounting to jurisdictional error are, with one exception,[142] those in which the conduct of a routine decision maker – that is, not the minister – could be characterized as hostile or misleading in the extreme. In *Re Refugee Review Tribunal; Ex parte Aala*,[143] writs were issued because the RRT member had found that Aala had concocted a story for his second hearing, on the basis that the story had never been mentioned before. In fact, Aala had given this account earlier at the Federal Court level. The RRT member had

---

be formally answered as the majority determined the case on the basis of breaches of natural justice. However, six members of the Court considered this practice and did not impugn it.

135 *Re Minister for Immigration and Multicultural Affairs; Ex parte Cassim*, [2000] H.C.A. 50.

136 *Re Minister for Immigration and Multicultural Affairs; Ex parte "A,"* [2001] H.C.A. 77. In this case, it was also relevant that the applicant had not indicated how access to the DFAT cable in question would have altered his own conduct and that the RRT had not in any way misled the applicant.

137 *Minister for Immigration and Multicultural Affairs v. Rajamanikkam*, [2002] H.C.A. 32. In a list of eight factors taken into account, two were considered to have no evidentiary basis.

138 *Minister for Immigration and Multicultural Affairs v. Yusuf; Minister for Immigration and Multicultural Affairs v. Israelian*, [2001] H.C.A. 30.

139 *Re Minister for Immigration and Multicultural Affairs; Ex parte PT*, [2001] H.C.A. 20.

140 *Minister for Immigration and Multicultural Affairs v. Jia; Minister for Immigration and Multicultural Affairs v. White*, [2001] H.C.A. 17. Both these applicants had had their visas revoked through an exercise of the minister's personal discretion on character grounds because of their criminal records. The Administrative Appeals Tribunal had previously considered their cases and found them to be of good character. In Jia's case, the minister made his decision shortly after discussing the applicant's circumstances on a radio program and after an exchange of letters with the president of the Administrative Appeals Tribunal. The Full Federal Court had found actual bias, in part perhaps because they no longer had the jurisdiction to make a finding of apprehension of bias.

141 *Re Minister for Immigration and Multicultural Affairs; Ex parte Epeabaka*, [2001] H.C.A. 23.

142 The exception is *Minister for Immigration and Multicultural Affairs v. Bhardwaj*, [2002] H.C.A. 11 [*Bhardwaj*]. Unlike the other cases, *Bhardwaj* falls strictly in the immigration realm, not the refugee realm. Here the Court held that the Immigration Review Tribunal could remake a decision when the first decision was considered to be an excess of jurisdiction. The opinions use a variety of wording to express this. I view this atypical judgment as an expression of the Court's frustration at the inflexibility of the *Migration Act* and the limited review provisions.

143 *Aala, supra* note 132.

assured Aala that she had reviewed all of his Federal Court papers. In *Minister for Immigration and Multicultural Affairs; Ex parte Miah*,[144] the first-instance decision maker had not given the applicant an opportunity to comment on information adverse to his claim regarding a change of government in Bangladesh that was vital, or even determinative, of the claim. In *Muin v. Refugee Review Tribunal; Lie v. Refugee Review Tribunal*,[145] differently constituted majorities found errors that mirrored the *Aala* and *Miah* grounds, that the applicant had been misled by the RRT's statements regarding information it was considering and that, in Muin's case, no notice was given of adverse information that the RRT intended to rely on in determining a crucial issue.

The relief granted in these cases did not, of course, guarantee any particular result to the applicants. Indeed, given the original jurisdiction setting of the decisions, these cases contain fewer broad statements of principle than is typically the case when the High Court is exercising its more familiar roles, determining appeals on the basis of special leave or ruling on matters of constitutional interpretation. In *Aala*, Justice Hayne began with a reminder that s. 75(v) is not a source of substantive rights but of jurisdiction,[146] a point that is vital in considering how the constitutional protections in Australia and Canada vary. Noteworthy also is Justice Kirby's observation that one part of the "context" that determines the applicable principles of natural justice for the first-instance decision is the humanitarian character of Australia's international obligations under the *Refugee Convention*.[147] This links humanitarianism to process rights in an important and novel way.

The most important decision regarding the constitutional writs was handed down in early 2003. In *Plaintiff S157/2002 v. Commonwealth of Australia*,[148] the High Court unanimously agreed that the privative clause the government had introduced in late 2001 could not be read as limiting its constitutional jurisdiction or, accordingly, as limiting the power of the Federal Court to review for jurisdictional error.[149] The clause is written in the strongest possible language, defining privative clause decisions as "any decision of an administrative character made, proposed to be made, or required to be made" under the Migration Act or regulations. The central provisions state that "a privative clause decision: (a) is final and conclusive; (b) must not be chal-

---

144 [2001] H.C.A. 22. This is a rare example of judicial review of a first-instance decision because the applicant's solicitor missed the deadline for applying for merit review in the RRT. The Court complained about the inflexibility of the *Migration Act* provisions in this regard, per Kirby J. at para. 223.

145 *Muin, supra* note 134.

146 *Aala, supra* note 132 at para. 155.

147 *Ibid.* at para. 186.

148 [2003] H.C.A. 2, handed down 4 February 2003.

149 Joint judgment of Gaudron, McHugh, Gummow, Kirby, and Hayne J.J. at para. 96. Gleeson C.J. and Callinan J. wrote separate concurring opinions.

lenged, appealed against, reviewed, quashed, or called in question in any court; and (c) is not subject to prohibition, mandamus, injunction, declaration or certiorari in any court or on any account."[150] The case proceeded as a preliminary matter, and therefore the individual whose claim grounded the arguments is absent from the reasons, save a brief note that the claim was similar to those of *Aala* and *Miah*, asserting that important information adverse to an applicant for refugee status was taken into account without giving the applicant an opportunity to address it. Each set of reasons stresses the importance of constitutionally protected judicial review to the rule of law, particularly in a federal system.[151] This situates the ruling as an important delineation of executive and judicial power, marking an assertion of judicial power that has been largely absent in this line of cases regarding community outsiders. It is notable, of course, that this kind of rights assertion occurs in a case where the applicant does not appear at all. The rights belong almost to the judiciary itself, in a scenario similar to the *Lim* decision.

The separate concurring judgments also emphasize the rule of law, but their reasoning has a broader reach. The interpretation of a privative clause in Australia proceeds on a case-by-case basis as a matter of statutory construction, beginning necessarily with the purpose of the act. Chief Justice Gleeson encapsulated the scheme of the *Migration Act* as "the making of decisions to grant or refuse visas, which enable a non-citizen lawfully to enter, or remain in, Australia," and followed this immediately by stating: "Unlawful entry into, or presence in, Australia, exposes a person to loss of liberty and compulsory removal."[152] Justice Callinan characterized access to the courts as a right of "citizens" and emphasized that "every nation insists upon the right to determine who may enter the country, who may remain in it, who may become one of its citizens, and who may be liable to deportation."[153] These judges expanded the reasoning in the case by reference to members and others.

150   *Migration Legislation Amendment (Judicial Review) Act 2001* (Cth.), altering s. 474 of the *Migration Act.*

151   After noting that neither the American nor Canadian constitutions has similar provisions, the joint judgment continues:

> The reservation to this Court by the Constitution of the jurisdiction in all matters in which the named constitutional writs or an injunction are sought against an officer of the Commonwealth is a means of assuring to all people affected that officers of the Commonwealth obey the law and neither exceed nor neglect any jurisdiction which the law confers on them. The centrality, and protective purpose, of the jurisdiction of the Court in that regard places significant barriers in the way of legislative attempts (by privative clauses or otherwise) to impair judicial review of administrative action. Such jurisdiction exists to maintain the federal compact by ensuring that propounded laws are constitutionally valid and ministerial or other official action lawful and within jurisdiction. (*Ibid.* at para. 104.)

152   *Ibid.* at para. 27.

153   *Ibid.* at paras. 111 and 112.

The story of the High Court of Australia cases from 1990 to 2003 is one of increasing restriction of procedural rights for refugee claimants. Procedural rights create a space for the identity of a refugee or other migration claimant to be articulated. In the High Court's ruling about *Kioa,* we learn a considerable amount about Mr. Kioa himself. While this is presented through the words of the original decision maker, the intense scrutiny of that decision makes it important to each opinion comprising the judgment. In contrast, we learn comparatively little about either Ms. Abebe or Mr. Eshetu, as the decisions had little to do with them. The restrictions that narrowed their procedural rights also narrowed the space for their identities to seep through into appellate judgment. The negotiated and malleable nature of legally constructed identity facilitates this restriction and calls to our attention how the court controls the appearance of the individual's identity to fit its jurisprudential objectives. In a parallel movement, the contrast between the individual and the nation is less evident in decisions such as *Guo, Abebe,* and *Eshetu,* and almost completely absent in the rush of original jurisdiction cases beginning in the year 2000. As the identity of the individual is diminished, that of the nation overwhelms the balance so that the contrast between the two, which situates what is at stake in these cases, is no longer visible. The tension between the individual and the state that is traditionally portrayed in process rights embodies a recognition of the individual. As alien outsiders disappear from the equation, they lose this recognition. Rights express a relationship between people on either side of the boundary created by the right. In this setting, the nation's boundary is at issue. When the right diminishes, its holder disappears from view. The nation is, as Fitzpatrick expresses, aspiring to unattainable universality.

These cases demonstrate the two ways in which process rights are substantive. First, procedural rights are the substance itself of liberal legalism. In the enduring logic of the legal system, nothing is more significant than the rights associated with being heard in a court. This is the core of the High Court's reasoning in *S157,* emphasizing the rule of law. The falseness of the dichotomy between procedural and substantive rights is seen in the relationship between them: procedural rights are integral to the system, substantive rights are viewed as some type of additional entitlement. Without the so-called procedural rights there is no access to the system and thus anything of substance cannot be called a right at all. Procedural rights are given effect within national legal systems. The cases delimiting these rights also, therefore, describe these systems. They depict the nation both explicitly and implicitly as its boundary is constructed through the decisions.

The second substantive aspect of procedural rights is the space they create for the emergence of identity. While identity as right holder is restrictive and carries with it constraints in the extra-legal sphere, within that sphere it is crucial. Being identified as a right holder is the first step in being identified as one who deserves justice rather than mere compassion. Here the function of rights as "islands of entitlement" is evident. As a right holder, one can assert a claim; without a right, one must beg the mercy of the state. Those who hold procedural rights are first identified as right holders and in consequence accorded a legal space in which to make arguments that enrich perceptions of their identity. The two steps are intertwined, another aspect of the substance of process rights.

It is arguably because of the substantive importance of procedural rights that both Australia and Canada have moved recently to keep migration claimants, and particularly refugee claimants, out of the courts. Additionally, procedural rights directly reduce the control of the executive over migration decision making as these rights are at the core of judicial function, as was articulated in *Lim, Abebe,* and *S157.* There is, therefore, a contrast to be drawn between Canada's move to institute the requirement that unsuccessful refugee claimants seek leave from the Federal Court and Australia's progressive ousting of jurisdiction. In this analysis, it is appropriate to understand the privative clause as expanding the realm of executive power. In the Canadian case, the procedural right remains with the claimant but its shape is altered. In Australia, the executive assumes control of as much of the process as it possibly can. The distinction drawn is another example of how a contrast in the self-perception of the nation is translated into legal effect in migration law decision making.

The Canadian Supreme Court cases illustrate the same story about the false dichotomy of procedural and substantive rights, and about the tension portrayed in these cases between the individual and the state. Like the Australian cases, these cases are replete with images of the nation, as the rights being articulated define the boundary between insider and outsider. In the Canadian context, however, contemporary arguments about rights entitlements are all contested either within or alongside the discourse of constitutionally entrenched rights. In the next section, I consider the role of the *Charter* in Canadian migration law and pay particular attention, as mandated by the jurisprudence, to the substance of process rights. This continues the story to this point and provides an avenue for assessing the potential of constitutional rights protections.

Testing the *Charter of Rights and Freedoms*
As Justice Wilson's statement in *Singh* suggests, interpretation of the *Canadian Charter of Rights and Freedoms* has provided a platform for articulating a vision of the political fabric of the Canadian nation. The requirement that all *Charter* rights are subject to the s. 1 provision of "such reasonable limits prescribed by law as can be demonstrably justified in a free and democratic society" has ensured that the vision of a free and democratic society, and of how Canada fulfills that description, is always in the background of *Charter*

rights analyses. The us–them setting of border law decision making reinforces the depiction of the nation as the relationship between insiders and outsiders is incessantly refined. An assessment of the value of these rights for those who are not full members of the Canadian community is complicated by the variety of circumstances in which the cases arise, and by the fact that to date there are only one or two leading cases in each of the key legal scenarios where a border is encountered (i.e., the refugee setting, extradition, deportation, removal, port of entry procedures). Despite these challenges for analysis, the picture that emerges is similar to that which developed in considering why refugee claims fail to be considered as rights claims and in analyzing the diminution of process rights for refugee claimants in Australia. That is, in an analysis of legal rights that by its structure pits the individual against the state, the greater the space retained for the development of individual identity, the more likely that the individual will succeed in asserting a rights claim.

In *Canadian Council of Churches v. Canada,* the Supreme Court of Canada rejected an argument that the Council, which has a long record of involvement in refugee advocacy, should be granted public interest standing to challenge a wide range of amendments to the *Immigration Act* that had been made in 1989.[154] The case is interesting both because of the procedural question it raises and because of the language used to quickly settle it. The issue of public interest standing arises in contexts where the classic opposition of the individual and the state breaks down for some reason. The refugee determination scenario fits this analysis well, as it casts the state in opposition to an individual who is not a member of the polity. This feature of the argument for the Council of Churches to represent refugee interests, however, was ignored by the Court in its reasoning. Despite noting at several instances that the *Charter* guarantees the rights of "Canadians" and "citizens,"[155] the Court did not note that those whose interests were being considered are not in this group. It is a curious omission given the attention the distinction between citizens and non-citizens had received in *Singh* seven years earlier. The Court explicitly rejected the argument that refugees as a group may have differing interests than individual claimants, or that they may face disadvantages in bringing litigation on their own behalf.[156] The case affirmed the ideological link of most *Charter* rights to individuals and ignored that rights function in part as a phenomenon of group identity, for example, by generating a group of refugees entitled to raise similar claims. This further diminishes the potential of the *Charter* in the migration setting, as the number of individuals inside Canada to assert these rights is much

154 *Canadian Council of Churches v. Canda* (1992), 88 D.L.R. (4th) 193, per Cory J. writing for a unanimous court.
155 *Ibid.* at 202-3.
156 *Ibid.* at 205.

smaller than the numbers outside the country who cannot claim *Charter* protection but who may be considered part of any number of groups constructed and then affected by immigration law. It also demonstrates that the logic of migration decision making falls apart when the legally constructed differences between citizens and those more distant from the core of the nation are not examined.

Identifying the differences between citizens and others does not guarantee any particular result, but shows that the Court is grappling with the significance of the distinction. The issue in *Chiarelli v. Canada (Minister of Employment and Immigration)* was whether a series of deportation provisions infringed s. 7 of the *Charter* by violating principles of fundamental justice.[157] Following the precedent that *Charter* rights must be interpreted in context,[158] Justice Sopinka stated that the fundamental principle of the immigration law context is "that non-citizens do not have an unqualified right to enter or remain in the country."[159] Given this context, he held that no principle of fundamental justice was infringed by deporting permanent residents convicted of serious crimes regardless of the circumstances of the offence or the actual sentence. Nor is fundamental justice disturbed by determining in camera that an individual may be someone who will likely be involved in organized crime and as a result of that determination removing the right held by other permanent residents facing deportation to launch an appeal based on humanitarian and compassionate considerations. The decision to situate the reasoning in this criminal deportation case in what the court called an "immigration context" rather than a "criminal context" was crucial to the outcome, as s. 7 has been repeatedly used to reshape Canadian criminal law. In the immigration context, it is possible to conclude that "deportation is not imposed as a punishment"[160] and therefore cannot be reviewed as to whether it is cruel and unusual, and that permanent residency is a conditional status.[161]

Section 7 of the *Charter* submerges the substantive rights–procedural rights distinction by its statement that "everyone has the right to life, liberty and security of the person and the right not to be deprived thereof except in accordance with the principles of fundamental justice." The so-called substantive rights in the first clause – life, liberty, and security of the person – are expressed in relation to the more likely procedural rights described by the principles of fundamental justice. Fundamental justice itself has sub-

---

157 *Chiarelli, supra* note 4, per Sopinka J. writing for a unanimous court.
158 *R. v. Wholesale Travel Group Inc.* (1991), 84 D.L.R. (4th) 161, which distinguished the *mens rea* for the criminal context from the *mens rea* for the regulatory context.
159 *Chiarelli, supra* note 4 at 303.
160 *Ibid.* at 305, paralleling the High Court of Australia's conclusion that "application detention" is not punitive. See *Lim, supra* note 103.
161 *Chiarelli, ibid.* at 304.

stantive elements, especially as it is to be determined in a given context. It is not contiguous with natural justice, which may, in Justice Sopinka's words, "inform principles of fundamental justice in a particular context."[162] The substance of procedural rights is reinforced by s. 7 of the *Charter* even in cases like *Chiarelli* where the Court makes every effort to focus on narrow procedural questions only, because the link to life, liberty, and security of person is always present in some degree.

In *Chiarelli*, Justice Sopinka used the rhetorical device familiar to *Charter* watchers of asserting that he need not decide whether deportation infringes the right to life, liberty, or security of person because he found no deviation from principles of fundamental justice.[163] This allowed him to circumvent the important question of the place of deportation itself in a rights discourse. It also ensured a focus on procedure rather than on the identity of the individual to whom a right to life, liberty, or security belongs. This rhetorical manoeuvre allowed Justice Sopinka not to look beyond the border of the nation and to focus his concerns exclusively on things happening in Canada. The identity of the other is suppressed in the rhetorical shift, which provides a concise illustration of how rights discourse narrows identities.

It is precisely on this point, whether to look beyond the border, that the majority and dissenting judgments in *Kindler v. Canada (Minister of Justice)*[164] can be distinguished. Kindler had fled to Canada from the United States after being convicted of first-degree murder, for which the jury had recommended the death penalty. The Canadian minister of justice proposed to extradite him without seeking assurances that the death penalty would not be imposed.[165] For the majority judges who held that extradition without assurances did not breach the *Charter*, the case was primarily about extradition. For the dissentients, the case was about the death penalty. In the first analysis, the sovereign nation and its border is central to the story; in the second, the border disappears as the relationship between what happens on either side of it becomes the focus. Writing one of the majority decisions, Justice La Forest stated that "the government has a right *and duty* to keep out and to expel aliens from this country if it considers it advisable to do so."[166] The link between extradition and the protection of the nation is underlined in his statement that Kindler and the appellant in the companion case, Ng, "would seem to me to be precisely the kinds of individuals the

---

162 *Ibid.* at 311.
163 *Ibid.* at 302.
164 *Kindler v. Canada (Minister of Justice)*, [1991] 2 S.C.R. 779, 84 D.L.R. (4th) 438 (SCC) [*Kindler*, cited to D.L.R.].
165 Article 6 of the *Extradition Treaty between Canada and the United States of America*, Can. T.S. 1976 No. 3, provides this possibility.
166 *Kindler, supra* note 164 at 448 [emphasis added].

Minister would wish to keep out of Canada for the protection of the public."[167] In her majority reasons, then-Justice McLachlin highlighted the uniqueness of the Canadian nation and judicial system as a justification for extradition: "The law of extradition must accommodate many factors foreign to our internal criminal law. While our conceptions of what constitutes a fair criminal law are important to the process of extradition, they are necessarily tempered by other considerations ... The simple fact is that if we were to insist on strict conformity with our own system, there would be virtually no state in the world with which we could reciprocate. Canada, unable to obtain extradition of persons who commit crimes here and flee elsewhere, would be the loser."[168] This reasoning highlights Canadian values and identity, as does the *Charter* test of cruel and unusual punishment, which is whether the punishment "'sufficiently shocks' the Canadian conscience."[169] For both of the justices who penned majority opinions, the need to protect Canada from an influx of people fleeing the American legal system was crucial.[170] Justice McLachlin referred explicitly to Canada's "long undefended common border with the United States,"[171] drawing on imagery of the legal nation and its boundedness and echoing a phrase familiar to generations of Canadian schoolchildren. That is, the decision taps directly into, and thereby reinforces, images of the nation.

For those judges who argued that extraditing Kindler to face the death penalty would offend s. 7 of the *Charter,* the Canadian nation held a different place in the analysis. Justice Cory viewed the argument that any cruel and unusual punishment would be applied not by Canada but by the United States as "an indefensible abdication of moral responsibility."[172] The existence of the border was irrelevant to his assessment of the punishment and of morality. For Justice Cory, the identity of the nation was a lesser value than the harm of the death penalty. Justice Cory also referred to the open border, but emphasized that to cross it a fugitive must first escape custody.[173] Justice Cory's presentation of Canadian values and identity situated these as belonging to the international community rather than being unique: "Canada has committed itself in the international community to the recognition and support of human dignity and to the abolition of the death penalty. These commitments were not lightly made. They reflect Canadian values and principles. Canada cannot, on the one hand, give an international commitment to support the abolition of the death penalty and at the same

167   *Ibid.* at 449. The companion case is *Reference Re Ng Extradition,* [1991] 2 S.C.R. 858.
168   *Ibid.* at 488.
169   *Ibid.* at 492. The "shock the conscience" test originated in *R. v. Schmidt* (1987), 39 D.L.R (4th) 18.
170   *Ibid.* at 450-51 and 495.
171   *Ibid.* at 495.
172   *Ibid.* at 479.
173   *Ibid.* at 480.

time extradite a fugitive without seeking the very assurances contemplated by the Treaty."[174] Canada is not a nation so unique that it must accept differences in order to make extradition function. Rather, it is a member of the community of nations and of values. The opinions in *Kindler* present a clear contrast of visions of the nation faced with giving meaning to fundamental justice at the border.[175] The tension in *Kindler* is a reflection of what Minow labels the instability of rights discourse that renders this discourse unable to give an adequate account of sameness and difference. In this instance, it is impossible for rights discourse to express in the same moment the importance of the boundary and the relationships between what happens on either side of it. In this tension, identity is manipulated and some parts of it are squeezed from the picture.

The illuminating tensions in the *Kindler* decision were again informative when, a mere decade later, the Supreme Court revisited the question of extradition to face the death penalty in *United States of America v. Burns*.[176] The unanimous, and unattributed, judgment stopped just short of formally overruling *Kindler*, instead confining it so narrowly to its facts that its outcome is unlikely to be repeated. The Court summed up its reasoning thus: "We agree that the Canadian *Charter of Rights and Freedoms* does not lay down a constitutional prohibition in all cases against extradition unless assurances are given that the death penalty will not be imposed ... We hold, however ... that such assurances are constitutionally required in all but exceptional cases."[177] The Court took great care to demonstrate that there had been a shift in international norms surrounding the death penalty in the intervening ten years. The contrast between the majority and dissenting judgments in *Kindler* was central to the outcome here. The result – refusal to extradite without seeking assurances against the death penalty – could have been achieved on the basis that Burns and Rafay were Canadian citizens whereas Kindler and Ng were not. Instead, the Court rejected this possibility[178] and made the case one about the death penalty, just as the dissentients in *Kindler* had. The judgment also places considerable emphasis on a series of high-profile wrongful convictions that the Canadian community

---

174 *Ibid.* at 481.
175 Justice Sopinka's brief dissent presents yet another variation on this theme as he focuses on the fact that the Canadian Parliament had voted just four years earlier not to reinstate the death penalty despite public opinion polls favouring it (see *ibid.* 452-55). In his analysis, the values of the community are reflected in the Parliament, whereas in the analysis of Justice La Forest, the opinion polls were influential (*ibid.* at 447).
176 [2001] 1 S.C.R. 283 [*Burns*].
177 *Ibid.* at 296.
178 As well as the related possibility of basing a ruling on s. 6 of the *Charter* guaranteeing citizens' right of entry. The Court stated: "The real issue here is the death penalty. The death penalty is overwhelmingly a justice issue and only marginally a mobility rights issue": *ibid.* at 317.

grappled with in the 1990s, arguing that rejecting the death penalty provides that "meaningful remedies for wrongful conviction are still possible."[179]

Despite the emphasis on the death penalty, there is an image of Canada as nation in the case. In this version of the nation, however, the Court emphasized Canada's role on the international stage rather than its domestic protection, just as Justice Cory had in *Kindler*. The Court noted that Canada has often been "in the forefront" on international initiatives to denounce the death penalty.[180] Their view of Canadian values regarding the death penalty was informed by the international sphere: "When they [international initiatives] are combined with other examples of Canada's international advocacy of the abolition of the death penalty itself ... it is difficult to avoid the conclusion that in the Canadian view of fundamental justice, capital punishment is unjust and it should be stopped."[181] The ruling in *Burns* effectively constitutionalized the exercise of ministerial discretion in questions of extradition. In doing so, the reasoning linked both the *Charter* and the death penalty to fundamental Canadian values, again portraying the nation. The Court stated that "the *Charter* does not give the Court a general mandate to set Canada's foreign policy on extradition. Yet the Court is the guardian of the Constitution and death penalty cases are uniquely bound up with basic constitutional values. While the death penalty arises as a possibility in only a fraction of the extradition cases dealt with by the Minister and departmental officials, it raises issues of fundamental importance to Canadian society."[182] The interpretation of fundamental principles of justice is thus linked both to Canadian values and to Canada's self-presentation on the international stage, and explicitly distanced from "opinion polls."[183] The exercise of ministerial discretion is constrained by procedural provisions of s. 7 and a robust understanding of the Canadian community, Canada's international image, and the death penalty itself injects substance into those rights.

Executive discretion and the *Charter* are also linked in two other Supreme Court of Canada decisions giving vital guidance to immigration decision makers in the area of procedural rights. In *Baker v. Canada (Minister of Citizenship and Immigration)*,[184] Justice L'Heureux-Dubé for the majority stated at the outset that the question of what standard of procedural fairness was required in determining a humanitarian and compassionate appeal did not raise any *Charter* questions[185] and thus there was no need to address the *Char-*

---

179   *Ibid.* at 337.
180   *Ibid.* at 332.
181   *Ibid.*
182   *Ibid.* at 310.
183   *Ibid.* at 324.
184   *Baker v. Canada (Minister of Citizenship and Immigration)*, [1999] 2 S.C.R. 817 [*Baker*].
185   *Ibid.* at para. 11. For a further discussion of humanitarian and compassionate appeals and *Baker* in particular, see Chapter 6.

ter arguments made in the case. The appeal was allowed due to breaches of the applicable principles of procedural fairness. Justice L'Heureux-Dubé held that a determination on a humanitarian and compassionate appeal "must be made following an approach that respects humanitarian and compassionate values."[186] While the decision to reject *Charter* arguments could have been made to avoid the overlap of substance and procedure that s. 7 entails, or to circumvent a determination that deportation affects life, liberty, or security of person, Justice L'Heureux-Dubé's reasoning belied her commitment to decide the case on purely procedural grounds. Humanitarian and compassionate values are clearly substantive. Furthermore, the influence of the approach to international human rights instruments that has evolved under the *Charter* seeped into the analysis of the *Convention on the Rights of the Child* despite her statement that this convention was inapplicable.[187] This case may signify the development of an approach to statutory interpretation in Canada that is influenced by the place the *Charter* has had in shifting the parameters of legal discourse in Canada.[188]

In contrast to the *Baker* decision, the linkage between discretionary decision making and the *Charter* is overt in *Suresh v. Canada (Minister for Citizenship and Immigration)*.[189] Suresh had refugee status in Canada but was facing deportation to Sri Lanka because of his links to the Liberation Tigers of Tamil Eelam, which the government believed engaged in terrorist activities. Suresh asserted, and the Court accepted, that he had established a *prima facie* case that he would face a substantial risk of torture in Sri Lanka. In its reasoning, Canada's ratification of the *Convention Against Torture*[190] was not determinative. Instead, the convention was read as part of the international law that informed Canada's constitutional norms.[191] The Court undertook a separate consideration of the "Canadian perspective" on the place of torture in relation to fundamental principles of justice.[192] In concluding that a

---

186 *Ibid.* at para. 74.
187 *Ibid.* at paras. 69-71. By this I mean that the *Charter* has been interpreted with reference to international conventions since its inception (see *Ward, supra* note 28, and *R. v. Keegstra,* [1990] 3 S.C.R. 697). This tradition of interpretation seems to have influenced Justice L'Heureux-Dubé to put more emphasis than would otherwise be possible on the weight of an unincorporated convention. It is precisely on this point that Justice Iacobucci disagreed with her (*ibid.* at paras. 78-81).
188 In this regard, the case is a contrast with another Supreme Court of Canada decision from the same time period, *Chieu v. Canada (Minister for Citizenship and Immigration),* [2002] 1 S.C.R. 82 (followed in *Al Sagban v. Canada [Minister for Citizenship and Immigration],* [2002] 1 S.C.R. 133), which was treated as a matter solely of statutory interpretation. I find little or no *Charter* influence on the *Chieu* reasoning.
189 *Suresh v. Canada (Minister of Citizenship and Immigration),* [2002] 1 S.C.R. 3 [*Suresh*].
190 *Convention Against Torture and Other Cruel, Inhuman or Degrading Treatment or Punishment,* 1984, 1464 U.N.T.S. 85 (entered into force 26 June 1987), which Canada acceded to in 1986.
191 *Suresh, supra* note 189 at para. 76.
192 *Ibid.* at paras. 48-58.

ministerial decision to deport an individual to face a substantial risk of torture would always involve a balancing of factors, the Court suggested more room for exceptions than it expressed in the *Burns* decision a year before. The Court stated:

> Canadian jurisprudence does not suggest that Canada may never deport a person to face treatment elsewhere that would be unconstitutional if imposed by Canada directly, on Canadian soil. To repeat, the appropriate approach is one of balancing. The outcome will depend not only on considerations inherent in the general context but also on considerations related to the circumstances and condition of the particular person whom the government seeks to expel. On the one hand stands the state's genuine interest in combatting terrorism, preventing Canada from becoming a safe haven for terrorists, and protecting public security. On the other hand stands Canada's constitutional commitment to liberty and fair process. This said, Canadian jurisprudence suggests that this balance will usually come down against expelling a person to face torture elsewhere.[193]

On the basis of its view of the relationship between the fundamental principles of justice and expulsion to face torture, the Court determined standards for procedural fairness in these cases and concluded that while not required to conduct a full oral hearing, the minister must at least inform individuals of the case to be met, provide materials relied upon (subject to privilege and public security), provide an opportunity to respond to the case and in particular to challenge the minister, and provide written reasons for her decisions. The Court emphasized that it is not constitutionalizing the common law of procedural fairness, but looking to the "common law factors not as an end in themselves but to inform the s. 7 procedural analysis."[194] Thus the common law of procedural fairness process rights is merged with substantive rights regarding protection against torture, to produce the constitutional outcome in *Suresh*.

The sum of these cases in the Supreme Court of Canada is not a compelling change in the debates or the outcomes of border law disputes under the influence of entrenched constitutional rights. The *Charter* has hastened acknowledgment of the falsity in the distinction between substantive and procedural rights, and has fostered the development of a jurisprudence that focuses overtly on national identity and values, but it has led to relatively minor changes for those crossing Canada's borders. Mr. Chiarelli, Mr. Kindler, the Canadian Council of Churches, and even Ms. Baker were all told that

193　*Ibid.* at para. 58.
194　*Ibid.* at para. 114.

the *Charter* did not assist them. Mr. Suresh was assisted in part by the *Charter* in being accorded the right to a new hearing, but the limits of this right were clear in the companion case of *Ahani v. Canada (Minister of Citizenship and Immigration)*,[195] where the Court was unconvinced that the applicant would face torture if deported. The most convincing and substantive *Charter* win in these border cases belongs to Mssrs. Burns and Rafay, Canadian citizens whose extradition was made conditional. Other less well known litigants such as Mr. Reza[196] and Mr. Delghani[197] have also found that the *Charter* has not changed their position before the Canadian courts. On the other hand, refugee claimants before the Supreme Court of Canada in the post-*Charter* era have met with considerable success. While *Singh* was not solely a *Charter* decision, its most memorable judgment does rely on the *Charter*, and its influence on refugee law in Canada has been far-reaching. Both *Ward* and *Pushpanathan* have extended the scope of refugee protection in Canada through their interpretations of the refugee definition. In *Ward* this was done explicitly with reference to *Charter* jurisprudence, even though the Court held that no *Charter* rights were engaged. In *Pushpanathan*, the *Charter* was not key to the Court's reasoning, but in the *Ward* decision it was, leading to a similar result.

Identity contributes to an understanding of these cases in two ways. First, the role of a refugee identity has considerable importance in these outcomes. While Pushpanathan and Ward had committed crimes similar to those of Chiarelli, the Court portrayed them as refugees rather than criminals. The importance of this distinction is highlighted by the dissent in *Pushpanathan* emphasizing drug trafficking: when the criminal identity predominates, a positive outcome is unlikely in the immigration setting. Suresh had not been convicted of any crime, and thus his identity as refugee could still play a role in the decision. This effect also points to how rights represent collective identities. The refugee exists not as the individual before the Court but as a group, a category, that could potentially be before a court. The *Canadian Council of Churches* decision rejects this view and thus amounts to a

---

195 [2002] 2 S.C.R. 72.
196 *Reza v. Canada* (1994), 116 D.L.R. (4th) 61. Reza, a refugee claimant who had exhausted all avenues of appeal under the *Immigration Act*, sought to commence an action in the Ontario Court (General Division) arguing that various sections of that act were inoperative under the *Charter*. The motions judge stayed his application. In a very brief judgment, the Supreme Court of Canada agreed.
197 *Delghani v. Canada (Minister of Employment and Immigration)* (1993), 101 D.L.R. (4th) 654. Delghani claimed refugee status at the airport and was denied counsel. He argued that his *Charter* right to counsel was infringed. The Supreme Court of Canada responded by stating that he had not been "detained" in the sense contemplated by the *Charter*, despite a line of cases establishing that secondary immigration examination, the process Delghani was involved in, constitutes detention in the case of Canadian citizens: *R. v. Greffe*, [1990] 1 S.C.R. 755.

statement of preference by the Court to determine the rights and identities of the refugee individually, fitting more directly into liberal rights discourse.

In the refugee cases, the influence of the *Charter* is covert. The *Charter* creates the space for an emerging and constitutionally legitimated discourse of human rights. This is a discourse in which the refugee identity can develop, in opposition to both a criminal identity and an identity as alien; it is an image of power. The *Charter*'s influence on these cases serves as a vehicle for incorporation by interpretive convention of international human rights discourse and for a jurisprudential reflection on what values a free and democratic society would like to be seen to embrace. A similar analysis holds for *Baker*, even though there the interpretive movement occurs implicitly. This may signify a maturing of the *Charter*'s role in this jurisprudence. As the critique of constitutional rights predicts, rights discourse tends to permeate all legal discourse once unleashed.

But considering the *Charter* in the migration setting, and especially in contrast to the Australian setting, allows a more textured analysis of the effect of rights discourses. The *Charter* has amplified the effect of procedural rights at the core of liberal legalism by emphasizing their substantive effects. This intertwining is seen plainly in the *Suresh* reasoning. The percolation of rights discourses in Canada, led by the *Charter*, creates a possibility of arguing about the refugee definition in fundamental human rights terms. While refugee claims do not function as rights claims, this discourse enlarges rather than constricts the potential for broad interpretations of the refugee definition's other, non-rights aspects. Finally, however limited rights discourses are, they contain a hierarchy of rights and therefore the potential for ascending that hierarchy. These cases certainly do not give rise to unbridled optimism but they do show that the potential of the *Charter* must be carefully assessed in each context, and that the identities at play are key to understanding those contexts and their particular power matrices. Legal argument can be manipulated by considering the rights–identity linkages to encourage given outcomes.

Considering identity in the analysis also calls our attention to how the potential of rights discourse is disappointed in these cases. In cases where the claimants are ultimately unsuccessful, they are portrayed as alien others whose interests are pitted against those of the nation. Their differences from members of the community are emphasized, as is the fact that the nation tolerates their presence generously and does not have the same responsibilities towards them that it does towards its citizens. Despite the potential for the development of robust substantive rights–procedural rights under the *Charter*, the s. 7 cases in the migration realm have been almost entirely unsuccessful. Even *Singh*, which led to the development of a hearing process for refugee determinations, does not explicitly require the full extent of procedural protections presently in place. Replacing the present process with interviews by bureaucrats could well come within the letter of the *Singh* ruling.[198] While substantive procedural developments in the laws of evidence and crime have been some of the most significant *Charter* results, changes resulting from s. 7 arguments about immigration law have been minimal. The message sent by the Supreme Court is that in spite of *Singh*, non-citizens have fewer rights protections than citizens in a variety of areas. While the *Suresh* decision may signal that the Court is prepared to extend *Charter* protections to some extent, it is also the decision where the terms "danger to the security of Canada" and "terrorism" were held not to be unconstitutionally vague.[199]

This result, then, is not so different from the result in the Australian High Court. Arguably, the *Charter* could be used to prevent the Canadian government from rolling back procedural protections to the same extent that the Australian government has done. While this would likely be the case, there is no way to conclusively state it, particularly recalling the strong similarities between *Singh* and *Kioa*. The biggest differences between the Australian and Canadian jurisprudence are not the result of the presence or absence of constitutionally entrenched rights, but rather relate to the respective governments' interactions with the courts in the area of migration law. The High Court's decision in *S157*, which defines the limits of rights erosion in Australia, relies on the separation-of-powers provisions of the Australian Constitution. The *Charter* is necessarily the vehicle by which immigrant rights arguments are brought before the Canadian courts. Nonetheless, the resulting jurisprudence is similar to that in Australia in that there have been no significant substantive rights victories since the mid-1980s. Even *Ward* and *Pushpanathan* are not strictly rights cases, but revolve around interpretations of narrow slices of the refugee definition. The jurisprudence in both countries portrays the nation itself. Differences in those portraits, in the national identities, do more to explain the differences in legal outcomes than the constitutional settings do.

Rights Discourses and the Liberal Nation

Rights discourses in migration law reflect the place of migration law in the

---

198 Such a proposal was made in *Building on a Strong Foundation for the 21st Century* (Hull, QC: Supply and Services Canada, 1999), c. 11, and has been repeated from time to time by members of the Canadian government.

199 The Court stated: "We conclude that the terms 'danger to the security of Canada' and 'terrorism' are not unconstitutionally vague. Applying them to the facts found in this case, they would *prima facie* permit the deportation of Suresh provided the Minister certifies him to be a substantial danger to Canada and provided he is found to be engaged in terrorism or a member of a terrorist organization": *Suresh, supra* note 189 at para. 99.

liberal nation. Analyzing the place of rights in the law and identity linkage is the final phase of my theoretical framework, tapping into some of the most extensive identity-based legal critiques and pulling the argument directly back to its foundation stone: the inability to establish a justice standard for evaluating liberal migration laws. Migration law constitutes the community and responds to the perceived needs of the nation, the national interest. The principal problem with using rights discourses to bring about changes in migration law is that a rights-based argument triggers a rights-based response. In this area of the law, the most unambiguous right is the right of the nation to exclude all outsiders. The tension between any rights claim brought in the migration area and this sovereign right to exclude is frequently the difference that splits judicial opinions, as the cases in this chapter illustrate. Rights exist in a hierarchy. The sovereign right to exclude the other is at the top of the hierarchy. Of the diverse rights that liberal legalism will recognize and put its considerable power behind, the right to exclude the other is paramount because the institution of liberal legalism is intertwined with the form of the liberal nation. It is for this reason that evaluations of migration laws are best made by comparing the national self-identifications they reflect, generate, and reify.

Images of the nation are present implicitly and explicitly in this jurisprudence. The nation is represented in its sovereign right to exclude, and in statements about the national interest or the values of the national community. The nation is also represented in the procedural rights that balance the interests of individual and state. While in theoretical terms we can postulate some generic state in this equation, the terms a court reasons with always put the interest of some particular individual against those of some existing state. Because of this, the attributes of the nation are always a backdrop to the discussion. The emotive content and sense of belonging permeate the state–individual dichotomy when it is brought into a real decision-making setting. These characteristics of migration law jurisprudence reinforce its role as a vital site for constituting the nation. The nation takes form, after all, as a myth. Understanding the diversity of factors that make the nation present in migration law jurisprudence helps us understand how migration law operates as a site for the construction and reconstruction of the national myth. The jurisprudence of the highest courts is particularly important because of its influence on lower courts and because of its role as a hegemonic social ordering discourse in legalistic societies such as Australia and Canada. The jurisprudence is not the extent of migration law's role in constituting the nation, but it is a vital part of it.

The central instability of rights discourse that Minow emphasizes is crucial in migration law as the needs of the nation are themselves unstable. One of the most important tricks of migration law is to create the appearance of stability, of a core of meaning, that grounds the appearance of the nation. Without borders, without some limit to the community, the nation could not assert existence. Accordingly, migration law, which posits some control over the border and the membership of the community, is essential to the enterprise. The framework of migration law allows adjustments in the national interest to be easily made into legal projections with a minimum of change. The need for an appearance of stability but an inherent flexibility is achieved through these mechanisms. Rights discourse runs a parallel course. In Minow's analysis, the inherent instability of rights discourse is due to the inability of rights to fully represent the relationship that they always express. In migration law, that relationship is between the insider and the outsider, the nation and the other. The right of one is always exercised against the right of the other, so that any expression of right somehow obscures the relationship between the two. The central instability is, then, a product of this relationship, a reaction to the contest that is set up by rights discourse.

In Minow's analysis of rights in other contexts, she focuses on the boundaries that are created in rights discourses and the identities on either side of those boundaries that rights discourses obscure. In the migration law setting, the boundary is that of the nation, and the relationship is between members and outsiders. Border law jurisprudence, as we have seen in the cases here, shows us again and again images of the nation and the other and manipulates them as a key reasoning technique. The manipulation of these images, the fact that the nation can be both the reason to reject extradition and the reason to permit it, shows us the instability that Minow discusses. Altering our perception of the other necessarily affects our perception of the nation, as the two are defined by their boundary. This explains why the outsider–refugee is disappearing from view in the jurisprudence of a progressive removal of procedural rights in Australia. As the space generated by process rights for the development of an identity for the refugee-outsider is squeezed smaller and smaller, the nation takes up all the imaginary space that is left.

Attention to identity helps us to focus on what rights discourses obscure. It helps us to understand their categories and hierarchies. In migration law, considering the overlapping effects of rights and identities reveals how the discourse of fundamental human rights can open a space for refugee claimants without making a refugee claim a rights claim. It demonstrates how gradations in procedural rights entitlements express gradations of attachment to the nation, of belonging, of identity, at the centre of which the identity of the nation and the individual overlap in the category of citizen. Considering identity helps build an understanding of when *Charter* rights are most effective, and when they are more likely to be overlooked. The migration law context brings together a number of rights discourses. Understanding the differences between them, and the ways in which they cross-cut and reinforce each other, enriches our understanding of migration law and of rights discourses themselves. Both are necessary to predict legal outcomes in this area, to strategize for legal change, and to theorize the relationship between migration law and the liberal nation.

8
Conclusions

There are three types of conclusions to this book. First, the analysis of humanitarian admissions to Australia and Canada contributes to the theoretical picture of the law and identity interrelationship. Second, conclusions can be drawn about the national self-identifications of the two nations, and about the meaning of humanitarianism in their respective laws. Third, this examination of the intertwining of migration law and the nation yields insights into how nations respond to contemporary globalizing forces.

The position of migration law and national identity in this analysis runs parallel to the intermediate position of law and identity theory generally as both constitutive and constituting. That is, migration law is affected by our perceptions of national identity and at other moments it influences those perceptions. Sometimes the most important insight gained by examining identity in migration law is that it is responding to a shift in the nation's view of its priorities and values, as in the recent shift towards preferring economic migrants. At other times, however, the perspicacity of the theory lies in demonstrating that the view of the nation written into the law constrains the law's application, as when humanitarian discretion is used to approve economic independence. The key to appropriate use of this type of intermediate theorization is to consider what is gained from the insights it generates and thereby avoid arriving at only the rather vacuous conclusion that law both constitutes and is constituting. The chapter-by-chapter conclusions in the second part of this book have therefore addressed how a focus on identity in migration law locates strengths and weaknesses in the refugee hearing process, how an understanding of the role and limits of humanitarianism as both jurisprudence and rhetoric can be built into law reform strategies, and how detailed analysis of rights discourses contributes to predicting successes in the courtroom and developing successful arguments for that setting.

The insights of law and identity scholarship can also be pushed further here to give an account of slippage between legal and popular discourse.

This is crucial in the realm of migration law because, in the absence of a liberal justice standard, the parameters for debate are purely political, above and beyond the way in which this is true for law generally. Law and identity scholarship draws our attention to the importance of who is constructing the legally positioned identity and for what purpose. This is central to the account of the negotiated and flexible quality of identity. In the realm of migration law, the malleability of identity is evident, and indeed forms a vital reason for using identity-based analyses in this setting. The dissonance between legal and popular or political discourses on questions such as the meaning of "refugee," the rights of citizens, or the identity of the nation is facilitated by the malleability of legally constructed identity. The identities that appear in legal discourses are linked to the purposes for which they are elaborated. This is no different in popular discourse. The slippages are explained by considering the purpose at issue. In legal discourse, "refugee" is defined primarily in order to limit access to the nation and to contain the responsibilities of the nation. In popular discourse, "refugee" is understood in a much broader way. The use of the legal label outside the law is a telling signifier of the hegemony of legal discourses in social and political arenas. The slippage in meaning points to the ends that are served by discursive transformations. These ends in turn lead us to an enhanced analysis of the ways in which migration law serves the needs of the nation. It becomes another dimension in the capacity of identity analysis to draw our attention to hidden dimensions of legal categories.

The use of this framework for analyzing migration law also highlights the relationship between identity as an individual phenomenon and as a group phenomenon, which is in turn important for using identity-based analyses in a liberal legal paradigm. Important parts of the analysis of refugee determination, of humanitarian acts of grace, and of rights allotments focus on individuals specifically. Nonetheless, because of its categorizing nature, the law creates group identities. This is a critical part of understanding how migration law affects the individuals who pass through it to join the nation. They become members of the social group of "immigrants," as "refugees," "dependent spouses," or "temporary workers." These labels affect their legal entitlements but go beyond that as well. Membership in these groups also affects how the community perceives individuals and how they form attachments with the nation. Identity is about individuals and groups at the same time. Both are relevant simultaneously, in a relationship which social psychology provides a matrix for understanding. The individual and group relevance of identity is important for having a full picture of the function of the law, and also for grasping the notion of national identity. The identity of the nation becomes important from time to time, in particular settings and in response to particular events or effects. There is no need for a collective mind or for the nation to function as an agent.

When identity is used to evaluate migration law, the power dynamic of identity becomes obvious. Some individuals choose identities and others are consigned to them. Not only do some choose their identities, but some have a wider range of choices. The availability of choice coincides with societal power. Further, the consequences of one's choices also leave an imprint of how powerful or powerless one is in a given setting. For many, fitting into the narrow strictures of a refugee identity or a deserving recipient of humanitarian consideration is the best outcome of their situation. Even these identities are not without some power, as they conform to legal categories where admission may be granted. That these narrow identity slots are also constraining reflects the limited power of these positions. For a tribunal member, there are also consequences of choosing how to position oneself within the parameters of that identity, but the consequences attached to the choice are different. You may feel better or worse about the job you are doing, and your prospects for continuing it may be altered, but your location as a privileged member of a prosperous nation is not affected. You have an enormous freedom in how you identify yourself as a tribunal member, or even whether you do so at all. Power is embedded in the identities located in the law. It becomes visible when we focus on how choices are made and how identities are negotiated.

Power is especially significant in considering the rights discourses of migration law. The discourse of rights does more than establish a simple binary code between right holders and non-right holders. Rights are hierarchically arranged. Those with more power have greater rights and a greater potential for accommodating the diversity of their identity within the discourse of rights. Examining the deployment of rights in migration law complicates our understanding of the relationship between rights and identities. The decisions of the highest courts of Australia and Canada demonstrate that holding rights creates a space for the flourishing of identities. Even being at the bottom of the hierarchy of rights is still to have some access to those "islands of empowerment" – to use Patricia Williams's words – and to have an identity that is intelligible to the law. The importance of dissecting rights discourses in this way is strategic. While much may be traded away to fit oneself or one's group into a narrow box at the bottom of the hierarchy, the trade-off may be worth it if the legal outcome is the best, or the only, outcome that is sought. Migration law provides stark evidence of the power of rights discourse to obscure the relationship between those on either side of the principal rights–non-rights boundary: the border of the nation. The line between members and others is about rights. The power that attaches to rights varies in the hierarchy of rights and helps us understand that rights discourses are perceived as monolithic only when viewed at a great distance. The detailed comparison of Australian and Canadian appellate jurisprudence also demonstrates the insidious and indirect role of rights. While differences in Australian and Canadian law are linked more to national self-interpretations than to the absence or presence of constitutional rights, Canada's constitutional rights form a backdrop to a more expansive reading of refugee identity. At the primary level, constitutional rights have meant little in the migration realm, but at this secondary level they have been important. This dual reading of the role of rights discourses is an important addition to a critical assessment of rights.

One of the consequences of the absence of a liberal justice standard in questions of migration is that it is impossible to conclude that Australian law is "better" than Canadian law or vice versa. Instead of this type of morally grounded comparison, the examinations here generate pictures of the laws in each place that tell us something about the way these nations understand themselves. Against these understandings, changes in the law can then be evaluated by whether they are in harmony with the nation's own internal values. The Australian law enshrines an ideology of control, with mechanisms such as application detention, inflexible target numbers, executive decision making, high-level location of discretionary decision making, and a progressive narrowing of rights for intending humanitarian migrants. These factors combine with language in ministerial statements, in policy guidelines, in discretionary decisions, and in judicial statements to present an image of Australia as a nation that guards its generosity closely, that picks migrants carefully, that feels vulnerable and needs to protect itself, isolated on its island continent. Australian migration law sends the message that this nation is distant from those migrants it has most affinity with and is surrounded by those whose values may threaten its control over its membership. Australia is more concerned with controlling its population than with humanitarian gestures, more concerned with efficiency than with the rights of outsiders. Similar elements appear in the Canadian law, but in a different mixture. Canada's law is filled with humanitarianism and with discretion. The impulse to control is weaker: targets are more flexible, discretion is more openly used, judicial decision making is given a wider scope. The law is constructed in such a way that more divergent meanings are generated. The balance in the refugee program is towards inland processing rather than the more easily controlled overseas cases. The jurisprudence of humanitarianism is revealingly counterintuitive, demonstrating both that the nation values economic self-sufficiency, social success, and small, independent families, and also that being perceived as humanitarian is vital. Canadian law and rhetoric displays more pride in the generosity of the nation, and therefore constructs a more generous mythology of nation.

For many concerned about people whose homelands are poor or dangerous or do not respect human rights, this makes the Canadian law and policy at least potentially better. But the hegemonic liberal theory that provides the standard for relationships between nations does not provide either a way of defending this statement or a vantage point from which to assert it. All it provides is a notion of humanitarianism that is vague enough that all nations can aspire to it while taking very different actions. It is thus a perfect fit with the political position of migration law. Humanitarianism runs into liberalism's threshold of heroism, and the principle that heroism is not required for moral action. The growing international commitment to human rights has likewise not generated a standard for assessing the behaviour of nations that refugees seek to resettle in, especially when those nations are far from the states refugees are fleeing. The discourse of fundamental human rights has made some inroads into influencing how we interpret what other countries do to refugees, but does not establish either an interpretation of humanitarianism or a right to enter another nation. In both liberal discourse and the overlapping discourse of fundamental human rights, those who argue that admitting refugees threatens the nation's self-interest, economic prosperity, job markets, and cultural protection can also find support.

This examination of the migration law–national identity relationship and its applications in Canada and Australia reveals a picture of nations strongly asserting their sovereignty. This picture is at odds with the views of at least some analysts of globalization who argue that the relevance or capacity, or both, of the nation-state is declining.[1] The relationship between migration law and the nation is key to understanding how globalization is affecting the state, and to evaluating the claims about the future of the nation that are contested in globalization theory.[2] While migration controls did not become standard until several centuries after the emergence of national sovereignty as a hegemonic political concept, control over the border is now, ironically, the essence of sovereignty in some accounts.[3] Even for theorists who do not define sovereignty in this way, accounts of the resilience of the nation-state in this era of globalization inevitably turn to facets of migration law to make their argument. In Hirst and Thompson's influential analysis on this point, it is people who "remain 'nationalized,' dependent on passports, visas

---

1 Examples of this view include Kenichi Ohmae, *End of the Nation State: The Rise of Regional Economies* (London: Harper Collins, 1995), and Robert B. Reich, *The Work of Nations: Preparing Ourselves for 21st Century Capitalism* (London: Simon and Schuster, 1983). For a counterargument, see Linda Weiss, *The Myth of the Powerless State: Governing the Economy in a Global Era* (Cambridge: Polity Press, 1998), and Paul Q. Hirst and Grahame Thompson, *Globalization in Question*, 2d ed. (Malden, MA: Polity Press, 1999).

2 I make this argument in more detail in "Making People Illegal" in Peter Fitzpatrick and Patricia Tuitt, eds., *Critical Beings: Law, Nation and the Global Subject* (Aldershot, UK: Ashgate Press, 2004). In "Illegal Migration and Sovereignty" in Catherine Dauvergne, ed., *Jurisprudence for an Interconnected Globe* (Aldershot, UK: Ashgate Press, 2003), I canvass and categorize trends in globalization theory.

3 Kim Rubenstein, "Citizenship in a Borderless World" in Anthony Anghie and Garry Sturgess, eds., *Legal Visions of the 21st Century* (The Hague: Kluwer Law International, 1998) 183 at 189. See also David Jacobson, *Rights Across Borders: Immigration and the Decline of Citizenship* (Baltimore and London: The John Hopkins University Press, 1996).

and residency and labour qualifications."[4] Each of the factors they refer to as evidence of the nation's continued importance is embedded in the texts of migration laws.

In my view, the increasing prevalence of illegal migration at the opening of the twenty-first century, as well the worldwide ratcheting up of legal provisions aimed at stopping it, are part of the globalization phenomenon, and can be explained within the migration law–national identity paradigm. The extent to which illegal migration is genuinely on the increase is by definition impossible to measure. What is certain, however, is that contemporary consciousness of it certainly is. At least weekly, stories of illegal arrivals play out in the international media. People running through the Channel Tunnel, crossing the Rio Grande, or being rescued in the waters north of Australia are all becoming familiar. Both the phenomenon of illegal migration and its worldwide visibility are effects of the technologies of globalization. People smugglers can now be increasingly organized, and those seeking to move can be increasingly well informed about their choices. The simultaneity of communication conveys to us that this is happening everywhere all the time – the compression of time and space that is a hallmark of globalization.

Around the world, national governments have responded to this by heightening legal sanctions against illegal migration. As this book has demonstrated, this is an important feature of recent alterations to Australian and Canadian migration regimes. It is also high on the agenda in the United States and the European Union. Such actions are taken in the name of defending the nation. These responses represent nations striving to shore up their borders, and thus their identities, in an area where both are increasingly challenged. In addition, the emergence of "illegal" as a pervasive identity category (that is, it now functions as a noun) allows the nation an avenue of control over its identity even when its borders are breached. When part of a nation's population is labelled "illegal," the line between "members" and "others" is shifted to function within the geographic nation as well as at its boundary. "Illegals" are named as transgressors, and thus do not trigger debates about membership, participation, and entitlement in the same way that guest workers or refugees historically have.

Contemporary responses to illegal migration reflect a moral panic. The crackdown on illegal migration is most insidious for humanitarian migrants. As the logic of humanitarianism necessarily implies, these migrants do not have rights of entry; they are instead recipients of mercy. For these migrants and potential migrants, there is often no way to enter the nation besides doing so outside the law. As such, they become – literally – illegal prior to having access to any other categorical identity. The effects of this are two-

4 Hirst and Thompson, *supra* note 1 at 171.

fold. First, they are associated with all the pejorative associations of illegality, which constrains even further their future identities within any new nation. Second, the crackdown provisions, as we have seen, directly affect the conditions of their lives and the conditionality of any humanitarian status they may eventually be granted. As "illegals" they are transgressors of "our" laws, and thus less worthy of our compassion. As the twentieth century was marked by national controls over migration that altered the nature of immigration and created the notion of humanitarian admissions, the twenty-first century may well be marked by increasing controls and attempted controls over illegal migration, which will again alter the relationship of humanitarianism and the nation.

Appendix A
Selected Immigration Statistics

Canada
Table A-1 has been compiled from information available on the Citizenship and Immigration Canada (CIC) website, <www.cic.gc.ca>. It reflects migration numbers published in *Facts and Figures: Immigration Overview* by CIC each year.

Table A-1

Canada: Migration numbers for 1998-2002

	2002	2001	2000	1999	1998
Economic	136,525	152,939	133,422	105,929	94,967
Family	65,277	66,644	60,541	55,266	50,880
Refugee	25,111	27,894	30,058	24,374	22,700
Total	226,913	227,477	224,021	185,569	168,547

Australia
This table is compiled from information available on the Government of Australia Department of Immigration and Multicultural and Indigenous Affairs website, <www.immi.gov.au/population/>. It reflects migration numbers published annually in *Population Flows* by the Government of Australia.

Table A-2

Australia: Migration numbers for 1998-99 to 2002-3

	2002-3	2001-2	2000-1	1999-2000	1998-99
Family	40,790	38,080	33,470	32,000	32,040
Skill	66,050	53,520	44,730	35,333	35,000
Humanitarian	12,525	12,349	13,733	15,860*	15,290
Total	119,365	103,949	91,933	83,193	82,330

* This figure includes 5,900 Safe Haven visas, comprising 4,000 grants to Kosovars offshore and 1,900 grants to East Timorese onshore.

United States

This table is compiled from information available on the United States Citizenship and Immigration Services website, <uscis.gov/graphics/shared/aboutus/statistics>. It reflects migration numbers published annually in the *Yearbook of Immigration Statistics* (formerly the *Statistical Yearbook* of the Immigration and Naturalization Service).

Table A-3

United States: Migration numbers for 1998-2002

	2002	2001	2000	1999	1998
Family*	673,029	675,178	583,150	475,467	474,848
Economic**	264, 564	280,371	200,295	128,241	126,455
Refugees and asylees	126,084	108,506	65,941	42,852	52,193
Total	1,063,677	1,064,055	849,386	646,560	653,496

* This category includes both family-sponsored immigrants and immediate relatives of US citizens.
** This category includes both employment-based immigrants and immigrants that the INS has placed in the "Other Immigrants" category.

United Kingdom

This table is compiled from information available on the UK government's Official Documents website, <www.official-documents.co.uk>. It reflects migration numbers published in the yearly *Control of Immigration: Statistics United Kingdom* by the Home Office.

Table A-4

United Kingdom: Migration numbers for 1998-2002

	2002	2001	2000	1999	1998
Family	52,765	56,810	53,040	42,115	39,615
Employment	19,800	15,255	15,610	11,480	11,230
Asylee and discretionary grants	40,845	34,755	56,440	43,480	18,935
Total	113,410	106,820	125,090	97,075	69,780

Appendix B
Court Hierarchies in Australia and Canada

Australia

High Court of Australia

Full Court – Federal Court of Australia

Federal Court of Australia

Administrative Appeals Tribunal   Migration Review Tribunal Refugee Review Tribunal

Canada

Supreme Court of Canada

Federal Court of Appeal

Federal Court

Immigration and Refugee Board Refugee Protection Division Refugee Appeal Division (implementation indefinitely delayed in 2002) Immigration Appeal Division Immigration Division

Bibliography

Table of Cases

A v. Veterans' Review Board (1995), 38 A.L.D. 315.
Abebe v. The Commonwealth; Re Minister for Immigration and Multicultural Affairs, [1999] H.C.A. 14.
Addai v. Minister for Immigration and Multicultural Affairs, [1999] F.C.A. 1702.
Ahani v. Canada (Minister of Citizenship and Immigration), [2002] 1 S.C.R. 72.
Al Sagban v. Canada (Minister of Citizenship and Immigration), [2002] 1 S.C.R. 133.
Andrews v. Law Society of British Columbia, [1989] 1 S.C.R. 143.
Applicant A and Another v. Minister for Immigration and Ethnic Affairs and Another (1997), 142 A.L.R. 331 (H.C.A.).
Applicant L.S.L.S. v. Minister for Immigration and Multicultural Affairs, [2000] F.C.A. 211.
Arkhanguelski v. Canada (Minister of Citizenship and Immigration), [1999] F.C.J. No. 1117.
Ates v. Minister of State for Immigration and Ethnic Affairs (1983), 67 F.L.R. 449.
Attorney-General for Canada v. Cain, [1906] A.C. 542 (P.C.).
Australia v. Applicant A, Communication No. 560/1993, UN Doc. CCPR/C/59/D/560/1993 (30 April 1997).
Baker v. Canada (Minister of Citizenship and Immigration), [1999] 2 S.C.R. 817.
Bhattachan v. Minister for Immigration and Multicultural Affairs, [1999] F.C.A. 547.
Birsan v. Canada (Minister of Citizenship and Immigration), [1998] F.C.J. No. 1861.
Bower v. Harwick (1986), 478 U.S. 186 (U.S.S.C.).
Burgos-Rojas v. Canada (Minister of Citizenship and Immigration) (1999) 162 F.T.R. 157.
Canada (Attorney-General) v. Ward (1993), 103 D.L.R. (4th) 1 (SCC).
Canada (Minister of Employment and Immigration) v. Hundal (1994), 167 N.R. 75.
Canadian Council of Churches v. Canada (1992), 88 D.L.R. (4th) 193.
Chan v. Canada (Minister of Employment and Immigration) (1995), 128 D.L.R. (4th) 213.
Chan v. Minister for Immigration and Ethnic Affairs (1989), 169 C.L.R. 379.
Chen Shi Hai v. Minister for Immigration and Multicultural Affairs, [2000] H.C.A. 19.
Cheung v. Canada (Minister of Employment and Immigration) (1993), 102 D.L.R. (4th) 214 (F.C.A.).
Chiarelli v. Canada (Minister of Employment and Immigration) (1992), 90 D.L.R. (4th) 289 (SCC).
Chieu v. Canada (Minister of Citizenship and Immigration), [2002] 1 S.C.R. 84.
Chirwa (1970), 4 I.A.C. 338.
Chu Kheng Lim and Ors v. Minister for Immigration, Local Government and Ethnic Affairs and Anor (1992), 176 C.L.R. 1.
Damouni and Anor v. Minister for Immigration, Local Government and Ethnic Affairs (1989), 87 A.L.R. 97 (F.C.).
Delgamuukw v. British Columbia, [1997] 3 S.C.R. 1010.
Delghani v. Canada (Minister of Employment and Immigration) (1993), 101 D.L.R. (4th) 654.

Dogra (unreported, Fed. Ct., Madgwick J., 28 April 1997).
Dolinovsky v. Canada (Minister of Citizenship and Immigration), [1999] F.C.J. No. 1784.
Dranichnikov v. Minister for Immigration and Multicultural Affairs, [2003] H.C.A. 26.
Dykon v. Canada (Minister of Employment and Immigration) (1994), 87 F.T.R. 98.
F v. Minister for Immigration and Multicultural Affairs, [1999] F.C.A. 947.
Fang v. Minister for Immigration and Ethnic Affairs (1996), 135 A.L.R. 583 (Full Court – Federal Court of Australia).
Gicu v. Canada (Minister of Citizenship and Immigration), [1999] F.C.J. 404.
Guo Ping Gui v. Minister for Immigration and Multicultural Affairs, [1998] 1592 F.C.A.
Herijanto v. Refugee Review Tribunal, [2000] H.C.A. 16.
Hossain v. Minister for Immigration and Multicultural Affairs, [1999] F.C.A. 957.
Hundal v. Canada (Minister of Employment and Immigration) (1994), 26 Imm. L.R. (2d) 47.
Kindler v. Canada (Minister of Justice) (1991), 84 D.L.R. (4th) 438 (SCC).
Kioa v. West (1985), 159 C.L.R. 550.
Kirpal v. Canada (Minister of Citizenship and Immigration) (1996), 35 Imm. L.R. (2d) 229.
Kuthyar v. Minister for Immigration and Multicultural Affairs, [2000] F.C.A. 110.
Lara v. Canada (Minister of Citizenship and Immigration), [1999] F.C.J. No. 264.
Lim v. Minister for Immigration (1992), 176 C.L.R. 1.
L.J. v. Canada (Minister of Citizenship and Immigration), [1996] F.C.J. No. 1042.
Mabo v. Queensland (No. 2) (1991), 175 C.L.R. 1.
McPhee and Ors v. Minister for Immigration and Ethnic Affairs (1988), 16 A.L.D. 77.
Magyari (unreported, Fed. Ct., O'Loughlin J., 22 May 1997).
Minister for Immigration and Ethnic Affairs v. Guo (1997), 144 A.L.R. 567 at 575.
Minister for Immigration and Ethnic Affairs v. Teoh (1995), 128 A.L.R. 353.
Minister for Immigration and Ethnic Affairs v. Wu Shan Liang (1996), 185 C.L.R. 259.
Minister for Immigration and Multicultural Affairs, Re: Ex parte Cassim, [2000] H.C.A. 50.
Minister for Immigration and Multicultural Affairs, Re: Ex parte Durairajassingham, [2000] H.C.A. 1.
Minister for Immigration and Multicultural Affairs, Re: Ex parte Epeabaka (2001), 179 A.L.R. 296.
Minister for Immigration and Multicultural Affairs, Re: Ex parte Fejzullahu, [2000] H.C.A. 23.
Minister for Immigration and Multicultural Affairs, Re: Ex parte Miah (2001), 179 A.L.R. 238.
Minister for Immigration and Multicultural Affairs v. Bhardwaj, [2002] H.C.A. 11.
Minister for Immigration and Multicultural Affairs v. Eshetu, [1999] H.C.A. 21.
Minister for Immigration and Multicultural Affairs v. Guan, [2000] F.C.A. 1033.
Minister for Immigration and Multicultural Affairs v. Gui, [1999] F.C.A. 1496.
Minister for Immigration and Multicultural Affairs v. Haji Ibrahim (2000), 204 C.L.R. 1; [2000] H.C.A. 55.
Minister for Immigration and Multicultural Affairs v. Jia, [2001] H.C.A. 17.
Minister for Immigration and Multicultural Affairs v. Khawar, [2002] H.C.A. 14.
Minister for Immigration and Multicultural Affairs v. Rajamanikkam, [2002] H.C.A. 32.
Minister for Immigration and Multicultural Affairs v. Singh, [2002] H.C.A. 7.
Minister for Immigration and Multicultural Affairs v. Thiyagarajah (2000), 199 C.L.R. 343.
Minister for Immigration and Multicultural Affairs v. Yusuf (2001), 180 A.L.R. 1.
Minister of Employment and Immigration v. Jiminez-Perez, [1984] 2 S.C.R. 565.
M.M.M. v. Minister for Immigration and Multicultural Affairs, [1998] 1664 F.C.A.
Mobil Oil Pty Ltd v. Federal Commissioner of Taxation (1963), 113 C.L.R. 475.
Muin v. Refugee Review Tribunal; Lie v. Refugee Review Tribunal, [2002] H.C.A. 30.
Muliadi v. Minister of Employment and Immigration (1986), 18 Admin. L.R. 243.
Musgrove v. Chun Teeong Toy, [1981] A.C. 272 (P.C.).
Muzychka v. Canada (Minister of Citizenship and Immigration), [1997] F.C.J. No. 279.
Nottebohm Case (Liechtenstein v. Guatemala), [1955] I.C.J. Reports 4.
Ozmanian v. Minister for Immigration, Local Government and Ethnic Affairs (1996), 137 A.L.R. 103.
Padfield v. Minister of Agriculture, Fisheries, and Food, [1968] AC997 (H.L.).

Parma v. Canada (Minister of Employment and Immigration) (1993), 21 Imm. L.R. (2d) 102.
Pizarro v. Canada (Minister of Employment and Immigration) (1994), 75 F.T.R. 120.
Plaintiff S157/2002 v. Commonwealth of Australia, [2003] H.C.A. 2.
Poll v. Lord Advocate, [1899] 1F.823 (Ct. Sess.).
Polyakov v. Canada (Minister of Citizenship and Immigration), [1996] F.C.J. No. 300.
Pushpanathan v. Canada (Minister of Citizenship and Immigration), [1998] 1 S.C.R. 982.
Qing Mei Fu, I.R.T. reference: N94/01303.
R. v. Big M Drug Mart, [1985] 1 S.C.R. 295.
R. v. Greffe, [1990] 1 S.C.R. 755.
R. v. Keegstra, [1990] 3 S.C.R. 697.
R. v. Kwok (1986), 31 C.C.C. (3d) 196 (Ont. C.A.).
R. v. Schmidt (1987), 39 D.L.R. (4th) 18.
R. v. Wholesale Travel Group Inc. (1991), 84 D.L.R. (4th) 161.
Re Australian Broadcasting Tribunal and Other; Ex parte 2H.D. Pty Ltd (1979), 27 A.L.R. 321 (H.C.A.).
Re Minister for Immigration and Multicultural Affairs and Anor; Ex parte SE, [1998] H.C.A. 72.
Re Minister for Immigration and Multicultural Affairs; Ex parte "A," [2001] H.C.A. 77.
Re Minister for Immigration and Multicultural and Indigenous Affairs; Ex parte Akapata, [2002] H.C.A. 34.
Re Minister for Immigration and Multicultural and Indigenous Affairs; Ex parte Applicant S154/2002, [2002] H.C.A. 39.
Re Minister for Immigration and Multicultural and Indigenous Affairs; Ex parte Applicants S134/2002, [2003] H.C.A. 1.
Re Minister for Immigration and Multicultural Affairs; Ex parte Epeabaka (2001), 179 A.L.R. 296.
Re Minister for Immigration and Multicultural Affairs; Ex parte Holland, [2001] H.C.A. 76.
Re Minister for Immigration and Multicultural Affairs; Ex parte Miah (2001), 179 A.L.R. 238.
Re Minister for Immigration and Multicultural Affairs; Ex parte P T, [2001] H.C.A. 20.
Re Minister for Immigration and Multicultural Affairs; Ex parte Te, [2002] H.C.A. 48.
Re Refugee Review Tribunal; Ex parte Aala (2000), 204 C.L.R. 82.
Re Refugee Review Tribunal; Ex parte H, [2001] H.C.A. 28.
Re Refugee Review Tribunal; Ex parte HB, [2001] H.C.A. 34.
Re Singh and the Minister of Employment and Immigration (1985), 17 D.L.R. (4th) 422.
Re S.S.W., [1998] C.R.D.D. 104 (No. U96-05945) at para. 43.
Reg v. I.A.T. ex parte Shah, [1999] 2 A.C. 629 (H.L.).
Reza v. Canada (1994), 116 D.L.R. (4th) 61.
Ruddock v. Vadarlis (includes Corrigenda dated 2 January 2002 and 2 January 2002), [2001] F.C.A. 1865.
S395/2002 v. Minister for Immigration and Multicultural Affairs, [2003] H.C.A. 71.
Sahra Abdullahi Elmi v. Minister for Immigration and Multicultural Affairs, [1998] 1442 F.C.A.
Serrano v. Canada (Minister of Citizenship and Immigration), [1999] F.C.J. 1203.
Shah v. Minister for Immigration and Multicultural Affairs, [2000] F.C.A. 489.
Suresh v. Canada (Minister of Citizenship and Immigration), [2002] 1 S.C.R. 3.
Talke v. Canada (Minister of Citizenship and Immigration), [2000] F.C.J. No. 1146.
Tchernilevski v. Canada (Minister of Citizenship and Immigration) (1995) 30 Imm. L.R. (2d) 67.
United States of America v. Burns, [2001] 1 S.C.R. 283.
Uppal v. Canada (Minister of Employment and Immigration) (1987), 2 Imm. L.R. (2d) 143 (Fed. C.A.).
Victorian Council for Civil Liberties Incorporated v. Minister for Immigration and Multicultural Affairs (and summary), [2001] F.C.A. 1297.
Vidal v. Canada (Minister of Employment and Immigration) (1990), 13 Imm. L.R. (2d) 123.
Voyvodov v. Canada (Minister of Citizenship and Immigration), [1999] F.C.J. 1417.
Wik Peoples v. Queensland (1996), 141 A.L.R. 248 (H.C.A.).
Xiang Sheng Li v. R.R.T. (unreported, F.C.A., 23 August 1996).
Yhap v. Canada (Minister of Employment and Immigration) (1990), 9 Imm. L.R. (2d) 243.

Legislation

Australian Citizenship Act 1948 (Cth.).
Canadian Bill of Rights, S.C. 1960, c. 44.
Citizenship Act, S.C. 1974-75-76, c. 108.
Immigration Act, R.S.C. 1985, c. I-2, repealed.
Immigration and Refugee Protection Act, S.C. 2001, c. 27.
Immigration and Refugee Protection Regulations, S.O.R/2002-227.
Immigration Regulations, 1978, repealed.
Indian Act, R.S.C. 1985, c. I-5.
Migration Act 1958 (Cth.).

Treaties

Cartagena Declaration, OR OEA/Ser.L/V/II.66/Doc. 10, rev.1 (1984).
Convention Against Torture and Other Cruel, Inhuman or Degrading Treatment or Punishment, 1984, 1464 U.N.T.S. 85 (entered into force 26 June 1987).
Convention Governing the Specific Aspects of Refugee Problems in Africa, 1969 1000 U.N.T.S. 46 (entered into force 20 June 1974).
Convention Relating to the Status of Refugees, 1951, 189 U.N.T.S. 150 (entered into force 22 April 1954).
International Covenant on Economic, Social and Cultural Rights, 1966, 973 U.N.T.S. 3 (entered into force 3 January 1976).
International Covenant on Civil and Political Rights, 1966, 999 U.N.T.S. 171 (entered into force 23 March 1976).
Montevideo Convention on Rights and Duties of States, 1933, 165 L.N.T.S. 19.
Protocol Relating to the Status of Refugees, 1967, 606 U.N.T.S. 267 (entered into force 4 October 1967).
Vienna Convention on the Law of Treaties, 1969, 1155 U.N.T.S. 331.

Secondary Materials

Adelman, Howard, et al., eds. *Immigration and Refugee Policy: Australia and Canada Compared* (Melbourne: Melbourne University Press, 1994).
Aleinikoff, T. Alexander. *Semblances of Sovereignty: The Constitution, the State and American Citizenship* (Cambridge, MA, and London: Harvard University Press, 2002).
–. "Theories of Loss of Citizenship" (1986) 84 Mich. L. Rev. 1471.
Allars, Margaret. *Introduction to Australian Administrative Law* (Sydney: Butterworths, 1990).
Anderson, Benedict. *Imagined Communities: Reflections on the Origin and Spread of Nationalism*, rev. ed. (London and New York: Verso, 1991).
Andrews, Geoff, ed. *Citizenship* (London: Lawrence and Wishart, 1991).
Anghie, Anthony, and Garry Sturgess, eds. *Legal Visions of the 21st Century: Essays in Honour of Judge Christopher Weeramantry* (The Hague: Kluwer Law International Publishers, 1998).
Bagambiire, David. "The Constitution and Immigration: The Impact of Proposed Changes to the Immigration Power under the *Constitution Act, 1867*" (1992) 15 Dal. L.J. 428.
Bakan, Joel. *Just Words: Constitutional Rights and Social Wrongs* (Toronto: University of Toronto Press, 1997).
Barbalet, J.M. *Citizenship: Rights, Struggle and Class Inequality* (Milton Keynes, UK: Open University Press, 1988).
Barry, Brian, and Robert Goodin, eds. *Free Movement: Ethical Issues in the Transnational Migration of People and Money* (University Park, PA: Pennsylvania State University Press, 1992).
Barsky, Robert I. *Constructing a Productive Other: Discourse Theory and the Convention Refugee Hearing* (Philadelphia: John Benjamins Publishing, 1994).
Bartholomew, Amy, and Alan Hunt. "What's Wrong with Rights?" (1990) 9 Law & Inequality 1.
Bellow, Gary, and Martha Minow, eds. *Law Stories* (Ann Arbor: University of Michigan Press, 1996).
Benhabib, Seyla. *The Culture of Claims: Equality and Diversity in the Global Era* (Princeton, NJ: Princeton University Press, 2002).

Berns, Sandra. "Law, Citizenship and the Politics of Identity: Sketching the Limits of Citizenship" (1988) 7 Griffith L.R. 1.

Bower, Lisa C. "Queer Acts and the Politics of 'Direct Address': Rethinking Law, Culture and Community" (1994) 28 Law & Soc'y Rev. 1009.

Brawley, Sean. *The White Peril: Foreign Relations and Asian Immigration to Australia and North America* (Sydney: UNSW Press, 1995).

Brownlie, Ian. *Principles of Public International Law,* 5th ed. (Oxford: Clarendon Press, 1998).

Brubaker, William Rogers. *Citizenship and Nationhood in France and Germany* (Cambridge, MA: Harvard University Press, 1992).

–. *Nationalism Reframed: Nationhood and the National Question in the New Europe* (Cambridge: Cambridge University Press, 1996).

–, ed. *Immigration and the Politics of Citizenship in Europe and North America* (Lanham, MD: University Press of America, 1989).

Calhoun, Craig, ed. *Social Theory and the Politics of Identity* (Oxford and Cambridge, MA: Blackwell, 1994).

Canada, Citizenship and Immigration Canada. *Building on a Strong Foundation for the 21st Century: New Directions for Immigration and Refugee Policy and Legislation* (Hull, QC: Minister of Supply and Services, 1999).

–. *Into the 21st Century: A Strategy for Immigration and Citizenship* (Hull, QC: Minister of Supply and Services, 1994).

Canada, Immigration Legislative Review Advisory Group. *Not Just Numbers: A Canadian Framework for Future Immigration* (Ottawa: Citizenship and Immigration Canada, 1997).

Carens, Joseph H. "Aliens and Citizens: The Case for Open Borders" (1987) 49 The Review of Politics 251.

–. *Culture, Citizenship, and Community* (Oxford: Oxford University Press, 2000).

–. "Dimension of Citizenship and National Identity in Canada" (1996-97) 28 Philosophical Forum 111.

–. "Liberalism and Culture" (1997) 4 Constellations 35.

–. "Open Borders and Liberal Limits" (2000) 34 International Migration Review 636.

–. "Refugees and the Limits of Obligation" (1992) 6 Public Affairs Quarterly 31.

–. "Who Belongs? Theoretical and Legal Questions about Birthright Citizenship in the United States" (1987) 37 U.T. Fac. L. Rev. 413.

Carrillo, Jo. "Identity as Idiom: Mashpee Reconsidered" (1995) 28 Ind. L. Rev. 511.

Cooper, Davina. "The Citizen's Charter and Radical Democracy: Empowerment and Exclusion within Citizenship Discourse" (1993) 2 Social and Legal Studies 149.

Crawford, James, and Patricia Hyndman. "Three Heresies in the Application of the Refugee Convention" (1989) 1 Int'l J. Refugee L. 152.

Creyke, Robin. "Restricting Judicial Review" (1997) 15 Australian Institute of Administrative Law Forum 22.

Crock, Mary. *Immigration and Refugee Law in Australia* (Sydney: Federation Press, 1998).

Cronin, Kathryn. "Concerning Equity and Control: A Look at the New Immigration Law" (1990) 28 Law Society Journal (June) 50.

Daley, Krista, and Ninette Kelley. "Particular Social Group: A Human Rights Based Approach to Canadian Jurisprudence" (2000) 12 Int'l J. Refugee L. 148.

Danielson, Dan, and Karen Engle, eds. *After Identity: A Reader in Law and Culture* (New York and London: Routledge, 1995).

Dauvergne, Catherine. "Amorality and Humanitarianism in Immigration Law" (1999) 37 Osgoode Hall L.J. 597.

–. "Beyond Justice: The Consequences of Liberalism for Immigration Law" (1997) 10 Can. J.L. & Jur. 323.

–. "Chinese Fleeing Sterilization: Australia's Response against a Canadian Backdrop" (1998) 10 Int'l J. Refugee L. 77.

–. "Citizenship, Migration Laws and Women: Gendering Permanent Residency Statistics" (2000) 24 Melbourne U.L. Rev. 280.

–. "Confronting Chaos: Migration Law Responds to Images of Disorder" (1999) 5 Res Publica 23.

–. "A Reassessment of the Effects of a Constitutional Charter of Rights on the Discourse of Sexual Violence in Canada" (1994) 22 Int'l J. Soc. L. 291.

–. "Sovereignty, Migration and the Rule of Law in Global Times" (2004) 67 Mod. L. Rev. 588.

–, ed. *Jurisprudence for an Interconnected Globe* (Aldershot, UK: Ashgate Press, 2003).

Dauvergne, Catherine, and Jenni Millbank. "Before the High Court: Applicants S396/2002 and S395/2002, a Gay Refugee Couple from Bangladesh" (2003) 25 Sydney L. Rev. 97.

–. "Burdened by Proof: How the Australian Refugee Tribunal Has Failed Lesbian and Gay Asylum Seekers" (2003) 31 Federal L. Rev. 299.

Dauvergne, Peter, ed. *Weak and Strong States in Asia Pacific Societies* (Sydney: Allen and Unwin, 1998).

Delgado, Richard. "The Ethereal Scholar: Does Critical Legal Studies Have What Minorities Want?" (1987) 2 Harv. C.R.-C.L.L. Rev. 301.

Dobson-Mack, Anne. "Independent Immigration Selection Criteria and Equality Rights: Discretion, Discrimination and Due Process" (1993) 34 Les Cahiers de Droit 549.

Dummett, Ann, and Andrew Nicol. *Subjects, Citizens, Aliens and Others: Nationality and Immigration Law* (London: Weidenfeld and Nicolson, 1990).

Dworkin, Ronald. *Law's Empire* (Cambridge, MA: Belknap Press, 1986).

Eliadis, F. Pearl. "The Swing from *Singh:* The Narrowing of Application of the Charter in Immigration Law" (1994) 26 Imm. L.R. (2d) 130.

Fishkin, James. *The Limits of Obligation* (New Haven, CT: Yale University Press, 1982).

Fitzpatrick, Peter. *Modernism and the Grounds of Law* (Cambridge: Cambridge University Press, 2001).

–. *The Mythology of Modern Law* (London and New York: Routledge, 1992).

–, ed. *Nationalism, Racism and the Rule of Law* (Aldershot, UK: Dartmouth Press, 1995).

Fitzpatrick, Peter, and Patricia Tuitt, eds. *Critical Beings: Law, Nation and the Global Subject* (Aldershot, UK: Ashgate Press, 2004).

Fudge, Judy. "The Effects of Entreating a Bill of Rights upon Political Discourse: Feminist Demands and Sexual Violence in Canada" (1989) 17 Int'l J. Soc. L. 445.

Fudge, Judy, and Harry Glasbeek. "The Politics of Rights: A Politics with Little Class" (1992) 1 Social and Legal Studies 45.

Fullerton, Maryellen. "A Comparative Look at Refugee Status Based on Persecution Due to Membership in a Particular Social Group" (1993) 26 Cornell Int'l L.J. 505.

Galloway, Donald. *Essentials of Canadian Law: Immigration Law* (Concord, ON: Irwin Law, 1997).

–. "Liberalism, Globalism and Immigration" (1993) 18 Queen's L.J. 266.

–. "Strangers and Members: Equality in an Immigration Setting" (1994) 7 Can. J.L. & Jur. 149.

–. "Three Models of (In)equality" (1993) 38 McGill L.J. 64.

Gellner, Ernest. *Nations and Nationalism* (Ithaca, NY: Cornell University Press, 1983).

Gibney, Mark, ed. *Open Borders? Closed Societies? The Ethical and Political Issues* (New York: Greenwood Press, 1988).

Glasbeek, Harry J. "From Constitutional Rights to 'Real' Rights: 'R-I-G-HTS FO-R-WA-RD-HO'!?" (1990) 10 Windsor Y.B. Access Just. 468.

Goodwin-Gill, Guy S. *The Refugee in International Law,* 2d ed. (Oxford: Clarendon Press, 1996).

Grant, George P. *Lament for a Nation: The Defeat of Canadian Nationalism* (Toronto: McClelland and Stewart, 1970).

Graves, Maureen. "From Definition to Exploration: Social Groups and Political Asylum Eligibility" (1989) 26 San Diego L. Rev. 740.

Habermas, Jurgen. *Between Facts and Norms: Contributions to a Discourse Theory of Law and Democracy* (Cambridge, MA: MIT Press, 1996).

Hall, Stuart M., and Martin Jacques, eds. *New Times: The Changing Face of Politics in the 1990s* (London: Lawrence and Wishart, 1989).

Hall, Stuart M., et al. *Policing the Crisis: Mugging the State and Law and Order* (London: Macmillan, 1978).

Hathaway, James C. *The Law of Refugee Status* (Toronto: Butterworths, 1991).

–. "Rebuilding Trust: Report of the Review of Fundamental Justice in Information Gathering and Dissemination at the Immigration and Refugee Board of Canada" (Paper presented to the Chair of the IRB, December 1993) [unpublished].

–. "Reconceiving Refugee Law as Human Rights Protection" (1991) 4 Journal of Refugee Studies 113.

–, ed. *Reconceiving International Refugee Law* (The Hague and Boston: M. Nijhoff, 1997).

Hathaway, James C., and Alexander Neve. "Making International Refugee Law Relevant Again: A Proposal for Collectivized and Solution-Oriented Protection" (1997) 10 Harv. Hum. Rts. J. 115.

Hathaway, James C., and Colin J. Harvey. "Framing Refugee Protection in the New World Disorder" (2001) 34 Cornell Int'l L.J. 257.

Hawkins, Freda. *Critical Years in Immigration: Canada and Australia Compared* (Sydney: UNSW Press, 1989).

Hawkins, Keith, ed. *The Uses of Discretion* (New York/Oxford: Clarendon Press/Oxford University Press, 1992).

Hirst, Paul Q., and Grahame Thompson. *Globalization in Question*, 2d ed. (Malden, MA: Polity Press, 1999).

Hobsbawm, Eric J. *Nations and Nationalism since 1780: Programme, Myth, Reality*, 2d ed. (Cambridge: Cambridge University Press, 1992).

Hobsbawm, Eric J. and Terence O. Ranger, eds. *The Invention of Tradition* (Cambridge: Cambridge University Press, 1983).

Hooson, David, ed. *Geography and National Identity* (Cambridge, MA: Blackwell, 1994).

Hunt, Alan. *Explorations in Law and Society: Toward a Constitutive Theory of Law* (London and New York: Routledge, 1993).

Hyndman, Patricia. "Refugees under International Law with a Reference to the Concept of Asylum" (1986) 60 Australian L.J. 148.

Ion, Shelley. "Benefits/Entitlements for Refugee Claimants: What They Get and Why They Get It" (Paper submitted in part completion of an LL.B. degree at the University of British Columbia, 1998) [unpublished].

Iyer, Nitya. "Categorical Denials: Equality Rights and the Shaping of Social Identity" (1993) 19 Queen's L.J. 179.

Jacobson, David. *Rights Across Borders: Immigration and the Decline of Citizenship* (Baltimore and London: The Johns Hopkins University Press, 1995).

Joel, Ardian. "The Edifice of Compassion" (1990) 28 Law Society Journal (June) 67.

Joppke, Christian. "Why Liberal States Accept Unwanted Immigration" (1998) 50 World Politics 266.

Jordens, Ann Marie. *Redefining Australians: Immigration, Citizenship and National Identity* (Sydney: Hale and Iremonger, 1995).

Jupp, James, and Marie Kabala, eds. *The Politics of Australian Immigration* (Canberra: Australian Government Publishing Service, 1993).

Kairys, David, ed. *The Politics of Law: A Progressive Critique* (New York: Basic Books, 1998).

Kelley, Ninette, and Michael Trebilcock. *The Making of the Mosaic: A History of Canadian Immigration Policy* (Toronto: University of Toronto Press, 1998).

Kennedy, Duncan. *Sexy Dressing, Etc.* (London: Harvard University Press, 1993).

Kline, Marlee. "Complicating the Ideology of Motherhood: Child Welfare Law and First Nation Women" (1993) 18 Queen's L.J. 306.

Kneebone, Susan. "The Refugee Tribunal and the Assessment of Credibility: An Inquisitorial Role" (1998) 5 Australian Journal of Administrative Law 78.

–, ed. *Administrative Law and the Rule of Law: Still Part of the Same Package?* (Canberra: Australian Institute of Administrative Law, 1999).

Kymlicka, Will. *Multicultural Citizenship: A Liberal Theory of Minority Rights* (Oxford: Clarendon Press, 1995).

–. *Recent Work in Citizenship Theory* (Toronto: Faculty of Law Workshop Series, University of Toronto, 1992).

Leader-Elliot, Ian. "Battered but Not Beaten: Women Who Kill in Self Defence" (1993) 15 Sydney L. Rev. 1.

Legomsky, Stephen H. *Immigration and the Judiciary: Law and Politics in Britain and America* (New York/Oxford: Clarendon Press/Oxford University Press, 1997).

Levinson, Sanford. "Constituting Communities through Words that Bind: Reflections on Loyalty Oaths" (1986) 84 Mich. L. Rev. 1440.

Macklin, Audrey. "*Canada (Attorney-General) v. Ward:* A Review Essay" (1994) 6 Int'l J. Refugee L. 362.

–. "Refugee Women and the Imperative of Categories" (1995) 17 Hum. Rts. Q. 213.

Mann, Bruce H. "Law, Legalism and Community before the American Revolution" (1986) 84 Mich. L. Rev. 1415.

Marrocco, Frank N., and Henry M. Goslett, eds. *The 2003 Annotated Immigration Act of Canada,* rev. ed. (Toronto: Carswell, 2002) (previous and subsequent editions also consulted).

Mathew, Pene. "Australian Refugee Protection in the Wake of the *Tampa*" (2002) 96 Am. J. Int'l L. 661.

–. "Conformity or Persecution: China's One Child Policy and Refugee Status" (2000) 23 U.N.S.W.L.J. 103.

Matsuda, Mari. "Looking to the Bottom: Critical Legal Studies and Reparations" (1987) 2 Harv. C.R.-C.L.L. Rev. 323.

Mawani, Nurjehan. "Introduction to the Immigration and Refugee Board Guidelines on Gender-Related Persecution" (1993) 5 Int'l J. Refugee L. 240.

–. (Speech to the Canadian Bar Association, Toronto, 1 March 1997).

Melandes, Goran. "The Protection of Refugees" (1974) 18 Scand. Stud. L. 153.

Mertz, Elizabeth. "Introduction to Symposium Issue: Legal Loci and Places in the Heart: Community and Identity in Sociolegal Studies" (1994) 28 Law & Soc'y Rev. 971.

Minow, Martha. "Identities" (1991) 3 Yale J.L. & Human. 97.

–. *Making All the Difference: Inclusion, Exclusion and American Law* (Ithaca, NY: Cornell University Press, 1990).

–. "Not Only for Myself: Identity, Politics and Law" (1996) 75 Or. L. Rev. 647.

Mnookin, Robert H., and Lewis Kornhauser. "Bargaining in the Shadow of the Law: The Case of Divorce" (1979) 88 Yale L.J. 950.

Morgan, Edward M. "Aliens and Process Rights: The Open and Shut Case of Legal Sovereignty" (1988) 7 Wis. Int'l L.J. 107.

Mosoff, Judith. "'Excessive Demand' on the Canadian Conscience: Disability, Family and Immigration" (1998-99) 26 Man. L.J. 149.

Ohmae, Kenichi. *End of the Nation State* (London: HarperCollins, 1995).

Peller, Gary. "Race Consciousness" (1990) Duke L.J. 758.

Perry, Richard Warren. "The Logic of the Modern Nation-State and the Legal Construction of Native American Tribal Identity" (1995) 28 Ind. L. Rev. 547.

Post, Robert. "Democratic Constitutionalism and Cultural Heterogeneity" (2000) 25 Australian Journal of Legal Philosophy 185.

Rajchman, John, ed. *The Identity in Question* (New York: Routledge, 1995).

Randall, Melanie. "Refugee Law and State Accountability for Violence against Women: A Comparative Analysis of Legal Approaches to Asylum Claims Based on Gender Persecution" (2002) 25 Harv. Women's L.J. 281.

Rawls, John. "Justice as Fairness: Political Not Metaphysical" (1985) 14 Philosophy and Public Affairs 223.

–. *The Law of the Peoples* (Cambridge, MA: Harvard University Press, 1999).

–. *Theory of Justice* (Oxford: Oxford University Press, 1971).

Razack, Sherene. "Domestic Violence as Gender Persecution: Policing the Borders of Nation, Race and Gender" (1995) 8 C.J.W.L. 45.

Reich, Robert B. *The Work of Nations: Preparing Ourselves for 21st Century Capitalism* (London: Simon and Schuster, 1983).

Rosenfeld, Michel. "The Identity of the Constitutional Subject" (1995) 16 Cardozo L. Rev. 1049.

Rotenberg, Cecil L. "Humanitarian and Compassionate" (1989) 8 Imm. L.R. (2d) 295.

Rothwell, Donald. "The Law of the Sea and the *MV Tampa* Incident: Reconciling Maritime Principles with Coastal State Sovereignty" (2002) 13 Public Law Review 118.

Rubenstein, Kim. *Australian Citizenship Law in Context* (Sydney: Law Book Company, 2002).

–. "Citizenship in Australia: Unscrambling Its Meaning" (1995) 20 Melbourne U.L. Rev. 503.

–. "Citizenship in a Borderless World" in Anthony Anghie and Garry Sturgess, eds., *Legal Visions of the 21st Century: Essays in Honour of Judge Christopher Weeramantry* (The Hague: Kluwer Law International Publishers, 1998).

–. "Citizenship, Sovereignty and Migration" (2002) 12 Public Law Review 102.

Ruddock, Philip. Address (Conference on Immigrant Justice, Sydney, 6 June 1997).

–. "Immigration Reform: The Unfinished Agenda" (Address at the National Press Club, Canberra, 18 March 1998) [notes available on the Department of Immigration and Multicultural and Indigenous Affairs website, <http://www.minister.immi.gov.au>].

–. "Narrowing of Judicial Review in the Migration Context" (1997) 15 Australian Institute of Administrative Law Forum 13.

Sarat, Austin, and Thomas R. Kearns, eds. *Legal Rights: Historical and Philosophical Perspectives* (Ann Arbor: University of Michigan Press, 1996).

Schwartz, Warren F., ed. *Justice in Immigration* (Cambridge and New York: Cambridge University Press, 1995).

Sheehy, Elizabeth, et al. "Defending Battered Women on Trial: The Battered Woman Syndrome and Its Limitations" (1992) 16 Criminal Law Journal 369.

Sinclair, Charles. *Who Would Want to Be a Refugee?* (Ph.D. thesis, University of New England, 1995) [unpublished].

Smart, Carol. *Feminism and the Power of Law* (London and New York: Routledge, 1989).

Smith, Anthony D. *The Ethnic Origins of Nations* (Oxford and New York: Blackwell, 1986).

–. *Myths and Memories of the Nation* (Oxford and New York: Oxford University Press, 1999).

–. *National Identity* (London and New York: Penguin, 1991).

–. *Nationalism: Theory, Ideology, History* (Cambridge, UK, and Malden, MA: Polity Press, 2001).

Staiger Gooding, Susan. "Place, Race and Names: Layered Identities in *United States v. Oregon*, Confederated Tribes of the Colville Reservation, Plaintiff, Intervenor" (1994) 28 Law & Soc'y Rev. 1181.

Thomas, Philip A., ed. *Socio-Legal Studies* (Aldershot, UK: Darmouth Press, 1997).

Thompson, Edward P. *Whigs and Hunters: The Origin of the Black Act* (London: Allen Lane, 1975).

Torpey, John. *The Invention of the Passport: Surveillance, Citizenship and the State* (Cambridge: Cambridge University Press, 2000).

Torres, Gerald, and Kathryn Milun. "Translating YONNONDIO by Precedent and Evidence: The *Mashpee India* Case" (1990) Duke L.J. 625.

Tuitt, Patricia. *False Images: Law's Construction of the Refugee* (London and East Haven, CT: Pluto Press, 1996).

Turner, John C. *Rediscovering the Social Group: A Self-Categorization Theory* (Oxford and New York: Blackwell, 1987).

–. *Social Influence* (Milton Keynes, UK: Open University Press, 1991).

Tushnet, Mark. "An Essay on Rights" (1984) 62 Tex. L. Rev. 1394.

Walzer, Michael. *Spheres of Justice: A Defense of Pluralism and Equality* (New York: Basic Books, 1983).

Weiss, Linda. *The Myth of the Powerless State: Governing the Economy in a Global Era* (Cambridge: Polity Press, 1998).

Williams, Patricia J. *The Alchemy of Race and Rights* (Cambridge, MA: Harvard University Press, 1991).

–. *The Rooster's Egg* (Cambridge, MA: Harvard University Press, 1995).

Young, Iris Marion. "Polity and Group Difference: A Critique of the Ideal of Universal Citizenship" (1989) 99 Ethics 250.

Index

LAW AND SOCIETY

Law and Society Series
W. Wesley Pue, General Editor